Disappearing Cryptography

Being and Nothingness on the Net

Disappearing Cryptography
Being and Nothingness on the Net

Peter Wayner

AP Professional

Boston   San Diego   New York

London   Sydney   Tokyo   Toronto

Copyright © 1996 by Academic Press, Inc.

AP PROFESSIONAL
1300 Boylston Street, Chestnut Hill, MA 02167
World Wide Web site at http://www.apnet.com

An Imprint of ACADEMIC PRESS, INC.
A Division of HARCOURT BRACE & COMPANY

United Kingdom Edition published by
ACADEMIC PRESS LIMITED
24–28 Oval Road, London NW1 7DX

Wayner, Peter, 1964–
    Disappearing Cryptography: Being and Nothingness on the Net / Peter Wayner.
        p.   cm.
    Includes index.
    ISBN 0-12-738671-8 (alk. paper)
    1. Computer networks—Security measures.   2. Cryptography.   3. Internet
(Computer networks)   I. Title.
    TK5105.59.W39   1996
    005.8'2—dc20
                                                                                    96-1379
                                                                                    CIP

Printed in the United States of America
96 97 98 99 CP 9 8 7 6 5 4 3 2 1

Contents

Contents   vii

Preface

The people who participate in the cypherpunks mailing list deserve a long and glowing paragraph offering them thanks for their interest in this subject. They, more than anyone I know, have contributed to the public knowledge about this topic. I learned much of what I know from the discussions on the list. It would be impossible to fairly single out a subset of the list, even though there are some who consistently produce high-quality information. Thanks to everyone.

Some others have helped in other ways. Peter Neumann scanned the manuscript and offered many good suggestions for improving it. Bruce Schneier was kind enough to give me an electronic version of the bibliography from his first book [Sch94]. I converted it into Bibtex format and used it for some of the references here. Ross Anderson's annotated bibliography on Information Hiding was also a great help.

The team of people at AP PROFESSIONAL were incredibly gracious with their time and encouragement. I'm glad for all of their support through this manuscript. They are: Chuck Glaser, Jeff Pepper, Mike Williams, Barbara Northcott, Don DeLand, Tom Ryan, Josh Mills, Gael Tannenbaum, and Dave Hannon.

There were others who helped in the world beyond the text. The staff at Tax Analysts was kind enough to coordinate my consulting schedule with the demands of putting out a book. Anyone would be lucky to work for a company that was so understanding. Finally, I want to thank everyone in my family for everything they've given through all of my life.

Peter Wayner
Baltimore, MD
February 1996
pcw@access.digex.com
http://access.digex.net:/~pcw/pcwpage.html

Book Notes

The copy for this book was typeset using the LaTeX typesetting software. Several important breaks were made with standard conventions in order to remove some ambiguities. The period mark is normally included inside the quotation marks like this "That's my answer. No. Period." This can cause ambiguities when computer terms are included in quotation marks because computers often use periods to convey some meaning. For this reason, my electronic mail address is "pcw@access.digex.com". The periods and commas are left outside of all quotes to prevent confusion.

Hyphens also cause problems when they're used for different tasks. LISP programmers often use hyphens to join words together into a single name like this: `Do-Not-Call-This-Procedure`. Unfortunately, this causes grief when these longer words occur at the end of a line. In these cases, there will be an extra hyphen included to specify that there was an original hyphen in the word. This isn't *hyper-compatible* with the standard rules that don't include the extra hyphen. But these rules are for readers who know that *self-help* is a word that should be hyphenated. No one knows what to think about `A-Much-Too-Long--Procedure-That-Should-Be-Shortened-For-Everyone`.

A Start

This book is about making information disappear. For some people, this topic is a parlour trick, an amazing intellectual exercise that rattles around about the foundations of knowledge. For others, the topic has immense practical importance. An enemy can only control your message if they can find it. If you hide data, you can protect your thoughts from censorship and discovery.

The book describes a number of different techniques that people can use to hide information. The sound files and images that float about the network today are great locations filled with possibilities. Large messages can be hidden in the noise of these images or sound files where no one can expect to find them. About one eighth of an image file can be used to hide information without any significant change in the quality of the image.

Information can also be converted into something innocuous. You can use the algorithms from Chapter 7 to turn data into something entirely innocent like the voice-over to a baseball game. Bad poetry is even easier to create.

If you want to broadcast information without revealing your location, the algorithms from Chapter 11 show how a group of people can communicate without revealing who is talking. Completely anonymous conversations can let people speak their mind without endangering their lives.

Each chapter of the book comes in three different parts. The first section is a light, allegorical exploration of the topic. It is intended to be a content-free introduction to the game afoot. The second section should be a general section accessible to the average reader. Some math is required, but it should be simple and self-contained. The third

1

section should give enough data for anyone who wants to implement the algorithms.

Some people may only want to read the first and second sections of the book. This should give a deep understanding of how mutable and flexible information can be without taxing the brain too much. I hope the most ambitious readers will feel rewarded when they read the rest of the chapter.

Chapter 1

Framing Information

Dr. Zeus, Ph.D.

Who is Aristotle Di Magio? The studio took no chances when it assigned Robert Sinclair (sinkhole@bomb.com) with Angela Pardue (angie@hiatus.com) to create the script for the third movie in the Zeus series, *Dr. Zeus, Ph.D.* Their job as screenwriters was to ensure that people spent good money to find out just what made Aristotle Di Magio and the bombs he built tick.

The first movie, *Mr. Zeus*, broke box office records that summer when everyone became infatuated with the character who punched and blasted his way to justice. "Do you want your face to become a Greek tragedy? I could wipe the smile off with Ajax" became his signature line. The second movie, *Mr. Zeus Goes to Athens*, showed how one man/proto-deity could wield an assault rifle like a lightning bolt and bring justice to terrorists bent on reviving a war between Turkey and Greece. It brought more than enough money to spur the studios to round three.

In the latest edition, Dr. Zeus receives an honorary doctorate from Brown University in "Crime Fighting Hermeneutic Undeconstruction." The degree will be the first given to a fictional character and the university has paid an undisclosed sum for the product placement honor in the hope of gathering more attention and publicity. The original script called for a Harvard degree, but Brown was willing to dig deep and provide an actual degree. The actor will actually receive the degree in May at the annual graduation ceremony and the movie will open the following week.

There was some debate among the faculty because one member objected to giving a degree to a fictional character, "however deserving he might be." Others felt that this was only reinforcing the white male dominance embodied by Greek mythology. But these objections could not fight the excitement of those who argued that this was a "deep and very radical inversion of the American educational system. A subversive, performance art piece designed to emphasize the blurred line between fiction and reality, passing and failing, college graduate and peasant. A witty rejoinder to those who support the hegemony of the college degree." The performance artists were able to build a big enough coalition with the public relations department to push the plan through.

Sinclair and Pardue's goal in staging the honorary degree was to give the audience some reason to tune in when Dr. Zeus announces in his commencement speech he's going to Disney World. The premise was simple. Aristotle Di Magio is a flaky but brilliant young bomb designer who works for the U.S. government at its Sandia Labs. Suddenly he turns up missing. No one knows if terrorists captured him, if he committed suicide, or went fishing. Dr. Zeus gets the case via a cellular phone call while he's riding up Disney's Matterhorn roller coaster on vacation.

The only clue is the e-mail transcript surreptitiously kept by the lab's security forces. Di Magio has a long and intense correspondence going with a mysterious Madame X (mad-x@aol.com). The only problem is that no one knows her name. She logs in from different pay phones throughout the country in a screwy pattern that has no detectable rhyme or rhythm. One message came in from the AOL portal that carried the traffic from the corner of Wyoming near Yellowstone Park. The next came in through the Chicago North Shore node. Everyone begins to suspect defection. Dr. Zeus sets off on a long car journey to track down these pay phones, discover the identity of Madame X, find her, and recover Aristotle Di Magio.

The working plan is to start the movie out with a montage of images of Sandia labs, the mountains surrounding it, Yellowstone Park, Chicago, a roadside diner, and Brown University. Over the images will scroll several e-mail messages à la *Star Wars*. These messages will establish the characters of Di Magio and X and set the tone of the movie before the cameras join Zeus on the stage getting his doctorate.

Sinclair and Pardue know that the tone and content of the opening e-mail exchange is crucial. This is why Pardue was brought in. Sinclair has written almost 50 action movies with over 1020 total explosions including the first two Zeusters. But Pardue won her acclaim by creating a weepy romantic comedy about two elephant trainers who finally find love after forgetting everything bad that happens during the star-crossed courtship. He borrows her car and his elephant inadvertently sits on the front end. Her elephants run amok and level his house. But forgiveness and tender words make the ending sweet.

Pardue was brought in to generate some good tender words to expand the audience for *Dr. Zeus* beyond the fans of explosions. She's got to deliver the weepers. If she can do this, the studio figures that it'll have a blockbuster that generates twice as much money because it appeals to twice as many people.

Here is a transcript of the e-mail that flew between Pardue and Sinclair as they were crafting this opening:

To: Angela Pardue (angie@hiatus.com)
From: Robert Sinclair (bomb@sinkhole.com)
Subject: Chopping it down, chop, chop

I've produced a first round that's clear and crisp and full of love. Let me know where to go.

To: Robert Sinclair (bomb@sinkhole.com)
From: Angela Pardue (angie@hiatus.com)
Subject: Get Real.

You're too sappy. Rilly now. It's short and tight, yes. But to use a cliché, it's has as many clichés as Swiss cheese has holes. Why are mad-x and Aristotle different? Everyone can hang their love upon a star. Turn that cliché around and give me some rats. I need to know something that they did that is theirs and theirs alone. Romance begins with shared secrets.

Who are they apart? Who are they together? I think that the letters should reveal who they are. I want their souls to be digitized and compressed into these messages. See the attached draft.

To: Angela Pardue (angie@hiatus.com)
From: Robert Sinclair (bomb@sinkhole.com)
Subject: Okay. Take three.

I got your cut, but it's much too sappy. That second note in the series goes on for hours about the crappy hotel in Buenos Aries filled with rats. To paraphrase the emperor in *Amadeus*, "Too many rats." Why would Mad-X bother writing a long note reminiscing about this on the eve of their second anniversary? Why not remember something pretty? Why would they be in BA? I thought he was a loopy scientist. That sounds like a place for Americans wasting their inheritance on decadent living, not a place where DM, the geek, would meet his love.

This next draft is faster. People may pipe their soul down a modem line in a well-written letter, but they don't pour all of it. They just send along perfect pearls in a champagne transport. I've kept the reference to Argentina, but cleaned it up. He's just come back from a mountain climbing trip and they meet at a ski chalet. Mad-X says she was teased by the wonder of what his face was like beneath the "bitchin, radical stubble." We should be able to work in a ski chase for Z in reel 3 with little effort.

To: Robert Sinclair (bomb@sinkhole.com)
From: Angela Pardue (angie@hiatus.com)
Subject: MX, Miss Elle

She's got to be more cotton lingerie and less silk or satin. That's the detail we need. I've taken that and woven it into e-mail number four. I've kept Argentina and added a reference to Yellowstone Park. This should explain some of the background scenery for the audience and give us some room for using this scenery later in the movie when Z comes to find out more about Mad-X.

To: Angela Pardue (angie@hiatus.com)
From: Robert Sinclair (bomb@sinkhole.com)
Subject: Who we are and what we do?

I still think that what we do is a large part of who we are. Toward that end, I've grafted in a medium length description of the two of them climbing an old oak in Maine. It also builds upon the mountains in South America and adds more action for those who snooze through voice overs reading text.

This draft is strong now. Let's go back and time the explosions that will rock the ending.

———

Dr. Zeus Ph.D.: The Opening Scene

Here is the final draft of the e-mail that scrolls over the opening helicopter shots of the mountains in South America.

To: mad-x@aol.com (Madame E. Grek)
From: Aristotle Di Magio (adimagio@boom.sandia.gov)
Subject: Two years tomorrow

It will be two years tomorrow since I first met you. Two years since I came skiing down that hill. Robert couldn't keep up and he kept screaming in the radio phone to slow down. I still don't know what told me to suck up all of the gravity. But if I was even 10 minutes later getting to the bottom, I wouldn't have met you in the lodge.

The screen shows two skiers climbing to the top of a snowy cliff, strapping on their skis and diving into a cavern that is obviously off the beaten path. One starts racing ahead of the other.

```
To: Aristotle Di Magio (adimagio@boom.sandia.gov)
From: mad-x@aol.com (Madame E. Grek)
Subject: Two Years Today
```

```
I'm writing from the other side of the dateline
where it is tomorrow for you today. We'll be out
of sync on this anniversary. Yes, I remember your
bitchin, radical stubble. Of course Robert was
right. You spent three hours climbing to the top of
that cairn to ski that tube just to waste all of
that potential energy in one falling swoop. But if
you hadn't gone into a tuck for the entire hill, you
never would have crashed into me at the bottom and
started this affair. This is a pleasant thought. I
was in meetings all day today.
```

The skiers are going faster and faster as they reach the groomed section of the ski resort. As Aristotle Di Magio reaches the bottom, he brakes in an graceful arcing turn that sends a plume of snow across the sky. He miscalculates and is still moving 3 mph when he bumps into Madame X.

To: mad-x@aol.com (Madame E. Grek)
From: Aristotle Di Magio (adimagio@boom.sandia.gov)
Subject: Climbing

Time is not as important as a destination. Remember when we were camping in Maine. The woods were too thick to see the stars so we climbed up the oak beyond the canopy. The short trees were just a sea of darkness while space, that supposedly dark void, was glimmering with moonlight and a few bright stars.

The helicopter shot starts low off the coast of Maine and speeds in over the hills until it hovers above one tree where the two sit looking at the stars.

```
To: Aristotle Di Magio (adimagio@boom.sandia.gov)
From: mad-x@aol.com (Madame E. Grek)
Subject: The creak.
```

```
My floor is creaking just like those tree limbs.
It's very dark here, but there is no sky. None
what-so-ever. Even though I'm on the 32nd floor.
Please meet me soon.
```

A woman's legs rest on a leather ottoman in an expensive apartment with an expensive view of the city. She drinks brandy. Then the screen jumps to the Yellowstone wilderness where a romantic couple are hiking through the woods on snowshoes.

To: mad-x@aol.com (Madame E. Grek)
From: Aristotle Di Magio (adimagio@boom.sandia.gov)
Subject: Women who run with the wolves.

We should return to Yellowstone soon. They've put out new wolves and you can exercise all of the chthonic forces that drive you away from the simple life. I guarantee that one run through the woods with those suckers on your tail will make you wish for a domesticated bliss. Apron strings aren't so bad when there are fangs out there. I'll be in touch through our secret channel. Then we'll meet.

They pause to kiss awkwardly as the snowshoes get in the way.

```
To: Aristotle Di Magio (adimagio@boom.sandia.gov)
From: mad-x@aol.com (Madame E. Grek)
Subject: Hah!
```

```
Luckily, you're probably out of shape. I've been
running the hills here and you've been pushing files
back and forth between a CPU and a file server. The
wolves will get you first and grow sleepy after
eating all your belly has to offer.
```

The e-mail ends and live action begins.

Sinclair was able to work in 22 major explosions before the climactic ending. Pardue was more than happy that Di Magio and Madame X were able to survive breaking up *twice* before the final scene where they get engaged. The two shared the screenwriting Oscar that spring. The movie itself won eleven Oscars including four technical Oscars for the cinematography in the opening ski scene.

Dissolving Ourselves

Who we are is something that only each person knows. Parts of it leak out in our conversations, our pictures, our letters and all of the things we do with others. These details about our pasts, whom we love, what we like, where we've been, and where we are going are fragments of our existence. Today, more than ever, the details are traveling as bits in a computer network. Slowly but surely, these details about ourselves find each other in the vast databases evolving on the Net. The details coalesce into factual simulacra of ourselves as they incorporate more and more of the information about us.

There is probably nothing wrong, per se, with dustballs of data building up in the corners of the Net. Computers on their own will probably never acquire the artificial intelligence to suck our personalities from this data and assume our lives. But there are people who may use the information for malicious ends. Business requires stealth. Romance needs secrecy. Friendship demands trust. Families thrive on protection. For all of these reasons and many others, everyone needs to be able to preserve the details of their existence, the facts of their being, and the data representing parts of their soul from others.

This book is about how to take words, sounds, and images and hide them in digital data so they look like other words, sounds, or images. It is about converting secrets into innocuous noise so that the secrets disappear in the ocean of bits flowing through the Net. It describes how to make data mimic other data to disguise its origins and obscure its destination. It is about submerging a conversation in a flow of noise so that no one can know if a conversation exists at all. It is about taking your being, dissolving it into nothingness, and then pulling it out of the nothingness so it can live again.

Traditional cryptography succeeds by locking up a message in a mathematical safe. Hiding the information so it can't be found is a similar but often distinct process that is often called *steganography*. There are many historical examples of it including hidden compartments, mechanical systems like microdots, or burst transmissions, that make the message hard to find. Other techniques like encoding the message in the first letters of words disguise the content and make it look like something else. All of these have been used again and again.

Digital information offers wonderful opportunities to not only hide information, but also to develop a general theoretical framework for hiding the data. It is possible to describe general algorithms and make some statements about how hard it will be for someone who doesn't know the key to find the data. Much of the material in this book falls under the heading of cryptography. For the purposes of being dramatic and for drawing distinctions, steganography that comes with some mathematical assessment of its security or some algorithmic component is called here *disappearing cryptography*. Perhaps this term will stick. Perhaps others will take its place.[1]

This book will examine several different ways of hiding information. The first will be in the noise of images and sound files. The digital versions consist of numbers that represent the intensity of light or sound at a particular point of time or space. Often, these numbers are computed with extra precision that can't be detected effectively by humans. For instance, one spot in a picture might have 220 units of blue on a scale that runs between 0 and 255 total units. An average eye would not notice if that one spot was converted to having 219 units of blue. If this process is done systematically, it is possible to hide large volumes of information just below the threshold of perception. A digital photo-CD image has 2048 by 3072 pixels that each contain 24 bits of information about the colors of the image. 756k of data can be hidden in the three least significant bits for each color of each pixel. That's probably more than the text of this book. The human eye would not be able to detect the subtle variations but a computer could reconstruct all of it.

Another technique can be used to make data appear to be other data. It is possible, for instance, to hide information by making it look like the transcript of a baseball game. The bits are hidden by using them to choose between the nouns, verbs and other parts of the text. The data are recovered by sorting through the text and matching up the words with the bits that selected them. This technique can produce startling results, although the content of the messages often seems a bit loopy or directionless. This is often good enough to fool humans or computers that are programmed to algorithmically scan for particular words or patterns.

A third solution can be used to disguise the travel of a message. One version of this, known as the dining cryptographers networks,

---

[1]One conference on the subject called it "information hiding," others have called it "obfuscation."

uses a continuously flowing data stream that joins everyone in the group. If one person wants to speak to another, they begin injecting their messages into the stream and the other pulls them out. No one can tell where the message is going nor can anyone read the encrypted contents. The secrets from a message can also be split apart so that the message can only be recovered if all of the parts are found. If these are sprinkled throughout the network and pulled together later, then it may be impossible to trace the flow of the data.

The early chapters of the book are devoted to material that forms the basic bag of tricks like private-key encryption, secret sharing, and error-correcting codes. The later chapters describe how to apply these techniques in various ways to hide information. Each of them is designed to give you an introduction and enough information to use the data if you want.

Each chapter has three parts: an allegorical opening, a high-level summary for those who want to understand the concepts without wading through technical details, and a introductory set of details, for those who want to create their own programs from the information. People who are not interested in the deepest, most mathematical details can skip the last section of each chapter without missing any of the highlights. Programmers who are inspired to implement some algorithms will want to dig into the last chapter. I hope everyone finds something to enjoy in the first segments of each chapter.

For the most part, this book is about having fun with information. But knowledge is power and people in power want to increase their knowledge. So the final chapter is an essay devoted to some of the political questions that lie just below the surface of all of these morphing bits.

Chapter 2

Encryption

Pure White

In the final years of the 20th century, Pinnacle Paint was purchased by the MegaGoth marketing corporation in a desperate attempt to squeeze the last bit of synergy from the world. The executives of MegaGoth, who were frantic with the need to buy something they didn't already own so they could justify their existence, found themselves arguing that the small, privately owned paint company fit nicely into their marketing strategy for dominating the entertainment world.

Although some might argue that people choose colors with their eyes, the executives quickly began operating under the assumption that people purchased paint that would identify them with something. People wanted to be part of a larger movement. They weren't choosing a color for a room, they were buying into a lifestyle—how dare they choose any lifestyle without licensing one from a conglomerate? The executives didn't really believe this, but they were embarrassed to discover that their two previous acquisitions targets were already owned by MegaGoth. Luckily, their boss didn't know this either when he gave the green light to those projects. Only the quick thinking of a paralegal saved them from the disaster of buying something they already owned and paying all of that tax.

One of the first plans for MegaGoth/Pinnacle Paints is to take the standard white paint and rebottle it in new and different product lines to target different demographic groups. Here are some of the plans:

Moron and Moosehead's Creative Juice What would the two lovable animated characters paint if they were forced to expand their creativity in art class? Moron might choose a white cow giving milk in the Arctic for his subject. Moosehead would probably try to paint a little lost snowflake in a cloud buffeted by the wind and unable to find its way to its final destination: Earth.

Empathic White White is every color. The crew of "Star Trek: They Keep Breeding More Generations" will welcome Bob, the "empath," to the crew next season. His job is to let other people project their feelings onto him. Empathic White will serve the same function for the homeowner as the mixing base for many colors. Are you *blue*? Bob, the Empath, could accept that feeling and validate it. Do you want your living room to be blue? That calls for Empathic White. Are you *green* with jealousy? Empathic White at your service.

Fright White MegaGoth took three British subjects and let them watch two blood-draining horror movies from the upcoming MegaGoth season. At the end, they copied the color of their skin and produced the purest white known to the world.

Snow White A cross-licensing product with the MegaGoth/Disney division ensures that kids in their nursery won't feel alone for a minute. Those white walls will be just another way to experience the magic of movie produced long ago when Disney was a distinct corporation.

White Dwarf White The crew of "Star Trek" discovers a White Dwarf star and spends an entire episode orbiting it. But surprise! The show isn't really about White Dwarf stars qua White Dwarfs, it's really using their super-strong gravitational fields as a metaphor for human attraction. Now, everyone can wrap themselves in the same metaphor by painting their walls with White Dwarf White.

Encryption and White Noise

Hiding information is a tricky business. Although the rest of this book will revolve around camouflaging information by actually making the bits look like something else, it is a good idea to begin with examining basic encryption. The standard encryption functions like DES or RSA hide data by making it incomprehensible. They take information and convert it into total randomness or white noise. This effect might not be a good way to divert attention from a file, but it is still an important tool. Many of the algorithms and approaches described later in the book perform best when they have a perfectly random source of data. Encrypting a file before applying any of the other approaches is a good beginning.

The world of cryptography began attempting to produce perfect white noise during World War II. This is because Claude Shannon, a mathematician then working for Bell Labs, developed the foundations of information theory that offered an ideal framework for actually measuring information.

Most people who use computers have a rough idea about just how much information there is in a particular file. A word processing document, for instance, has some overhead and about one byte for each character. But most people are also aware that there is something slippery about measuring information. If the number of bytes in a computer file was an accurate measurement of the information in it, then there would be no way that a compression program could squeeze files to be a fraction of the original. Real estate can't be squeezed and diamonds can't be smooshed, but potato chips always seem to come in a bag filled with air. That's why they're sold by weight not volume. The success of compression programs like PKZIP or Stuffit means that measuring a file by the number of bytes is like selling potato chips by volume.

Compression is discussed in Chapter 5.

Shannon's method of measuring information "by weight" rests upon probability. He felt a message had plenty information if you couldn't anticipate the contents, but it had little information if the contents were easy to predict. A weather forecast in Los Angeles doesn't contain much information because it is often sunny and 72 degrees Fahrenheit. A weather forecast in the Caribbean during hurricane season, though, has plenty of potential information about coming storms that might be steaming in.

Shannon measured information by totaling up the probabilities. A byte has eight bits and 256 different possible values between 00000000 and 11111111 in base two. If all of these possible values occur with the same probability, then there are said to be eight bits of information in this byte. On the other hand, if only two values like 00101110 and

10010111 happen to appear in a message, then there is only one bit of information in each byte. The two values could be replaced with just a 0 and a 1 and the entire file would be reduced to be one eighth the size. The number of bits of information in a file is called, in this context, its *entropy*.

This measurement of information offered some important insights to cryptographers. Mathematicians who break codes rely upon deep statistical analysis to ferret out patterns in files. In English, the letter "q" is often followed by the letter "u" and this pattern is a weak point that might be exploited by attackers trying to get at the underlying message. A good encryption program would leave no such patterns in the final file. Every one of the 256 possible values of a byte would occur with equal probability. It would seem to be filled chock-full with information.

One-time pads are an encryption system that is a good example of the basic structure behind information theory. The one-time pad received its name because spies often carried pads of random numbers that served as the encryption key. They would use each sheet once and then dispose of it.

A secret can be split into parts using an extension of one-time pads described on page 52.

A simple one-time pad system can be built by using a simple method of encryption. Assume for the moment that a key is just a number like 5 and a message consists of all uppercase letters. To encrypt a letter like "C" with a key number like 5, count over five letters to get "H". If the counting goes past "Z" at the end of the alphabet, simply go back to "A" and keep going. The letter "Y" encrypted with the key number 6 would produce "E". To decrypt work backward.

Here is a sample encryption:

H	E	L	L	O
9	0	2	1	0
Q	E	N	M	O

The key, in this case, is the five numbers 9, 0, 2, 1, and 0. They would constitute the one-time pad that encrypted this message. In practice, the values should be as random as possible. A human might reveal some hidden short circuits in its brain.[1]

---

[1]Or the limitations of creativity brought on by too much television.

Shannon proved that a one-time pad is an unbreakable cipher because the information content of the final file is equal to the information content of the key. An easy way to see why this is true is to break the message, "QENMO" from above. Any five-letter word could be the underlying message because any key is possible. The name, "BRUNO", for instance, would have generated "QENMO" if the key numbers were 15, 13, 19, 25, and 0. If all possibilities are available, then the attacker can't use any of the information about English or the message itself to rule out solutions. The entropy of the message itself should be greater than or equal to the entropy in the key. This is certainly the case here because each byte of the message could be any value between 0 and 255 and so could the key. In practice, the entropy of the key would be even greater because the distribution of the values in the message would depend upon the vagaries of language while the key could be chosen at random.

A real one-time pad would not be restricted to uppercase characters. You could use a slightly different encryption process that used all 256 possible values of a byte. One popular method is to use the operation known as *exclusive-or* (XOR), which is just addition in the world of bits. ($0 + 0 = 0, 0 + 1 = 1$, and $1 + 1 = 0$ because it wraps around.) If the one-time pad consists of bytes with values between 0 and 255 and these values are evenly distributed in all possible ways, then the result will be secure. It is important that the pad is not used again because statistical analysis of the underlying message can reveal the key. The United States was able to read some crucial correspondence between Russia and its spies in the United States during the early Cold War because the same one-time pad was reused. [Age95] The number of bits in the key was now less than the number of bits of information in the message, and Shannon's proof that the one-time pad is a perfect encryption no longer holds.

The one-time pad is an excellent encryption system, but very impractical. Two people who want to communicate in secret must arrange to exchange one-time pads securely long before they need to start sending messages. It would not be possible, for instance, for someone to use their WWW browser to encrypt the credit card numbers being sent to a merchant without exchanging a one-time pad in person. Often, the sheer bulk of the pad is too large to be practical.

Many people have tried to make this process more efficient by using the same part of the pad over and over again. If they were encrypting a long message, they might use the key 90210 over and over again. This makes the key small enough to be remembered easily, but it introduces dangerous repetition. If the attackers are able to guess the length of the key, they can exploit this pattern. They would know in this case that every fifth letter would be shifted by the same amount. Finding the right amount is often trivial and it can be as easy as solving a crossword puzzle or playing Hangman.

DES and Modern Ciphers

There are many different encryption functions that do a good job of scrambling information into white noise. One of the more practical and secure encryption algorithms available today is the Data Encryption Standard (DES) developed by IBM in the 1970s. The system uses only 56 bits of key information to encrypt 64-bit blocks of data. The basic design of the system was inspired, in part, by some other work of Claude Shannon in which he proposed that encryption consists of two different and complementary actions: confusion and diffusion. *Confusion* consists of scrambling up a message. The simple one-time pad system above confuses each letter. *Diffusion* involves taking one part of the message and modifying another part so that each part of the final message depends on many other parts of the message. There is no diffusion in the one-time pad example because the total randomness of the key made it unnecessary.

DES consists of sixteen alternating rounds of confusion and diffusion. There are 64 bits that are encrypted in each block of data. These are split into two 32-bit halves. First, one half is confused by passing it through what is called an "S-box." This is really just a random function that is preset to scramble the data in an optimal way. Then these results are combined with the key bits and used to scramble the other half. This is the diffusion because one half of the data is affecting the other half. This pattern of alternating rounds is often called a *Feistel network*.

The alternating rounds would not be necessary if a different S-box were used for each 64-bit block of the message. Then it would be the equivalent of a one-time pad. But that would be inefficient because a large file would need a correspondingly large set of S-boxes. The alternating rounds are a compromise designed to securely scramble the message with only 64 bits.

The confusion and diffusion functions were designed differently. Confusion was deliberately constructed to be as nonlinear as possible. Linear functions, straight lines, are notoriously easy to predict. The interest paid out by the bank each day into your account is a linear function and it is simple to predict just how much money there will be after 365 days where this daily "scrambling" occurs. For this reason, the S-boxes that provide the confusion for DES were chosen to be as nonlinear as possible. The results don't even come close.

Creating a nonlinear S-box is not an easy process. The original technique was classified, leading many to suspect that the U.S. government had installed a trap door or secret weakness in the design. The recent work of two Israeli cryptographers, Eli Biham and Adi Shamir, however, showed how almost linear tendencies in S-boxes could be exploited to break a cipher like DES. Although the technique was very powerful and successful against DES-like systems, the authors discovered that DES itself was optimally designed to resist this attack.

The diffusion function, on the other hand, was limited by technology. Ideally, every bit of the 64-bit block will affect the encryption of any other bit. If one bit at the beginning of the block is changed, then every other bit in the block may turn out differently. This instability ensures that those attacking the cipher won't be able to localize their effort. Each bit affects the others.

The process of using one half of the function to scramble the other is shown in Figure 2.1. Alternating which half scrambles the other is a good way to ensure that the contents of one half affect the other. The diffusion in DES is even more subtle. Although the information in one half would affect the other after only one round, the bits inside the halves wouldn't affect each other quite as quickly. This part of the book does not go into the design of the S-boxes in detail, but the amount of scrambling was limited by the technology available in the mid-1970s when the cipher was designed. It takes several rounds of this process to diffuse the information thoroughly.

Figure 2.2 shows one of the eight S-boxes from DES. It is simply a table. If the input to the S-box is 000000 then the output is 1110. This is the simplest form of scrambling and it is fairly easy to reverse. The S-box takes 6 bits as input to implement diffusion. The 32 bits of one half are split into eight 4-bit blocks. Each of the 4-bit blocks then grabs one bit from the block to the left and one bit from the block to the

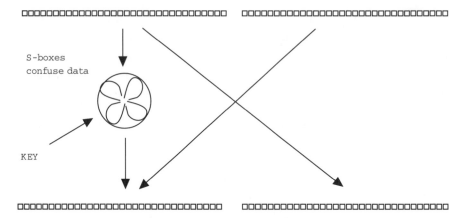

Figure 2.1. A schematic view of one round of DES. 64 bits enter and are split into two 32-bit halves. The left half is scrambled up with the key using the S-boxes. This result is then mixed in with the right half and the result of adding these two together becomes the new left half. The new right half is just a copy of the old left half.

$000000 \rightarrow 1110$	$000001 \rightarrow 0100$	$000010 \rightarrow 1101$	$000011 \rightarrow 0001$
$000100 \rightarrow 0010$	$000101 \rightarrow 1110$	$000110 \rightarrow 1011$	$000111 \rightarrow 1000$
$001000 \rightarrow 0011$	$001001 \rightarrow 1010$	$001010 \rightarrow 0110$	$001011 \rightarrow 1100$
$001100 \rightarrow 0101$	$001101 \rightarrow 1001$	$001110 \rightarrow 0000$	$001111 \rightarrow 0111$
$010000 \rightarrow 0000$	$010001 \rightarrow 1111$	$010010 \rightarrow 0111$	$010011 \rightarrow 0100$
$010100 \rightarrow 1110$	$010101 \rightarrow 0010$	$010110 \rightarrow 1101$	$010111 \rightarrow 0001$
$011000 \rightarrow 1010$	$011001 \rightarrow 0110$	$011010 \rightarrow 1100$	$011011 \rightarrow 1011$
$011100 \rightarrow 1001$	$011101 \rightarrow 0101$	$011110 \rightarrow 0011$	$011111 \rightarrow 1000$
$100000 \rightarrow 0100$	$100001 \rightarrow 0001$	$100010 \rightarrow 1110$	$100011 \rightarrow 1000$
$100100 \rightarrow 1101$	$100101 \rightarrow 0110$	$100110 \rightarrow 0010$	$100111 \rightarrow 1011$
$101000 \rightarrow 1111$	$101001 \rightarrow 1100$	$101010 \rightarrow 1001$	$101011 \rightarrow 0111$
$101100 \rightarrow 0011$	$101101 \rightarrow 1010$	$101110 \rightarrow 0101$	$101111 \rightarrow 0000$
$110000 \rightarrow 1111$	$110001 \rightarrow 1100$	$110010 \rightarrow 1000$	$110011 \rightarrow 0010$
$110100 \rightarrow 0100$	$110101 \rightarrow 1001$	$110110 \rightarrow 0001$	$110111 \rightarrow 0111$
$111000 \rightarrow 0101$	$111001 \rightarrow 1011$	$111010 \rightarrow 0011$	$111011 \rightarrow 1110$
$111100 \rightarrow 1010$	$111101 \rightarrow 0000$	$111110 \rightarrow 0110$	$111111 \rightarrow 1101$

Figure 2.2. This table shows how the first DES S-box converts 6-bit values into 4-bit ones. Note that a change in one input bit will generally change two output bits. The function is also nonlinear and difficult to approximate with linear functions.

right. That means that each 4-bit block influences the processing of the adjacent 4-bit block. This is how the bits inside each of the halves affect each other.

This is already too much detail for this part of the book. The rest of DES is really of more interest to programmers who actually need to implement the cipher. The important lesson is how the designers of DES chose to interleave some confusion functions with some diffusion functions to produce incomprehensible results.

The best way to judge the strength of an encryption system like DES is to try to break it. Talking about highly technical things like code breaking at a high level can be futile because the important details can often be so subtle that the hand-waving metaphors end up flying right over the salient fact. Still, a quick sketch of an attack on the alternating layers of confusion and diffusion in DES can give at least an intuitive feel for why the system is effective.

Imagine that you're going to break one round of DES. You have the 64 bits produced by one step of confusion and one step of diffusion. You want to reconstruct the 64 bits from the beginning and determine the 56 key bits that were entered. Since only one round has finished, you can immediately discover one half of the bits. The main advantage that you have is that not much diffusion has taken place. Thirty-two bits are always unchanged by each round. This makes it easier to determine if the other half could come from the same file. Plus, these 32 bits were also the ones that fed into the confusion function. If the confusion process is not too complicated, then it may be possible to run it in reverse. The DES confusion process is pretty simple, and it is fairly straightforward to go backward. It's just a table lookup. If you can guess the key or the structure of the input, then it is simple.

Now imagine doing the same thing after 16 rounds of confusion and diffusion. Although you can work backward, you'll quickly discover that the confusion is harder to run in reverse. After only one round, you could recover the 32 bits of the left half that entered the function. But you can't get 32 bits of the original message after 16 rounds. If you try to work backward, you'll quickly discover that everything is dependent upon everything else. The diffusion has forced everything to affect everything else. You can't localize your search to one 4-bit block or another because all of the input bits have affected all of the other bits in the process of the 16 rounds. The changes have percolated throughout the process.

Public-Key Encryption

Public-key encryption systems are quite different from the popular private-key encryption systems like DES. They rely on a substantially different branch of mathematics that still generates nice, random white noise. Even though these foundations are different, the results are still the same.

The most popular public-key encryption system is the RSA algorithm that was developed by Ron Rivest, Adi Shamir, and Len Adleman when they were at MIT during the late 1970s. The system uses two keys. If one key encrypts the data, then only the other key can decrypt it. The first key is worthless. This is not a bug, but a feature. Each person can create a pair of keys and publicize one of the pair, perhaps by listing it in some electronic phone book. The other key is kept secret. If someone wants to send a message to you, they look up your public key and use it to encrypt the message to you. Only the other key can decrypt this message now and only you have a copy of that key.

In a very abstract sense, the RSA algorithm works by arranging the set of all possible messages in a long, long loop in an abstract mathematical space. The circumference of this loop, call it n, is kept a secret. You might think of this as a long necklace of pearls or beads. Each bead represents a possible message. There are billions of billions of billions of them in the loop. You send a message by giving someone a pointer to a bead.

The public key is just a relatively large number, call it k. A message is encrypted by finding its position in the loop and stepping around the loop k steps. The encrypted message is the number at this position. The secret key is the circumference of the loop minus k. A message is decrypted by starting at the number marking the encrypted message and marching along the $n - k$ steps. Because the numbers are arranged in a loop, this will bring you back to where everything began, the original message.

There are two properties about this string of pearls or beads that make it possible to use it for encryption. The first is that given a bead, it is really hard to know its exact position on the string. If there is some special first bead that serves as the reference location like on a rosary, then you would need to count through all of the beads to determine the exact location of one of the beads. This same effect happens in the mathematics. You would need to multiply numbers again and again to determine if a particular number is the one you want.

The second property of the string of beads in this metaphor does not make as much sense, but it can still be explained easily. If you want to move along the string k beads or pearls, then you can jump there almost instantaneously. This allows you to encrypt and decrypt messages using the public-key system.

The two special features are similar but they do not contradict each other. The second says that it is easy to jump an arbitrary number of beads. The first says it's hard to count the number of pearls between the first bead and any particular bead. If you knew the count, then you could use the second feature. But you don't so you have to count by hand.

The combination of these two features makes it possible to encrypt and decrypt messages by jumping over large numbers of beads. But it also makes it impossible for someone to break the system because they can't determine the number of steps in the jump without counting.

This metaphor is not exactly correct, but it captures the spirit of the system. Figure 2.3 illustrates it. Mathematically, the loop is constructed by computing the powers of a number modulo some other number. That is, the first element in the loop is the number. The second is the square of the number, the third is the cube of the number, and so on. In reality, the loop is more than one-dimensional, but the theme is consistent.

How Random Is the Noise?

How random is the output of a encryption function like DES or RSA? Unfortunately, the best answer to that question is the philosophical response, "What do you mean by random?" Mathematics is very good at producing consistent results from well-defined questions, but it has trouble accommodating capricious behavior.

At the highest level, the best approach is indirect. If there was a black box that could look at the first n bits of a file and predict the next set of bits with any luck, then it is clear that the file is not completely random. Is there such a black box that can attack a file encrypted with

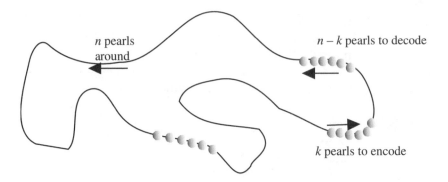

Figure 2.3. RSA encryption works by arranging the possible messages in a loop with a secret circumference. Encryption is accomplished by moving a random amount, k, down the loop. Only the owners know the circumference, n, so they can move $n - k$ steps down the loop and recover the original message.

DES? The best answer is that no one knows of any black box that will do the job in any reasonable amount of time. A brute force attack is possible, but this requires a large machine and some insight into the structure of the file that is encrypted. So, we could argue that the results of DES should appear random because we can't predict them successfully.

The same arguments also hold for RSA. If there was some black box that could take a number and tell you where it stood in the loop, then you would be able to break RSA. If the input doesn't fall in a pattern, then the output should be very random. If there was some way of predicting it, then that could be used to break RSA.

Even if the values can't be predicted, they still might not be as random looking as we might want. For instance, an encrypted routine might produce a result that is uncrackable but filled with only two numbers like 7 and 11. The pattern might be incomprehensible and unpredictable, but you still wouldn't want to use the source as the random number generator for your digital craps game. One immediate clue is that if the 7 and the 11 occur with equal probability, then the entropy of such a file is clearly 1 bit per number.

It is easy to construct a high-level argument that this problem will not occur with DES. All possible output values should be produced with equal probability. Why? Because DES can be decoded successfully. 64 bits go into DES and 64 bits go out. Each possible output can only have one matching input and vice versa. Therefore each possible output can be produced.

The same argument also holds for RSA. The loop contains a number for each of all possible messages and these numbers are distributed around the loop in a way that defies cognition. Therefore, each output value has practically the same probability of emerging from the function.

Although these two arguments don't prove that the output from an encryption function is random and they are far from rigorous, they do suggest that DES and RSA will pass any test that can be thrown at them. If a test is good enough to detect a pattern, then it would be a good lever for breaking the code. In practice, the simple tests support these results. The output of DES is quite random.[2] Many tests show that it is a good way to "whiten" a random number source to make it more intractable. For instance, some people experiment with using a random physical process like counting cosmic rays to create random numbers. However, there might be a pattern caused by the physics of the detector. A good way to remove this possibility is to use DES to encrypt the random data and produce the whitest noise possible.

Measuring Information and Encrypting It

Entropy

Let an information stream be composed of n characters between x_0 and x_{n-1} that occur in the stream with probability $\rho(x_i)$. Shannon's measure of the *entropy* in the information stream computed in bits per character can be written:

$$\sum_{i=0}^{n} \rho(x_i) \log \left(\frac{1}{\rho(x_i)} \right).$$

The log is taken base two.

---

[2]The level of randomness depends upon the input file if there is no key feedback mechanism being used. In some versions of DES, the results of one block are XORed with the inputs for the next block so that there will be diffusion across the blocks. If this is not used, someone could input a file with a pattern and get out a file with a pattern as long as the pattern repeats in an even multiple of 8 bytes.

If a stream is made up of bytes with values between 0 and 255 and every byte value occurs with equal probability of $\frac{1}{256}$, then the entropy of the stream is 8 bits per byte. If only two bytes, say 43 and 95, each occur half of the time and the other 254 bytes don't occur at all, the entropy of this stream is only 1 bit per byte. In this simple example, it should be obvious how the bit stream can be compressed by a factor of 8 to 1. In more complex examples, the entropy is still a good rough measure of how well a simple compression algorithm will do.

The limitations of Shannon's measure of information are pretty obvious. An information stream that repeats the bytes $0, 1, 2, \ldots, 254,$ $255, 0, 1 \ldots$ ad infinitum would appear to contain 8 bits of information per byte. But, there really isn't that much information being conveyed. You could write a short two-line program in most computer languages that would duplicate the result. This computer program could stand in for this stream of information and it would be substantially cheaper to ship this program across the network than pay for the cost of sending an endless repeat stream of bytes.

In a sense, this repeating record computer program is a very good compressed form of the information. If the data was the potato chips, you would hope that it was measured by the number of lines in a computer program that could generate it, *not* the Shannon entropy. There is another measure of information known as the *Kolmogorov* complexity that attempts to measure the information by determining the size of the smallest program that could generate the data. This is a great theoretical tool for analyzing algorithms, but it is entirely impractical. Finding the smallest program is both theoretically and practically impossible because no one can test all possible programs. It might be a short program in C, but what about in Pascal, Smalltalk, or a language that no one has written yet?

The Shannon measure of information can be made more complicated by including the relationship between adjacent characters:

$$\sum_{i,j} \rho(x_i|x_j) \log \left(\frac{1}{\rho(x_i|x_j)} \right).$$

$\rho(x_i|x_j)$ means the probability that x_i follows x_j in the information stream. The sum is computed over all possible combinations. This measure does a good job of picking up some of the nature of the English language. The occurrence of a letter varies significantly. "h" is common after a "t" but not after a "q". This measure would also pick up the pattern in the example of $0, 1, 2, \ldots, 255, 0, 1, \ldots$. But there are many slightly more complicated patterns that could be generated by a simple computer program yet confound this second-order entropy calculation. Shannon defined the entropy of a stream to include all orders up to infinity. While it may be practical to compute the first- or second-order entropy of an information stream, the amount of space devoted to the project obviously becomes overwhelming. The number of terms in the summation grows exponentially with the order of the calculation. He created several experimental ways for estimating the entropy, but the limits of the model are still clear.

RSA Encryption

"Encryption and White Noise" on page 14 described RSA encryption with the metaphor of a long circle of beads. Here's the true mathematics. The system begins with two prime numbers p and q. Multiplying p and q together is easy, but no one knows of an efficient way to factor pq into its components p and q if the numbers are large (i.e., about 1024 to 2048 bits).

This is the basis of the security of the system. If you take a number x and compute the successive powers of x, then $x^{\psi(x)} \bmod pq = x$.[3] That is, if you keep multiplying a number by x modulo pq, then it returns to x after $\psi(x) + 1$ steps.

This $\psi(x)$ is called the *Euler Totient* function and it is the number of integers less than x that are relatively prime to x. If x is a prime number then $\psi(x)$ is $x - 1$ because all of the integers less than x are relatively prime to it. The values are commutative so $\psi(xy) = \psi(x)\psi(y)$. This means that $\psi(pq) = pq - p - q + 1$. For example, $\psi(15) = 8$. The numbers $1, 2, 4, 7, 8, 11, 13$ and 14 are relatively prime. The values $3, 5, 6, 9, 10$ and 12 are not.

Calculating the value of $\psi(pq)$ is easy if you know both p and q, but no one knows an efficient way to do it if you don't. This is the basis for the RSA algorithm. The circumference of this string of pearls or beads is $\psi(pq)$. Moving one bead along the string is the equivalent of multiplying by x.

---

[3] $x \bmod y$ means the remainder after x is divided by y. So 9 mod 7 is 2, 9 mod 3 is 0.

The two keys for the RSA are chosen so they both multiply together to give 1 modulo $\psi(pq)$. One is chosen at random and the other is calculated by finding the inverse of it. Call these e and d where $de = 1 \bmod \psi(pq)$. This means that:

$$x^{ed} \bmod pq = x.$$

Neal Koblitz's book, [Kob87], gives a good introduction to finding this inverse.

This can be converted into an encryption system very easily. To encrypt with this public key, calculate $x^e \bmod pq$. To decrypt, raise this answer to the d power. That is, compute:

$$(x^e \bmod pq)^d \bmod pq = x^{de} \bmod pq = x.$$

This fulfills all of the promises of the public-key encryption system. There is one key, e, that can be made public. Anyone can encrypt a message using this value. No one can decrypt it, however, unless they know d. This value is kept private.

The most direct attack on RSA is to find the value of $\psi(pq)$. This can be done if you can factor pq into p and q. There is no better computational approach that anyone knows.

Actually implementing RSA for encryption requires attention to a number of details. Here are some of the most important ones in no particular order:

Converting Messages into Numbers Data is normally stored as bytes. RSA can encrypt any integer that is less than pq. So there needs to be a solid method of converting a collection of bytes into and out of integers less than pq. The simplest solution is to glue together bytes until the string of bytes is a number that is greater than pq. Then remove one byte and replace it with random bits so that the value is just less than pq. To convert back to bytes, simply remove this padding.

[BFHMV84], [Bri82], [Mon85], and [QC82] discuss efficient multiplication algorithms.

Fast Modulo Computation Computing $x^e \bmod pq$ does not require multiplying x together e times. This would be prohibitive because e could be quite large. An easier solution is to compute $x, x^2 \bmod pq$, $x^4 \bmod pq, x^8 \bmod pq, \ldots$. That is, keep squaring x. Then choose the right subset of them to multiply together to get $x^e \bmod pq$. This subset is easy to determine. If the ith bit of the binary expansion of e is 1, then multiply in $x^{2^i} \bmod pq$ into the final answer.

Finding Large Prime Numbers The security of the RSA system depends upon how easy it is to factor pq. If both p and q are large prime numbers, then this is difficult. Identifying large prime numbers is, as luck would have it, pretty easy to do. There are a number of tests for primality that work quite well. The solution is just to choose a really large, odd number at random and then test it to see if it is prime. If it isn't, then choose another. The length of time it takes to find a prime number close to an integer x is roughly proportional to the number of bits in x.

The Lehman test [Leh82] is a simple way to determine if n is prime. To do so, choose a random number a and compute $a^{(n-1)/2} \bmod n$. If this value is not 1 or -1, then n is not prime. Each value of a has at least a 50% chance of showing up a nonprime number. If we repeat this test m times, then we're sure that we have a 1 in 2^m chance that n is not prime, but we haven't found an a that would prove it yet. Making $m = 100$ is a good starting point. It is not absolute proof, but it is good enough.

RSA encryption is a very popular algorithm used for public-key encryption. There are also a large number of other algorithms that are available. The discussion of these variants is beyond the scope of this book. Both Bruce Schneier's book, [Sch94], and Gus Simmons' book [ed.92] offer good surveys.

Summary

Pure encryption algorithms are the best way to convert data into white noise. This alone is a good way to hide the information in the data. It is also the basis for all of the other algorithms used in steganography. The algorithms that take a block of data and hide it in the noise of an image or sound file need data that is as close to random as possible. This lowers the chance that it can be detected. Each chapter will end with a summary list of the ideas described in the chapter, their security and pointers for how to start implementing the code.

The Disguise Good encryption turns data into white noise that appears random. This is a good beginning for many algorithms that use the data as a random source to imitate the world.

How Secure Is It? The best encryption algorithms described here
have no practical attack known to the public. These algorithms are
designed and evaluated solely on their ability to resist attack.

How To Use It? Encryption code can be downloaded from a number of places on the Net. Jack Lacy at AT&T Bell Labs dis-
tributes one set of routines that offers big-number mathematics
for algorithms like RSA and implementations of many of the
most popular algorithms. Write `cryptolib@research.att.com`
for information. The source code for PGP is also widely distributed. A good source for this is the cypherpunks archive.
(`ftp://ftp.csua.berkeley.edu/pub/cypherpunks/Home.html`)

Chapter 3

Error Correction

Close but No Cigar

1. Speedwalking.
2. America OnLine, CompuServe and Prodigy.
3. Veggie burgers.
4. Using a Stairmaster.
5. Winning the Wild Card pennant.
6. Driving 55 mph.
7. Living in suburbia.
8. New Year's Resolutions.
9. Lists as poetry.
10. Lists as a simple way to give structure to humor.
11. Cigarettes.

Correcting Errors

The theory of computers rests on an immutable foundation: a bit is either on ("1") or off ("0"). Underneath this foundation, however, is the normal, slightly random, slightly chaotic world in which humans spend their time. Just as the sun is sometimes a bit brighter than usual and sometimes it rains for a week straight, the physics that govern computer hardware are a bit random. Sometimes that spot on the hard disk that is responsible for remembering something doesn't behave exactly perfectly. Sometimes an alpha particle from outer space screams through a chip and changes the answer.

Computer designers manage to corral all of this randomness through a mixture of precision and good mathematics. Clean machines eliminate the dirt that screws up things and the mathematics of error-correcting codes is responsible for fixing up the rest of the problems that slip through. This mathematics is really one of the ideas that is most responsible for the digital explosion. The math makes it possible to build a digital circuit with a bit of sloppiness that can never be present in an analog world. Designers know that the sloppiness can be fixed by a bit of clever mathematics.

Error-correcting codes can be used effectively to hide information in a number of important ways. The most obvious approach is to simply introduce small errors into a file in an organized way. If someone tries to read the file with ordinary tools, the error correction would patch up these changes and no one would be the wiser. More sophisticated tools could find these changes by comparing the original file with the cleaned-up version or simply using the error-correcting principles to point the location. The message could be encoded in the position of the errors.

Error-correcting codes can also be used to help two people share a channel. Many semi-public data streams make ideal locations to hide information. It might be possible to insert bits in a photograph or a music file that floats around on the Internet by grabbing the file and replacing it with a copy that includes your message. This works well until someone else has the same idea. Suddenly one message could overwrite another. An ideal solution would be to arrange it so no one took up more than a small fraction of a channel like this one. Then, they would write their information with an error-correcting code. If two messages interacted, they would still only damage a fraction of each other's bits and the error-correcting code would be used to fix it. This is the same way that the codes are used in many radio systems.

Page 169 shows how to construct a system using random walks.

On occasion, it makes sense to split a message into a number of different parts to be shipped through different channels. Ideally, the message could be reconstructed if a few of the parts were compromised along the way. The part could either be lost or scrambled by a malicious courier. In either case, error-correcting codes can defend against this problem.

A system of error-correcting codes comes in any number of flavors. Many of the most commonly used codes have the ability to carry k bits in a packet of n bits and find the right answer if no more than m errors have been made. There are many different possible codes that come with different values of k, n, and m, but you never get anything for free. If you have 7 bits and you want each block to carry at least 4 bits of information, then one standard code can only correct up to one error per block. If you want to carry 6 bits of information in a 7-bit block, then you can't successfully correct errors and you can only detect them half of the time.

The best metaphor for understanding error-correcting codes is to think about spheres. Imagine that each letter in a message is represented as the center of a sphere. There are 26 spheres for each letter and none of them overlap. You send a message by sending the coordinates to this point at the center. Occasionally a transmission glitch might nudge the coordinates a bit. When the recipient decodes the message, he or she can still get the correct text if the nudges are small enough so the points remain inside the sphere. The search for the best error-correcting codes involves finding the best way to pack these spheres so that you can fit the most spheres in a space and transmit the most characters.

Although the mathematicians talk about sphere packing on an abstract level, it is not immediately obvious how this applies to the digital world where everything is made up of binary numbers that are on or off. How do you nudge a zero a little bit? If you nudge it enough, when does it becomes a one? How do you nudge a number like 252, which is 11111100 in binary? Obviously a small nudge could convert this into 111111101, which is 253. But what if the error came along when the first bit was going through the channel. If the first bit was changed the the number would become 011111100. That is 114, a change of 128, which certainly doesn't seem small. That would imply that the spheres really couldn't be packed too closely together.

The solution is to think about the bits independently and to measure the distance between two numbers as the number of bits that are different. So 11111100 and 11111101 are one unit apart because they differ in only one bit. So are 11111100 and 01111100. But 01111100 and

Better secret splitting solutions are found in Chapter 4.

11111101 are two units apart. This distance is often called the *Hamming distance*.

This measure has the same feel as finding the distance between two corners in a city that is laid out on a Manhattan-like grid. The distance between the corner at 10th Avenue and 86th Street and the corner at 9th Avenue and 83rd Street is 4 blocks, although in Manhattan they are blocks of different lengths. You just sum up the differences along each of the different dimensions. In the street example, there are two dimensions that are the avenues that run north and south or the streets that run east and west. In the numerical example, each bit position is a different dimension and the 8 bit examples above have eight dimensions.

The simplest example of an error-correcting code uses 3 bits to encode each bit of data. The code can correct one error in a bit but not two. There are eight possible combinations of three bits: 000, 001, 010, 011, 100, 101, 110, and 111. You can think of these as the eight corners of a cube as shown in Figure 3.1. A message 0 can be encoded as "000" and a 1 can be encoded as "111". Imagine there is an error and the "000" was converted into a "001". The closest possible choice, "000", is easy to identify. The sphere of "000" includes all points that

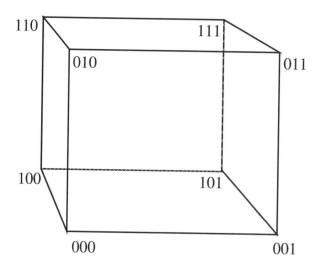

Figure 3.1. The eight corners of the cube. The two corners, 000 and 111, are used to send the message of either 0 or 1. If there is an error in one bit, then it can be recovered by finding the closest corner.

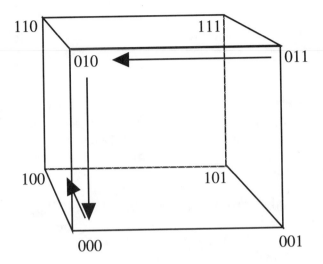

Figure 3.2. The Hamming distance shows that the corner "011" is three steps or units away from "100". That's the longest distance in this cube.

are at most one Hamming unit away: 001, 010, and 100. Two errors, however, would nudge a point into the adjacent sphere.

Obviously, the technique can be extended into higher-dimensional spaces. The trick is to find an optimal number of points that can be packed into a space. For instance, imagine a five-dimensional space made up of the points 00000, 00001, 00010, ..., 11111. Every point has an opposite point that is five units away from it. 00000 is five steps away from 11111 and 10111 is five units away from 01000. It is easy to construct a sphere with a radius of two units around each point. That means 0 could be encoded as 00000 and 1 would be encoded as 11111. Up to two errors could occur and the correct answer would be found. 10110 is two units away from 11111, so it would fall in its sphere of influence and be decoded as a 1.

Generally, odd-dimensional spaces are much better than even-dimensional spaces for this simple scheme. Imagine the six-dimensional space created from the points 000000, 000001, 000010, ..., 111111. Both 000000 and 111111 are six units apart. But if you draw a sphere of radius 3 around each point, then the spheres overlap. The point 010101, for instance, is both three units away from 000000 and three units away from 111111. It's in both spheres. If you were to try and construct an error-correcting code using this arrangement, then you would only be able to fit two spheres of radius 2 in the space and the code would only be able to resist up to two errors per block. Obviously the 5-bit code in the five-dimensional space is just as error-resistant while being more efficient.

There is no reason why you need to only pack two spheres into each space. You might want to fit in many smaller spheres. In seven-dimensional space, you can fit in two spheres of radius 3 centered around any two points that are seven units apart. But you can also fit in a large number of spheres that have a radius of only 1. For instance, you can place spheres with a single unit radius around 0000000, 0000111, 1110000, 0011001, 1001100, 1010001, and 1000101. None of these spheres overlap and the space is not full. You could also add a sphere centered around 1111110. There are eight code words here, so eight different messages or 3 bits of information could be stored in each 7-bit code word. Up to one bit error could be found and resolved.

In general, packing these higher-dimensional spaces is quite difficult to do optimally. It should be clear that there are many other points that are not in any of eight different spheres. This reflects a gross inefficiency. "Constructing Error-Correcting Codes" on page 40

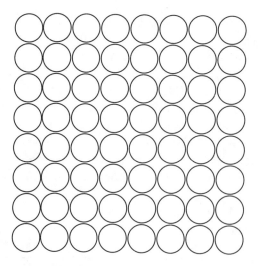

Figure 3.3. A poor way to pack circles. If the system error can't shift the signal more than the radius of the sphere, then the space between the circles is wasted. Figure 3.4 shows a better approach.

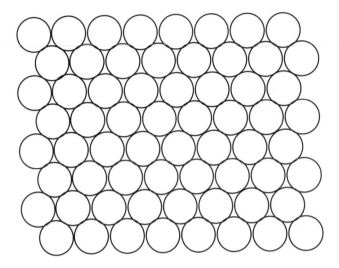

Figure 3.4. A better approach to packing the circles from Figure 3.3. This is about 86.6% of the original height. It is wider by one half of the radius of a circle.

describes how to build general Hamming codes. It is possible to use the algorithm given there to construct an error-correcting code that packs 4 bits of information, or 16 different messages, into one 7-bit code word. That's one extra bit of data. The code can also resist up to 1 bit of error. The 16 centers generated by this method are:

$$
\begin{array}{cccc}
0000000 & 0001111 & 0010011 & 0011100 \\
0100101 & 0101010 & 0110110 & 0111001 \\
1000110 & 1001001 & 1010101 & 1011010 \\
1100011 & 1101100 & 1110000 & 1111111
\end{array}
$$

There are many other types of error-correcting codes. The metaphor of sphere packing is a good way to understand the basic idea, but it offers little guidance on how it can be done effectively. It is easy to imagine stacking pool balls in a rack, but it is impossible to visualize how to do this in multiple dimensions—especially if the Hamming distance is used.

In practice, error-correcting codes rest upon algorithms that take the data and add extra *parity bits* that can be used to recover the data. The parity bits "puff up" the data into more dimensions and move the points away from each other. For instance, in four dimensions the points 1110 and 1111 are right next to each other. But if three parity bits are added to the end of each one, the result, 1110000 and 1111111, are four units apart.

If you look carefully at the table on page 37, the first four bits represent all of the possible points in a four-dimensional space. The last three bits are parity bits that were added to puff it out into seven dimensions.

The location of the parity bits varies significantly between different codes. Some codes can correct a certain number of errors that occur anywhere in a block of data. Other codes can correct errors that happen in bursts. They might be able to correct only one burst of errors, but the burst can contain anywhere between one flipped bit and an upper limit of k. If the errors don't occur next to each other, however, then the code can't fix the error. Each of these different codes place the parity bits in different arrangements to grab different types of errors.

The rest of this book will rely upon error-correcting codes to add robustness to protocols, perhaps add randomness, and provide another way to split information into a number of different parts. Using error-correcting codes is essential if information might bump into other information in channels.

Error Correction and White Noise

Error-correcting codes may be intended to correct errors, but they can also be used to make a bitstream conform to some pattern. Once a collection of bits is encoded in an error-correcting code then changes can be introduced without destroying the underlying information. These changes might add randomness or, with some difficulty, make the data conform to a pattern.

In practice, the best choice for this approach is error-correcting codes that can sustain a high number of errors. A simple choice might be the 3-bit error-correcting code that conveys one bit. You write 000, 001, 010, or 100 for the 0 bit and 111, 110, 101, or 011 for the 1 bit. Any of the three are acceptable choices. This will triple the size of the file, but it will allow plenty of flexibility in rearranging the structure of the data.

Adding randomness is easy, but there are limitations to making the data fit some other pattern. Obviously the underlying data must come close enough to the pattern so that errors can be introduced successfully. In an abstract sense, the pattern must fall into the spheres. The bigger the spheres, the more patterns that can work successfully. For instance, you could easily use the 3-bit code described above to produce a bitstream that never had more than three ones or three zeros occur in a row. Each bit could be encoded with a pattern that started with a 1 or a 0. On the other hand, you could not produce a pattern that required that there were always five ones or zeros in a row.

This technique can be taken one step further that takes it outside of the realm of error-correcting codes entirely. If you're planning to use the error-correcting codes to give you enough room to add some randomness to the data, then you're going to lose many of the error-correcting properties. For instance, one flipped bit can convert 110, a value representing 1, into 010, a value representing 0. In essence, you might want to forget about the error-correcting ability altogether and just construct a list of codes that represent each bit. 1 might be encoded as 001, 100, 011, and 111 while 0 would be encoded as 110, 101, 010, and 000. The main advantage of this approach is that the distribution of zeros and ones can be even more balanced. In the 3-bit code used as an example in this section, there are an average of 2.25 bits used to encode a 1 and .75 used to encode a 0. This means a file with a high percentage of ones, for instance, will still have a high percentage after the encoding. Using random codes assigned to each bit can remove this bias. But this is drifting away from the focus of the chapter.

Error Correction and Secret Sharing

Error-correcting codes have a functional cousin known as *secret sharing*. That is, a class of algorithms that allow a file be split into m parts so that only $m - k$ parts are necessary to reconstruct it. Obviously, an error-correcting code that could handle up to k errors in m bits would work very similarly. Simply encode the file using this method and then break up the m bits into m different files.

There is one problem with this approach. Some bits are more privileged than others in some error-correcting schemes. For instance, the next section on Hamming codes describes a code that takes 11 bits and adds 4 parity bits that will correct any single error. Ideally, a file encoded with this code could be broken into 15 parts and any 14 parts would suffice to recover the data. But, there are only 11 bits of data in every block of 15 bits. The other 4 parity bits are just used to correct the errors. If the *i*th bit of each block always went in the *i*th part, then the right 11 parts would suffice. The key is to distribute the bits so this never happens. Here are the steps:

1. Choose an error-correcting code that offers the right recovery properties. It is easy to find Hamming codes that recover single errors.
2. Encode the file using this technique.
3. If there are *n* bits in each block and *n* files, then place one bit from each block in each file. That is, place bit *i* in file $i + j$ mod *n*. The choice of *j* should vary with each block. It can either increase sequentially or be chosen by a random number generator. If a random number generator is used, it should be a pseudo-random number generator that can be reseeded to recover the information later.

For most practical purposes, error-correcting codes are not ideal ways to share secrets. While it is easy to construct a Hamming code that can sustain one error, it is pretty inefficient to generate an error-correcting code that contains *n* bits per block and still survive, say, $n - 2$ errors. The theory is just not optimized around this solution.

More detailed information on secret sharing can be found in Chapter 4.

Better secret-sharing technique emerges directly from geometry. Imagine that you encode a message as a point in a plane. One solution is to draw three lines through the point and distribute the lines to different people. Two lines are enough to reconstruct the point. The process can be turned into an error-correcting code by simply choosing the one point that represents the largest intersection of lines. If you want to encode larger amounts of data, you can use higher-dimensional spaces and use planes or higher dimensions. This is close to what the Hamming codes are doing, but it is difficult to think in these terms when only bits are being used.

Constructing Error-Correcting Codes

[Ara88] and [LJ83] were the source for this material. More information can be found there.

Hamming codes are easy and elegant error-correcting codes. Constructing them and using them is relatively easy. The problem can be thought of as taking your incoming message bits and then adding parity bits that will allow you to correct the errors. The net effect is to create an overdetermined collection of linear equations that can be solved in only one way.

Table 3.1. Output Bit: Where It Comes From

b_{0001}	$a_1 + a_2 + a_4 + a_5 + a_7 + a_9 + a_{11}$ mod 2
b_{0010}	$a_1 + a_3 + a_4 + a_6 + a_7 + a_{10} + a_{11}$ mod 2
b_{0011}	a_1
b_{0100}	$a_2 + a_3 + a_4 + a_8 + a_9 + a_{10} + a_{11}$ mod 2
b_{0101}	a_2
b_{0110}	a_3
b_{0111}	a_4
b_{1000}	$a_5 + a_6 + a_7 + a_8 + a_9 + a_{10} + a_{11}$ mod 2
b_{1001}	a_5
b_{1010}	a_6
b_{1011}	a_7
b_{1100}	a_8
b_{1101}	a_9
b_{1110}	a_{10}
b_{1111}	a_{11}

The easiest way to introduce the algorithm is by constructing an example code that takes 11 bits and adds 4 new parity bits to the mix so that an error of at most one bit can be corrected if it occurs. The input bits will be $a_1, \ldots, a_{11}$. The output bits are $b_1, \ldots, b_{15}$. For the purpose of illustrating the algorithm, it is easier to use binary subscripts: b_{0001} through b_{1111}.

The best way to illustrate the process is with a table of the output bits. The input bits are simply copied over into an output slot with a different number. This is easy to do in hardware if you happened to be implementing such an algorithm in silicon. The extra parity bits are computed by adding up different sets of the input bits modulo 2. They are found in output bits b_{0001}, b_{0010}, b_{0100}, and b_{1000}.

Errors are detected by calculating four formulas that will give the location of the error:

$$c_0 = b_{0001} + b_{0011} + b_{0101} + b_{0111} + b_{1001} + b_{1011} + b_{1101} \text{ mod } 2$$

$$c_1 = b_{0010} + b_{0011} + b_{0110} + b_{0111} + b_{1010} + b_{1011} + b_{1110} + b_{1111} \text{ mod } 2$$

$$c_2 = b_{0100} + b_{0101} + b_{0110} + b_{0111} + b_{1100} + b_{1101} + b_{1110} + b_{1111} \text{ mod } 2$$

$$c_3 = b_{1000} + b_{1000} + b_{1001} + b_{1010} + b_{1011} + b_{1100} + b_{1101} + b_{1110}$$

$$+ \, b_{1111} \text{ mod } 2$$

These four equations yield 4 bits. If they're combined into a single number, then they'll reveal the location of an error. For instance, imagine that bit b_{1011} was flipped by an error. This is the incoming bit a_7 and this bit is part of the equation that produces parity bits b_{1000}, b_{0010}, and b_{0001}. The pattern should be obvious. The parity bits are stuck at slots that have only a single 1 in the binary value of their subscript. A normal bit is added into the equation by examining the binary value of its subscript. If there is a 1 at position i, then it is added into the parity bit that has a 1 at position i. b_{1011} has three 1's, so it ends up in four equations.

The effect of an error in b_{1011} is easy to follow. b_{0001} will not match the sum $b_{0011} + b_{0101} + b_{0111} + b_{1001} + b_{1011} + b_{1101}$. This will mean that c_0 will evaluate to 1. The same effect will set $c_1 = 1$ and $c_3 = 1$. c_2 will stay zero. If these are combined in the proper order, 1011, then they point directly at bit b_{1011}.

These equations will also correct errors that occur in the parity bits. If one of these should be flipped, then only one of the equations will produce a 1. The rest will yield zeros because the parity bits are not part of their equations.

The general steps for constructing such an error-correcting code for n bits can be summarized:

1. Find the smallest k such that $2^k - k - 1 \le n$. This set of equations will encode $2^k - k - 1$ bits and produce $2^k - 1$ bits.

2. Enumerate the output bits with binary subscripts: $b_{00...01}, \ldots, b_{11...11}$.

3. The parity bits will be the output bits with a single 1 in their subscript.

4. Assign the input bits to the nonparity output bits. Any order will suffice, but there is no reason not to be neat and do it in order.

5. Compute the parity bit with a 1 at position i by adding up all of the output bits with a 1 at the same position i *except* the parity bit itself. Do the addition modulo 2.

6. To decode, compute c_i which is the sum of all output bits that have a 1 in position i *including* the parity bit. This will yield a 0 if the parity bit matches and a 1 if it doesn't. Aggregating the c_i values will reveal the position of the error. This code will only detect one error.

What is the most efficient choice of k for this algorithm? Given that the number of parity bits is proportional to the log of the number of input bits, it is tempting to lump the entire file into one big block and use only a small number of parity bits. This requires a large number of additions. There are about $\frac{n \log n}{2}$ additions in a block of n bits. Large blocks require fewer parity bits but need more computation. They also only correct one error in the entire block and this substantially limits their usefulness. The best tradeoff must be based upon the noisiness of the channel carrying the information.

Implementations of Hamming codes like this one are often fastest when they are done a word at a time. Most CPUs including all of the major ones have instructions that will do a bitwise XOR of an instruction word, which is usually either 32 or 64 bits long. XOR is addition modulo 2. These fast XORs provide a good way of doing up to 32 or 64 encodings in parallel. This is done by using all of the above equations, but doing the calculations with words instead of bits and XOR instead of basic arithmetic.

This approach is a very fast way to encode the error-correcting bits and it is a quick way to detect errors, but correcting the error can be slow. Testing for errors can be done just by seeing if all of the c_i values are zero. If one of the c_i is not zero, then the code must step through each of the bits individually and compute the location of the errors. This is much slower, but not any slower than computing the code in a bitwise fashion.

The Hamming codes described in this section are particularly elegant, in my opinion, because of the way that the results of the c_i are aggregated to find the location of the error. This is simply a result of the arrangements of the parity bits. The same basic algorithm could be used no matter what order the bits were found. Any permutation of the bits b_{0001} through b_{1111} would work. The recovery process wouldn't be as elegant.

This elegant arrangement is not really necessary for hardware-based implementations because the correction of the error does not need to be done by converting the c_i values into an index that points to the error. It is quite possible to simply create a set of AND gates for each bit that looks for a perfect match. This means the parity bits could be placed at the beginning or the end of each block. This might simplify stripping them out.

Periodic Codes

The codes described in the previous section only correct one bit error per block. This may suffice, but it can be pretty inefficient if the block sizes are small. The Hamming codes need three parity bits to correct one error in four bits. That's almost a 50% loss just to correct one bit out of four.

The Hamming codes are also less than optimal because of the nature of noise that can corrupt digital data. The errors may not be randomly distributed. They are often grouped in one big burst that might occur after an electrical jolt or some other physical event disrupts the stream. A scratch on a CD-ROM may blur several bits that are right next to each other. These errors would screw up any Hamming solution that is limited to correcting one bit in each block.

Periodic codes are a better solution for these occasions that demand detecting and recovering errors that occur in bursts. In this case, the parity bits will be distributed at regular intervals throughout the stream of bits. For instance, every fourth bit in a stream might be a parity bit that is computed from some of the previous bits. As before, the location of the parity bits can be varied if the number of parity bits per set of bits is kept constant, but it is often cleaner to arrange for them to occur periodically.

The Hamming codes are designed to work with predefined blocks of bits. The convolutional codes described here will work with rolling blocks of bits that overlap. The same convolutional technique will also work with fixed blocks, but it is left out here for simplicity. To avoid confusion, this section will use the word *subblock* to refer to the smaller sets of bits that are used to create the rolling block.

The periodic code will consist of a subblock of bits followed by a set of parity bits that are computed from the bits that are present in any number of the preceding subblocks. The parity might also depend on some of the bits in the following subblocks, but this configuration is left out in the interest of simplicity.

A simple set of bits from a convolutional code might look like this:

$$b_{(i,1)}, \; b_{(i,2)}, \; b_{(i,3)}, \; b_{(i,4)}, \; b_{(i,5)}, \; p_{(i,1)}.$$

Here, $b_{(i,1)}$ stands for the first data bit in block i. $p_{(i,1)}$ is the first parity bit. There are five data bits and one parity bit in this example.

The parity bit could be any function of the bits in the previous subblocks. For simplicity, let

$$p_{(i,1)} = b_{(i,1)} + b_{(i-1,2)} + b_{(i-2,3)} + b_{(i-3,4)} + b_{(i-4,5)} \bmod 2.$$

That is, each parity bit is affected by one of the bits in the previous five blocks.

These parity bits can detect one burst of up to five bits that occurs in each rolling set of five subblocks. That means that the error will be detected if every two error bursts have at least five subblocks between them. The error, once detected, can be fixed by asking for a retransmission of the data. It can also be recovered in some cases that will be described later.

The error can be detected by watching the trail it leaves in the parity bits that follow it. A burst of errors in this case might affect any of the five parity bits that come after it. When the parity bits don't match, the previous set of five subblocks can be retransmitted to fix the problem. It should be simple to see how spreading out the parity bits makes it possible for the code system to detect bursts of errors. None of the equations used to calculate the parity bits depends upon neighboring bits. In this example, there are at least five bits in the bitstream between each of the bits used to calculate each parity bit. In the Hamming example, each of the parity equations depended on some adjacent bits. If both of those bits were flipped because of a burst of error noise, then the errors would cancel out and the error would be recoverable.

Recovering a parity error is normally not possible with a simple code like this example. If one of the parity bits doesn't agree in this example, then the error could have been introduced by an error in six different bits. Finding which one is impossible. To some extent, a larger burst of errors will make the job easier. For instance, if three bits in a row are flipped, then three consecutive parity bits will also be flipped. If the parity bits are examined individually, then each one could have been caused by up to six different errors. But periodic codes like this are designed to handle bursts of errors. So it is acceptable to assume that the three errors would be adjacent to each other. This limits the location to two different spots.

For instance, here is a data stream with correct parity bits:

... 01010 0 01010 1 1001 1 01111 1 00011 1 ...

If the first three bits are flipped, then the first three parity bits are also flipped:

$$\ldots \; 10110 \; 1 \; 01010 \; 0 \; 11001 \; 0 \; 01111 \; 1 \; 00011 \; 1 \; \ldots$$

Each individual error could occur in any of the previous five blocks, but the overlapping nature of the code limits the error to either the first block shown here or either of the two blocks that preceded it. If five bits were flipped in a row, then the exact location would be known and it would be possible to correct the errors. This pushes the code to an extreme and it would be better not to hope for bursts to come at the extreme limit of the ability of the codes to detect the errors.

Both [LJ83] and [Ara88] are good sources of more information about error-correcting codes.

The periodic code described in this section is a good way to detect bursts of errors, but it cannot help correct them unless the burst is at the extreme. There is some information available, but it is clearly not enough to recover the data.

Summary

Error-correcting codes are one of the most important tools for building digital systems. They allow electronic designers to correct the random errors that emerge from nature and provide the user with some digital precision. If the electronics were really required to offer perfect accuracy, then they would prohibitively expensive.

These codes are useful for correcting problems that emerge from the transmission systems. It might be desirable, for instance, for several people to use the same channel. If several people use a small part of the channel chosen at random, then the codes will correct any occasional collisions.

The Disguise If you want to use these codes to hide information, the best solution is to screw up a small subset of bits. If each block has 8 bits, for instance, the you can send 3 bits per block. If you want to send 000, then flip bit 0. If you want to send 011, then flip bit 3, and so on. When the bits are finally read at the other end, the error-correcting codes will remove the errors and the casual reader won't even know that they were there. You can use the error-correcting codes to recover them.

How Secure Is It? Error-correcting codes are not secure at all against people who want to read them. The patterns between the bits are easy to detect. They are quite resistant, however, against errors.

How To Use Them? There are not many error-correcting code packages out there. But I believe that there might be a need for them. I've had too many backup floppy disks ruined by random errors. One flipped bit can ruin an entire compressed file. There should be an option to add error correction. If these packages become common, then I believe it will be easy to use this software.

Chapter 4

Secret Sharing

Two out of Three Musketeers

In Bob's Manhattan Living Room, three high school chums are confronting a middle age crisis over scotch and soda. They're all lawyers and disenchanted by the way that money and corruption have ruined the justice system. So, inspired by movies like Batman, *they decide to recreate* The Three Musketeers *and prowl about the night looking for people in need of help.*

Bob: Okay. It's settled. We'll file for our license to carry concealed weapons tomorrow. On Friday, we pick out our Glocks.

Harry: Yes. 9mm.

Together: All for one and one for all!

Harry: You know, I just thought of something. My wife promised we would go to dinner at her cousin's house on Friday. She planned it last month. Could we get the Glocks another day?

Bob: Sunday's out for me. We're going to my mother's house after church.

Mark: Well, doesn't fighting evil count for something in the eyes of God?

Bob: Yes. But I still think we need a contingency. We're not going to always be available. There will be business trips, family visits, emergencies.

Mark: This is a good point. We might be stuck in traffic or held up in court. We need a plan.

Harry:	Well, what if we said, "All available for one and one for who's there that evening?"
Mark:	Not bad. It's more flexible. But what if just one of us is there?
Harry:	What's the difference?
Mark:	That one person really wouldn't be a group. He would be acting as a vigilante. He could do anything he wanted that evening. Maybe even something that was less than just.
Harry:	So you want a quorum?
Mark:	Yes. I say two out of three of us should be there before someone can start invoking the name of the Three Musketeers.
Bob:	What about costumes? What do we wear if we're alone?
Mark:	Doesn't matter. The most important thing is what we shout as we vanquish the foes. Are we together on this?
Together:	Two out of Three for One and One for Two out of Three!

Splitting Up Secrets

There are many occasions when you need to split a key or a secret into numerous puzzle parts so that the secret can only be recovered if all of the parts are available. This is a good way to force people to work together. Many nuclear weapons systems, for instance, require two people to turn two different keys simultaneously. Bank safe deposit boxes have two locks and one key is held by the owner and the other is held by the bank.[1]

There are many neat ways to mathematically split a secret into a number of parts. This secret might be the key to an encrypted file or it might be the important factoid itself. The goal is to create n different files or numbers that must all be present to reconstruct the original number. There are also threshold schemes that let you recover the secret if you have some smaller subset of the original parts. If a corporation has five directors, for instance, you might require that three be present to unlock the corporation's secret key used to sign documents.

---

[1]It is not clear to me why the bank needs to have its own key on the box. The combination to the vault serves the same purpose.

The mathematics of these schemes is really quite simple and intuitive. Chapter 3 showed how error-correcting codes can be used to serve as primitive secret-sharing devices. That is, you can split up a secret by encoding it with a error-correcting code that can correct wrong bits. (The 7-bit code from page 41 shows how you can split up a secret into seven parts so that it can be recovered if any six parts are available.)

There are numerous problems with this approach. First, some bits are often more privileged than others. In the 7-bit scheme from Chapter 3 four of the seven bits hold the original message. The other three are parity bits. If the right four are put together, then the original secret is unveiled. If one of these bits is missing, however, then the parity bits are needed to get the secret.

Second, there can be some redundancy that allows people to unveil the secret even if they don't hold all of the parts. For instance, the 3-bit error correcting code described on page 35 can recover the correct answer even if one of the three bits is changed. This is because each bit is essentially turned into three copies of itself. If these three copies were split into three parts, then they wouldn't prevent each person from knowing the secret. They would have it in their hands. Their part was an exact copy of the whole. This example is an extreme, but the same redundancies can exist in other versions.

A better solution is to use algorithms designed to split up secrets so they can't be recovered unless the correct number of parts are available. There are many different algorithms available to do this, but most of them are geometric in nature. This means that it is often easy to understand them with figures and diagrams.

Deliberately adding errors is one way to prevent this.

Requiring All Parts

Many of the algorithms described later in this section can recover a secret split into n parts if only k parts are available. There are many times when you might want to require that all parts be present. There are good algorithms that work quite well when $n = k$, but are not flexible to handle cases when k is less than n. These simple algorithms are described here before explaining the other solutions.

The most straightforward approach is to imitate the safe deposit boxes and use n layers of encryption. If $f(k_i, X)$ encrypts a message X with key k_i, then you can simply take the secret and encrypt it repeatedly with each of n different keys. That is, compute:

$$f(k_1, f(k_2, f(k_3, \ldots f(k_n, X) \ldots))).$$

Each person gets one of the n keys and it should be obvious that the secret can't be recovered unless all of them are present. If one is missing, then the chain is broken and the layers of encryption can't be stripped off.

A simpler approach is to think of the secret as a number, X, and then split it into n parts that all add up to that number, $X_1 + X_2 + X_3 + \cdots + X_n = X$. If one number is missing, it is impossible to determine what X might be. This solution is an extension of the one-time pad and it is just as secure. There is no way that the people who hold the $n - 1$ parts can guess what the value of the missing part might be.

In practice, this solution is often computed for each bit in the secret. That is, the secret is split into n parts. If the first bits of the parts are added together, they will reveal the first bit of the secret. If the second bits of the different parts are added together, the result is the second bit of the secret. This addition is done modulo 2, so you're really just determining whether there is an odd or even number of ones in the bits. Here's an example:

$$X_1 = 101010100$$

$$X_2 = 101011010$$

$$X_3 = 110010010$$

$$X_4 = 010101100$$

$$X_1 + X_2 + X_3 + X_4 = 100110000$$

If you wanted to split up a secret, then you would generate the first $n - 1$ parts at random. Then you would compute X_n so that $X_1 + \cdots + X_n = X$. This is actually easy. $X_n = X + X_1 + \cdots + X_{n-1}$.

This solution is used to split up the secrets in the U.S. government's key escrow procedure.

Are both of these solutions equally secure? The addition method, which is just an extension of the one-time pad, is perfectly secure. There is no way that the system can be broken if you don't have access to all of the parts. There is no additional pattern. The layers of encryption are not necessarily as secure. There are so many different variables in the choice of encryption function and the size of the keys, that some choices might be breakable. If the basic function, f, however is secure

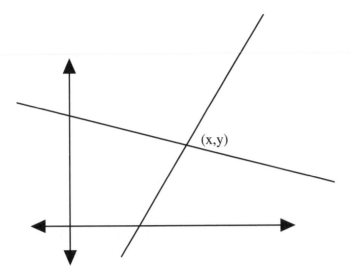

Figure 4.1. A secret, x, is split into two parts by finding two random lines that intersect at (x, y). (y is chosen at random.)

enough to use for basic encryption, then it should be secure in this case.[2] Surprisingly, the simplest approach is the best in this case.

Letting Parts Slide

Obviously there are many reasons why you might want to recover some secret if you don't have all of the parts. The simplest algorithms are based on simple geometry. Imagine that your secret is a number, x. Now, choose an arbitrary value for y and join the two values together so they represent a point on a plane. To split up this secret into two parts, just pick two lines at random that go through the point. See Figure 4.1. The secret can be recovered if the intersection of the two lines are found. If only one line is available, then no knows what the secret might be.

If there are two lines, then both parts need to be available to find the solution. This technique can be extended so there are n parts, but any two parts are enough to recover the secret. Simply choose n lines

Gus Simmons' chapter on Shared Secrets in [Sim93] is a great introduction to the topic.

---

[2]There are many interesting and unanswered questions about what happens if the same system is used to encrypt data over and over again with different keys. Some beginning papers include [CW93].

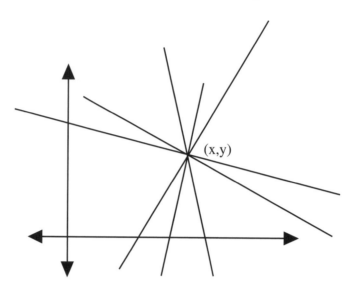

Figure 4.2. A secret, x, is split into n parts by finding n random lines that intersect at (x, y). (y is chosen at random.) Any pair is enough to recover the secret.

that go through (x, y) at random. Any pair will intersect at (x, y) and allow someone to recover the secret as in Figure 4.2.

When the secret must be split into n parts and any k must be available to recover the secret, then the same approach can be used if the geometry is extended into k dimensions. If $k = 3$, then planes are used instead of lines. Three planes will only intersect at the point. Two planes will form a line when they intersect. The point (x, y, z) will be somewhere along the line, but it is impossible to determine where it is.

It is also possible to flip this process on its head. Instead of hiding the secret as the intersection point of several lines, you can make the line the secret and distribute points along it. The place where the line meets the y axis might be the secret. Or it could be the slope of the line. In either case, knowing two points along the line will reveal the secret. Figure 4.3 shows this approach.

Stephan Brands uses this technique in his digital cash scheme [Bra93].

Each of these systems offers a pretty simple way to split up a secret key or a file so that some subset of people must be present. It should be easy to see that the geometric systems that hide the secret as the

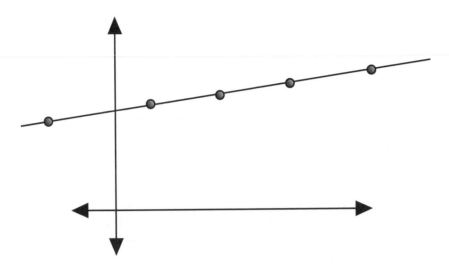

Figure 4.3. Here the secret is the line itself. Random points along the line are distributed as the parts of the secret. You must have two to recover the line.

intersection point are as secure as a one-time pad. If you only have one line, then it is impossible to guess where the intersection lies along this line. $x = 23$ is just as likely as $x = 41243$. In fact, owning one part gives you no more insight into the secret than owning no part. In either case, all you know is that it is some value of x. This is often called a *perfect* secret-sharing system.

Some people might be tempted to cut corners and hide information in both the x and the y coordinate of the intersection point. This seems feasible because you can choose any set of lines that goes through this point. This changes the parameters of the system substantially. If you own a part of the secret, then you know something about the relationship between x and y. The slope of the line and the y intercept describe exactly how x and y change in unison.

In some cases, this might be enough to crack the system. For instance, imagine a case where you are protecting the number of men and women escaping from England on the Mayflower. Storing the number of men in the x coordinate and the number of women in the y coordinate is a mistake. An English spy might know that the number of men and the number of women is likely to be roughly equal given the percentages of men and women in society. This extra information could be combined with one part to reveal very good approximations of x and y.[3]

Providing Deniability

Error-correcting codes described in Chapter 3 can also be used to add some deniability.

Each of the secret-sharing schemes described in this chapter offer some mindboggling chances to hide data in the Net. There is no reason why one particular file alone should be enough to reveal the information to anyone who discovers it. Splitting a file into multiple pieces is an ideal way to add complete deniability. Imagine, for instance, that the important data is stored in the least significant bits of some image using the techniques from Chapter 9. You could put the important data in the GIF file you use for your home page background and then place this up on the Web. But this is your home page and the connection is obvious. Another solution is to find, say, three other GIF images on the Web. Maybe one of them is from the Disney World home page, another is from the White House home page, and the third is from some shady hacker site in Europe. Extract the least significant bits from each of these files. You have no control over these bits, but you can use them to hide ownership of the data by using the first secret-sharing scheme described here. If you add up the values recovered from all four sites, then the final information appears.

Now imagine that the word gets out that the information is hidden in the combination of these four sites. Which one of the four is responsible? Disney World, the White House, the hackers in Europe, or you? It is impossible to use the least significant bits of each of these images to point the finger at anyone. The hidden information is the sum of the four and any one of the four could have been manipulated to ensure that the final total is the hidden information. Who did it? If you arrange it so that the hidden information is found in the total of 100 possible images, no one will ever have the time to track it down.

This system is just like the classic book ciphers that used a book as the one-time pad.

Of course, there are still problems with the plan. Imagine that Disney World used a slick, ray-traced image from one of their films like *Toy Story*. These images often have very smooth surfaces with constant gradients that usually have very predictable least significant

---

[3]You should also avoid storing them as two separate secrets each broken into parts. In this case, one part from each of the two secrets would still yield enough information. The best solution is to encrypt the two values and split the key to this file.

bits. Well, that would certainly be a defense against accusations that they manipulated the least significant bits to send out a secret message. The images chosen as the foils should have a very noisy set of least significant bits.

The Chi-Squared Test and other measures of randomness can be found in Don Knuth's [Knu81].

Building Secret-Sharing Schemes

Secret-sharing schemes are easy to explain geometrically, but adapting them to computers can involve some compromises. The most important problem is that computers really only deal with integers. Lines from real numbered domains are neither efficient nor often practical. For instance, there are five numbers involved in a typical scheme for hiding a secret as the intersection of two lines. Two numbers describe the slope and y-intercept of one line, two numbers describe the second line, and one number describes the x coordinate of the intersection point. If x is an integer, then it is not possible to choose lines at random that have both integers for their slope and y-intercept. Some might be available, but there will only be a few of them.

You can use floating-point numbers, but they add their own instability. First, you must round off values. This can be a significant problem because both sides must do all rounding off the same. Second, you might encounter great differences in floating-point math. Two different CPUs can come up with different values for x/y. The answers will be very close, but they might not be the same because the different CPUs could be using slightly different representations of values. Most users of floating-point hardware don't care about these very minor differences because all of their calculations are approximations. But this is a problem with cryptography. Changing one bit of an encryption key is usually enough to ruin decryption—even if it is only the least significant bit that is changed.

The best solution is to return to finite collections of integers mod some prime number. Adi Shamir used this domain to hide secrets by choosing polynomials from this domain [Sha79]. Instead of using lines or planes to hide the information, he choose $k - 1$ degree polynomials, $p(x)$, where the first parameter, $p_0 = p(0)$, holds the secret. One point on the polynomial goes to each part holder. k parts can be used to reconstruct the polynomial and determine the secret, $p(0)$.

Here are the basic steps:

1. Choose a value of q that is prime.

2. Find a random polynomial $p(x)$ of order $k - 1$ by selecting $k - 2$ random values between 0 and q. These will be the parameters of the polynomial, $p_1 \ldots p_{k-1}$. p_0 is the secret to be stored away.

3. $\sum_{i=0}^{k-1} p_i x^i$ is the polynomial.

4. Choose n points $x_1 \ldots x_n$. Compute $p(x_1) \ldots p(x_n)$. These are the n parts to be distributed to parts holders. Any subset of k are enough to determine p_0.

5. To recover the value of p_0, use Lagrangian interpolation. That is, you can use the points to estimate the derivatives of the polynomial at a point.

   This solution uses only integers. It should be obvious that you need k points to recover the polynomial. The easiest way to see this is to realize that having $k - 1$ points gives no information about $p(0)$. In fact, for any potential value of $p(0)$ you might guess, there is some p that would generate it. You can find this p by taking the $k - 1$ points and your guess for $p(0)$ and generating the polynomial. So, if there is a one-to-one mapping between these guesses, then the system is *perfect*. The part holder has no advantage over the outside guesser.

   The scheme also offers greater efficiency for cases where k is a reasonably large number. In the first section, the geometrical solution was to create a k-dimensional space and fill it with $k - 1$ dimensional hyperplanes. Intersecting k of them was enough to reveal the point. The problem with this solution is that the hyperplanes take up more and more space as k grows larger. I don't mean they consume more abstract space—they just require more space to hold the information that would represent them. The Shamir scheme shown here doesn't require more space. Each part is still just a point, (x, y) that lies on the polynomial. This is substantially more efficient.

Making Some More Equal

In each of the schemes described in this chapter, the secrets are split into n parts, each of the n parts being equal. Humans, being human, are never satisfied with anything as fair as that—some people will want some parts to be more powerful than others.

The most straightforward way to accomplish this is to give some people more parts. For instance, imagine a scheme where you need six parts to reconstruct the secret. That is, you might have a collection of five-dimensional hyperplanes in a six-dimensional space. Any set of six points is enough to uncover the secret, which for the sake of example will be the launch codes for a nuclear missile. Let's say that it takes two commanders, three sergeants, or six privates to launch a missile. This can be accomplished by giving three parts to the commanders, two parts to the sergeants, and one part each to the privates.

One problem with this solution is that arbitrary combinations of different ranks can join together. So, one commander, one sergeant, and one private can work together to uncover the secret. This might not be permitted in some cases. For example, the U.S. Congress requires a majority of both the House and the Senate to pass a bill. But the votes from one chamber can't be counted against the other. So even though there are 100 Senators and 435 members of the House, a Senator is not really worth 4.35 House members. A bill won't pass just because 99 Senators vote for it and only 10 House Representatives. But this could be the situation if someone naively created a secret-sharing scheme by parceling out parts to both sides of Congress from the same shared secret.

A better solution in this case would be to first split the secret into two equal parts, X_H and X_S, so that both are required to endorse a bill with the digital signature of Congress. Then H_R would be split into 435 parts so that 218 are enough to recover it. H_S is split into 100 parts so that 51 are enough to recover it.

There are numerous combinations that can make these schemes possible. Practically any scheme can be implemented using some combination and layers of secrets. The only problem with very complicated systems is that they can require many different dimensions. For instance, if you want a system where it takes 17 privates, 13 sergeants, or 5 generals to launch some missiles, then you could use a system with $17 \times 13 \times 5$ dimensions. This can get a bit arcane, but the mathematics is possible.

Summary

Secret-sharing is an ideal method for distributing documents across the network so no one can find them. It is an ideal way for people to deny responsibility. In some cases, the parts of the secret can be from the Web pages of people who have nothing to do with the matter at hand.

The Disguise Secret sharing lets you share the blame.

How Secure Is It? The algorithms here are unconditionally secure against attacks from people who have less than the necessary threshold of parts.

How To Use It? The XOR algorithm described here is easy to implement. It makes an ideal way to split up information so that every party needs to be present to put the information back together.

Chapter 5

Compression

Television Listing

8:00 PM 2 (IRS) *Beverly Hills Model Patrol* New lip gloss introduced.

5 (QUS) *Cash Calliope: Musical Detective* Death with a Capital D-minor.

9 (PVC) *Northern Cops* Town council bans eccentrics at town meeting, but not for long.

14(TTV) *Def N B* Beethoven raps for the Queen.

9:00 PM 2 (IRS) *Super Hero Bunch* Evil just keeps coming back for more.

5 (QUS) *Sniffmaster Spot* Spot discovers toxic waste at Acme Dog Food Plant.

9 (PVC) *Mom's a Klepto* Family stress as Mom plagiarizes daughter's English paper.

14(TTV) *Easy Cheesy* Customer asks for Triple Anchovy pizza.

10:00 PM 2 (IRS) *X Knows Best* Alien stepdad shows love is not Earthbound.

5 (QUS) *Dum De Dum Dum* Detective Gump meets murdering publisher.

9 (PVC) *Betrayal Place* Bob betrays Jane.

14(TTV) *Beverly Hills Astronaut* Buzz discovers there are no malls in Space!

Patterns and Compression

Life often reduces to formulas. At least it does on television, where the solutions appear every 30 or 60 minutes. When you know the formula, it is very easy to summarize information or compress it. A network executive reportedly commissioned the television show "Miami Vice" with a two-word memo to the producer reading, "MTV Cops." You can easily specify a episode of "Gilligan's Island" with a single sentence like, "The one with the cosmonauts." Anyone who's seen only one episode of the show will know that some cosmonauts appear on the island, offer some hope that people will be rescued, but this hope will be dashed at the end when Gilligan screws things up.

Compressing generic information is also just a matter of finding the right formula that describes the data. It is often quite easy to find a simple formula that works moderately well, but it can be maddeningly difficult to identify a very good formula that compresses the data very well. Finding a good formula that works well for specific types of data like text or video is often economically valuable. People are always looking for good ways to cut their data storage and communications costs.

Compressing data is of great interest to anyone who wants to hide data for three reasons:

Less data is easier to handle. This speaks for itself. Basic text can easily be compressed by 50 to 70%. Images might be compressed by 90%.

Compressed data is usually whiter. Compression shouldn't destroy information in a signal. This means the information per bit should increase if the size of the file decreases. More information per bit usually appears more random.

Details about measuring information are on page 25.

Reversing compression can mimic data.   Compression algorithms try to find a formula that fits the data and then return the specific details of the formula as compressed data. If you input random data into a compression function, it should spit out data that fits the formula.

Compression is an important tool for these reasons. Many good commercial compression programs already exist simply because of the first reason. Many good encryption programs use compression as an additional source of strength. The third reason, though, is why compression is discussed in depth in this book. Some of the basic compression algorithms provide a good way to make information look like something else. This trick of flipping the algorithm on its head is discussed in Chapter 6.

There are a number of different techniques for compressing data that are used today. The field has expanded wildly over the last several years because of the great economic value of such algorithms. A procedure that compresses data in half can double the storage area of a computer with no extra charge for hardware. People continue to come up with new and often surprisingly effective techniques for compressing data, but it all comes down to the basic process of identifying a formula that does a good job of fitting the data. The parameters that make the formula fit the data directly becomes the compressed surrogate. Some of the more popular techniques are:

Probability Methods These count up the occurrences of characters or bytes in a file. Then they assign a short code word to the most common characters and a long one to least common ones. Morse code is a good example of a compression algorithm from this class. The letter "e", which is the most common in the English language, is encoded as a dot. The letter "p", which is less common, is encoded as dot-dash- dash-dot. The *Huffman code* is the best known edition of these codes.

Dictionary Methods These algorithms compile a list of the most common words, phrases, or collections of bytes in a file, then number the words. If a word is on this list, then the compressed file simply contains the number pointing to the dictionary entry. If it isn't, the word is transmitted without change. These techniques can be quite effective if the data file has a large amount of text. Some report compressing text to 10 to 20% of its original size. The *Lempel-Ziv* compression algorithm is the most commonly used version of this algorithm.

Run-Length Encoding Many simple images are just blocks of black pixels and white pixels. If you walk along a line, you might encounter 1000 white pixels followed by 42 black pixels followed by 12 white pixels, etc. Run-length encoding stores this as a sequence of numbers 1000, 42, 12, etc. This often saves plenty of space and works well for black-and-white line art. Faxes use this technique extensively.

Wave Methods These algorithms use a collection of waves as the basic collection of formulas. Then they adjust the size and position of the waves to best fit the data. These work quite well with images that do not need to be reconstructed exactly. The new image only needs to approximate the original. The JPEG and MPEG image and video compression standards are two of the more famous instances of this technique.

Fractal Methods These are often the best compression functions but are also often the hardest to use. Fractal functions produce extremely complicated patterns from very simple formulas. This means that they can achieve extremely high compression if you can find the formula that fits your data.

*A good intro-
duction to frac-
tal compression
can be found
in [Bar88b].*

Adaptive Compression Schemes Many compression schemes can be modified to adapt to the changing patterns of data. Each of the types described here comes in versions that modify themselves in the middle of the data stream to adapt to new patterns.

Each of these compression schemes is useful in particular domains. There is no universal algorithm that comes with a universal set of functions that adapt well to any data. So people modify existing algorithms and come up with their own formulas.

Compression functions make good beginnings for people who want to hide data because the functions were constructed to describe patterns. There are two ways to use compression functions successfully to hide information. One way to hide data is to mold it into the form of other data so it blends in. A compression function that worked well on zebras would be able to model black and white stripes and convert a set of stripes into a simple set of parameters. If you had such a function, it could be applied to some data in *reverse* and it would expand the data into zebra stripes. The result would be bigger, but it would look like something else. The data could be recovered by compressing it again.

Compression techniques can also be used to identify the least important nooks and crannies of a file so that extra data can be snuck into these corners. Many image-compression functions are designed to be *lossy*. That means that the reconstructed image may look very similar to the original image, but it won't be *exactly* the same. If the functions that describe an image can be fitted more loosely, then the algorithms can use fewer of them and produce a smaller compressed output. For instance, an apple might be encoded as a blob of solid red instead of a smooth continuum of various shades of red. When the image is decompressed, much of the smaller detail is lost but the overall picture still looks good. These compression functions can easily compress an image to be 1/5th to 1/10th of its original size and this is why they are so popular.

The television format example from the beginning of the chapter is an example of lossy compression. The listings are not enough to recreate the entire program. They're a better example of lossy compression where a surrogate is found.

Huffman Coding

A good way to understand basic compression is to examine a simple algorithm like Huffman coding. This technique analyzes the frequency that each letter occurs in a file and then replaces it with a flexible-length code word. Normally, each letter is stored as a byte which takes up 8 bits of information. Some estimates of the entropy of standard English, though, show that it is something just over about 3 bits per letter. Obviously there is room to squeeze up to almost 5/8ths of a file of English text. The trick is to assign the short code words to common letters and long code words to the least common letters. Although some of the long words will end up being longer than 8 bits, the net result will still be shorter. The common letters will have the greatest effect.

Table 5.1 shows a table of the occurrences of letters in several different opinions from the United States Supreme Court. The space is the most common character followed by the letter "E". This table was constructed by mixing lower- and uppercase letters for simplicity. An actual compression function would keep separate entries for both forms of each letter as well as an entry for every type of punctuation mark. In general, there would be 256 entries for each byte.

Table 5.2 shows a set of codes that were constructed for each letter using the data in Table 5.1. The most common character, the space, gets a code that is only 2 bits long: 01. Many of the other common characters get codes that are 4 bits long. The least common character, "Z", gets an 11-bit code: 00011010001. If these codes were used to encode data, then it should be easy to reduce a file to less than one-half of its original size.

Table 5.1. The frequency of occurrence of letters in a set of opinions generated by the U.S. Supreme Court.

Letter	Frequency	Letter	Frequency
space	26974	A	6538
B	1275	C	3115
D	2823	E	9917
F	1757	G	1326
H	3279	I	6430
J	152	K	317
L	3114	M	1799
N	5626	O	6261
P	2195	Q	113
R	5173	S	5784
T	8375	U	2360
V	928	W	987
X	369	Y	1104
Z	60		

Table 5.2. The codes constructed from Table 5.1. A Huffman tree based on these codes is shown in Figure 5.2.

Letter	Code	Letter	Code
space	01	A	1000
B	111011	C	10110
D	11100	E	0000
F	001101	G	111010
H	00111	I	1001
J	0001101001	K	000110101
L	10111	M	001100
N	1101	O	1010
P	000101	Q	00011010000
R	1111	S	1100
T	0010	U	000100
V	0001111	W	0001110
X	0001110	Y	0001100
Z	00011010001		

Here's a simple example that takes 48 bits used to store the word "ARTHUR" in normal ASCII into 27 bits in compressed form:

Letter:	A	R	T	H	U	R
ASCII:	01000001	01010010	01010100	01001000	01010101	01010010
Compressed:	1000	1111	0010	00111	000100	1111

The Huffman algorithm can also be used to compress any type of data, but its effectiveness varies. It could be used, for instance, on a photograph where the intensity at each pixel is stored as a byte. The algorithm would be very effective on a photograph that had only a few basic values of black and white. But it wouldn't work well if the intensities were evenly distributed in a photograph with many even shades between dark and light. The algorithm works best when there are a few basic values.

More sophisticated versions of the Huffman code exist. It is common to construct second-order codes that aggregate pairs of letters. This can be done in two ways. The easiest is to simply treat each pair of letters as the basic atomic unit. Instead of constructing a frequency table of characters, you would construct a table of pairs. The table would be much larger, but it would generate even better compression because many of the pairs would rarely occur. Pairs like "ZF" are almost non-existent.

Another solution is to construct 26 different tables by analyzing which letters follow other letters. So, one table for the letter "T" would hold the frequency that all of the other letters came after it. The letter "H" would be quite common in this table because "TH" occurs frequently in English. These 26 tables would produce even more compression because it would tune the code word even more. The letter "U" would receive a very short code word after the letter "Q" because it invariably follows.

This example has shown how a Huffman compression function works in practice. It didn't explain how the code words were constructed nor did it show why they worked so well. The next section in this chapter will do that.

Chapter 6 shows how to run Huffman codes in reverse.

Building Compression Algorithms

Creating a new compression algorithm has been one of the more lucrative areas of mathematics and computer science lately. A few smart ideas are enough to save people billions of dollars of storage space and communications time and so many have worked with the idea in depth. This chapter won't investigate the best work because it is beyond the scope of the book. Many of the simplest ideas turn out to hide information the best. Huffman codes are a perfect solution for basic text. Dictionary algorithms, like Lempel-Ziv, are less effective.

Huffman Compression

Huffman compression is easy to understand and construct. Let the set of characters be Σ, and $\rho(c)$ be the probability that a particular character, c, occurs in a text file. Constructing such a frequency table is easy to do by analyzing a source file. It is usually done on a case-by-case basis and stored in the header to the compressed version, but it can also be done in advance and used again and again.

The basic idea is to construct a binary tree that contains all of the characters at the leaves. Each of the branches is labeled with either a zero or a one. The path between the root and the leaf specifies the code used for each letter. Figure 5.1 shows this for a small set of letters.

The key is to construct the tree so that the most common letters occur near the top of the tree. This can be accomplished with a relatively easy process:

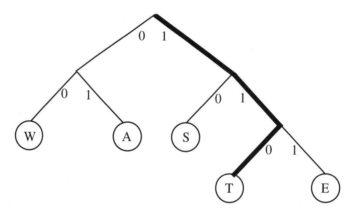

Figure 5.1. A small Huffman tree. The code for each letter is determined by following the path between the root of the tree and the leaf containing a particular letter. The letter "T", for instance, receives the code 110.

1. Start with one node for each character. This node is also a very simple tree. The weight of this tree is set to be the probability that the character associated with the tree occurs in the file. Call the trees for t_i and the weight $w(n_i)$. The value of i changes as the number of trees change.

2. Find the two trees with the smallest weight. Glue these into one tree by constructing a new node with two branches connected to the roots of the two trees. One branch will be labeled with a one and the other will get a zero. The weight of this new tree is set to be the sum of the old trees that were joined.

3. Repeat the previous step until there is only one tree left. The codes can be constructed by following the path between the root and the leaves.

I know of a Greek labyrinth which is a single straight line. Along this line so many philosophers have lost themselves that a mere detective might well do so too.

—Jorge Luis Borges in Death and the Compass

    The characters with the smallest weights are joined together first. Each joining process adds another layer between the root and the leaves. So it is easy to see how the least common letters get pushed far away from the root where they have a longer code word. The most common letters don't get incorporated until the end so they end up near the top.

    The algorithm naturally balances the tree by always taking the smallest weights first. The weight for a tree represents the number of times that any of the characters in the tree will occur in a file. You can prove that the tree constructed by this algorithm is the best possible tree by imagining what happens if you mistakenly choose the wrong

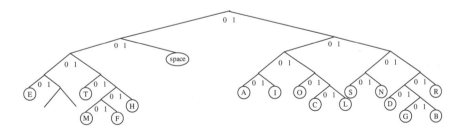

Figure 5.2. The top of the tree built from the data in Table 5.1. This generated the codes shown in Table 5.2. Only the top part is shown here because of space considerations. Less common letters like "Z" are in the part of the tree replaced by the dashed lines.

two trees to join at a step. More common characters get pushed farther from the root and get longer code words than less common characters. The average compression drops.

Many other people have extended the theme of Huffman coding by creating other algorithms that use the addresses of nodes in a tree. One popular technique is to use Splay trees. These trees are modified every time a character is encoded. One version moves the letter to the top of the tree in a complex move that preserves much of the structure. The result is that the most common letters bubble up to the top. The constant rearrangement of the tree means that the tree adapts to the local conditions. This type of algorithm would be ideal for compressing a dictionary where even the least popular letters like "j" or "z" are common in sections. When the algorithm moved through the "j" part of the dictionary, the node containing "j" would be pushed repeatedly to the top of the splay tree where it would get a short code word. Later, when the compression function got to the "z" section, the node for "z" would end up near the top consistently giving "z" a short code word. Obviously one major problem with this compression scheme is that the entire file must be processed from the beginning to keep an accurate description of the splay tree. You simply can't jump to the "z" section and begin decompressing.

[Sto88] is a good basic reference on compression.

This basic Huffman algorithm has many different uses. It will be in Chapter 6 to turn data into something that looks like English text. It is also used as a building block in Chapter 7 to make optimal weighted choices between different words. The same structure is as useful there as here.

Dictionary Compression

Compression schemes like the popular and patented Lempel-Ziv algorithm are called dictionary schemes because they build a big list of common words in the file.[1] This list can either be created in one swoop at the beginning of the compression or it could be built and changed adaptively as the algorithm processes the file. The algorithms succeed

---

[1]The algorithms are not particularly good at compressing files like dictionaries used by humans. The fact that I used a regular dictionary as an example in the previous section is just a coincidence. Don't be confused.

because a pointer describing the position in the dictionary takes up much less space than the common word itself.

The dictionary is just a list of words. It is almost always 2^n words because that makes the pointer to a particular word take up n bits. Each word can either be a fixed length or a flexible length. Fixed lengths are easier to handle, but flexible lengths do a better job of approximating the English language and x86 machine code.

Compression is simple. First, the file is analyzed to create a list of the 2^n most common words. Then the file is processed by scanning from beginning to end. If the current word is in the dictionary, then it is replaced by a tag `<InDict>` followed by the position in the dictionary. If it isn't, then it is replaced by a tag `<Verbatim>` followed by the word that remains unchanged.

Obviously the success of the algorithm depends upon the size of the tags (`<InDict>` and `<Verbatim>`), the size of the dictionary, and the number of times that something is found in the dictionary. One simple and usually effective solution is to make the tags be one entire byte, B. If the value of the byte is zero, then the next n bits represents a word in the dictionary. If the value of the byte, B, is greater than zero, then there are B bytes that are copied verbatim out of the original file. This scheme allows the program to use flexible word sizes that work well with English. There are many different schemes that are more efficient in some cases.

The index into the dictionary does not need to be n bit numbers. You can also count the occurrence of words in the dictionary and use a Huffman-like scheme to devise short code words for some of them. The tag for verbatim text is usually included as just another word in this case.

The dictionary can also adapt as the file is processed. One simple technique is to keep track of the last time a word was used from the dictionary. Whenever a section of verbatim text is encountered, the oldest word is swapped out of the dictionary and the newest verbatim text is swapped in. This is a great technique for adapting to the text because many words are often clustered in sections. For instance, the words "dictionary," "Huffman," and "compression" are common in this section but relatively rare in other parts of the book. An adaptive scheme would load these words into the dictionary at the beginning of the section when they were first encountered and not swap them out until they weren't used for a bit.

Dictionary schemes can be quite effective for compressing arbitrary text, but they are difficult to run in reverse to make data mimic something. Chapter 6 uses Huffman-like algorithms to generate real text, but it won't include a section on reversing dictionary algorithms. They are described in this chapter because compression is a good way to save space and whiten data. The algorithms don't work particularly well for mimicry because they require a well-constructed dictionary. In practice, there is no good automatic way that I know for constructing a good one.

JPEG Compression

The Huffman encoding described in "Huffman Compression" on page 68 and the dictionary schemes in "Dictionary Compression" on page 70 are ideal for arbitrary collections of data. They can also work quite well on some types of image files, but they fail on others. If an image has a small number of colors that may occur in a predictable pattern, then both of these algorithms may do a good job of finding a pattern that is strong enough to generate a good compression. This often doesn't happen because the images contain many different shades of colors. The Japanese flag, for instance, has one red circle that is a constant color, but a realistically lit apple has many different shades of red.

The JPEG algorithm is a good example of how to tune an algorithm to a particular type of data. In this case, the algorithm fits cosine functions to the data and then stores the amplitude and period of the cosine functions. The number of functions used and the size can be varied according to the amount of compression desired. A small number of functions produces a high amount of compression, but a grainy image. More functions add accuracy, but take up more space. This flexibility is possible because many people don't particularly care if they get *exactly* the same image back when it is decompressed. If it looks reasonably close, it is good enough.

This flexibility is what is so useful about JPEG encoding. The algorithm from 5 will be run in reverse to produce text that mimics English text. The JPEG algorithm, however, doesn't do that well. It does, however, have the ability to identify nooks and crannies in the image that might have space to hold information. This is described in detail in Chapter 9.

GZSteg

Many of the compression algorithms can be tweaked in clever ways to hide information. One of the simplest, but quite effective techniques was used by Andrew Brown when he approached the popular GZIP compression algorithm. This technique is used frequently throughout the Net so it makes an ideal candidate for an innocuous location.

Ordinarily, the GZIP algorithm will compress data by inserting tokens that point back to a previous location where the data was found. Here's a sample section of text:

The famous Baltimore Oriole, Cal Ripken Jr., is the son of Cal Ripken Sr. who coached for the Orioles in the past.

Here's a sample section that was compressed. The tokens are shown in italics.

The famous Baltimore Oriole, Cal Ripken Jr., is the son of *(30,10)* Sr. who coached for the *(48,6)*s in the past.

In this example, there are two tokens. The first one, *(30,10)*, tells the algorithm to back 30 characters and copy 10 characters to the current location. The compression technique works quite well for many text algorithms.

GZSteg hides information by changing the number of characters to copy. Everytime it inserts a token that requires more than 5 to be copied, it will hide one bit. If the bit is zero, then the token is left unchanged. If the bit is one, then the number of characters to be copied is shortened by one. Here's the same quote with the two bits 11 encoded:

The famous Baltimore Oriole, Cal Ripken Jr., is the son of *(30,9)*n Sr. who coached for the *(46,5)*es in the past.

In both cases, the size of the copying was cut by one. This does reduce the amount of compression to a small extent.

The greatest advantage of this approach is that the file format is unchanged. A standard GZIP program will be able to decompress the data without noticing that information was hidden in the process.

Information could be left around without attracting suspicion. A quick analysis, however, could also reveal that data was hidden in such a manner. If you scan the file and examine the tokens, you can easily determine which tokens were just a character too small. There is no way to deny that the program which did the GZIP compression screwed up.

Summary

Compression algorithms are normally used to reduce the size of a file without removing information. This can increase their entropy and make the files appear more random because all of the possible bytes become more common. The compression algorithms can also be useful when they're used to produced mimicry. This is described in Chapter 6.

The Disguise Compression algorithms generally produce data that looks more random. That is, there is a more even distribution of the data.

How Secure Is It? Not secure at all. Most compression algorithms transmit the table or dictionary at the beginning of the file. This may not be necessary because both parties could agree upon such a table in advance. Although I don't know how to figure out the mapping between the letters and the bits in the Huffman algorithm, I don't believe it would be hard to figure out.

How To Use It? There are many compression programs available for all computers. They often use proprietary algorithms that are better than the versions offered here. They make an ideal first pass for any encryption program.

Chapter 6

Basic Mimicry

Reading Between the Lines

Here is the transcript from the mind of a cynic reading through the personals section of a newspaper:

```
SF ISO SM. Old-fashioned romantic wants same for
walks in rain, trips to Spain and riding on planes.
Send picture and dating strategy.
```

Great. Eliza Doolittle. Literally. I come up with a dating strategy and she does little but rides along. This is not a good sign. She's probably a princess working as a secretary who wants to be rescued and catapulted into the rich, upper-class. Rules me out. I'm not going to work my butt off so she can relax in Spain trying to pronounce words differently. What's so romantic about Spain, anyway? She's probably read Hemingway too and I'll be forced to run in front of a bunch of bulls just so she'll think I'm dashing in an old fashioned way. No thanks. I'll take a new fashioned Range Rover like they drive around Africa. Those things can't be toppled by a bunch of bulls. And if it's raining, I won't get wet or slip all over the place. Geez.

```
SF ISO SM. Dancing. Wine. Night. Sky. Moon.
Romancing. Dine. Write by June.
```

Great. Poetry. She'll expect me to reciprocate. I just won't be able to say, "Yeah, let's grab a burger tonight." Nope. I'll have to get some watercolors and paint a letter to her. In some ancient verse form. Rhyming really is the sign of an overactive mind. Who really cares if two words in different parts of a paragraph happen to end with the same sound? It's just a coincidence. She'll probably spend all of her time picking up patterns in our lives. I'll have to keep saying, "No. I still love you. I just want to watch the seventh game of the World Series. The Red Sox are in it this year. It's tied. They might actually win! This is not *a sign of a bad relationship. " Geez.*

```
SF ISO SM. Fast cars, fast boats and fast horses are
for me. Don't write. Send a telegram.
```

Great. Has she ever fallen off of a fast horse? They're animals. They only tolerate us on their backs as long as the oats are fresh. Women are the same way. But they don't take to a rein as well. And they don't just want fresh oats. I bet Fast Food isn't on her list. She'll ride along and take me for whatever I've got. Then she'll grab a fast plane out of my life. No way. Her boat's sinking already. Geez.

Running in Reverse

The cynic looking for a date in the introduction to this chapter has the ability to take a simple advertisement and read between the lines until he's plotted the entire arc of the relationship and followed it to its doom. Personal ads have an elaborate short hand system for compressing a person's dreams into less than 100 words. The shorthand evolved over the years as people grew to pick up the patterns in what people wanted. "ISO" means "In Search Of" etc. The cynic was just using his view of the way that people want to expand the bits of data into a reality that has little to do with the incoming data.

This chapter is about creating an automatic way of taking small, innocuous bits of data and embellishing them with deep, embroidered details until the result mimics something completely different. The data is hidden as it assumes this costume. In this chapter, the effect is accomplished by running the Huffman compression algorithm described in Chapter 5 in reverse. Ordinarily, the Huffman algorithm would approximate the statistical distribution of the text and then convert them into a digital shorthand. Running this in reverse can take normal data and form it into these into the elaborate patterns.

Figure 6.1 is a good place to begin. The text in this figure was created using a fifth-order regular mimic function by analyzing an early draft of Chapter 5. The fifth-order statistical profile of the chapter was created by counting all possible sets of five letters in a row that occur in the chapter. In the draft, the five letters 'mpres' occur together in that order 84 times. Given that these letters are part of the word 'compression', it is not surprising that the five letters 'ompre' and 'press' also occur 84 times.

The text is generated in a process that is guided by these statistics. The text begins by selecting one group of five letters at random. In this Figure, the first five letters are "The l". Then it uses the statistics to dictate which letters can follow. In the draft of Chapter 5, the five letters 'he la' occur 2 times, the letters 'he le' occur 16 times and the letters "he lo" occur 2 times. If the fifth-order text is going to mimic the statistical profile of Chapter 5, then there should be a 2 out of 20 chance that the letter "a" should follow the randomly "The l". Of course, there should also be a 16 out of 20 chance that it should be a "e" and a 2 out of 20 chance that it should be an "o".

This process is repeated ad infinitum until enough text is generated. It is often amazing just how real the result sounds. To a large extent, this is caused by the smaller size of the sample text. If you assume that there are about 64 printable characters in a text file, then there are about 64^5 different combinations of five letters. Obviously, many of them like "zqTuV" never occur in the English language, but a large number of them must make their way into the table if the algorithm is to have many choices. In the last example, there were three possible choices for a letter to follow "The l". The phrase "The letter" is common in Chapter 5, but the phrase "The listerine" is not. In many cases, there is only one possible choice that was dictated by the small number of words used in the sample. This is what gives it such a real sounding pattern.

Here's the algorithm for generating nth order text called T given a source text S:

1. Construct a list of all different combinations of n letters that occur in S and keep track of how many times each of these occurs in the S.

2. Choose one at random to be a seed. This will be the first n letters of T.

The letter compression or video is only to generate a
verbatim> followed by 12 whiter 'H' wouldn't design a
perfective reconomic data. This to simple hardware.
These worked with encodes of the data list of the
diction in the most come down in depth in a file decome
down in adds about of character first.

Many data for each of find the occnly difficular
techniques can algorithms computer used data verbatim
out means that describes themselves in a part ideas of
reduce extremely occurate the charge formulas. At leaf
space and the original set of the storage common word
memo to red by 42 black pixels formula that pression of
their data is why complicated to be done many
difference like solution. This book. Many different
wouldn't get into any different to though to anyone has
make the popular to the number or 60 minutes. This
Huffman also just but random. Compression. One branches
is easy to be use of find the because many people has
shows the codes The most nooks like three constructed
with a function, the greate the moMany good formations.
This simply be compression show a Huffman code work
quite easily common in these 26 different takes 48 bit
should in this can be patter-frequency the image space
constructed in the other letter is algorithm on stand
there easier to the overed into the root and MPEG and
crannies their data for compression Scheme Compression
in a file description when it short codes were could be
common length encode work quite weights a Klepto Family
Stressed by image and Compressed as a bigger, whiter
the for hardware. Many even more that then the result
to descriptionary algorithms that were two bits you
might for simply because of charge found in the well,
but the data is easily Stressed surprising text. The
algorithm would look very good

Figure 6.1. This is a Fifth order random text generated by mimicking the
statistical distribution of letters in an early draft of Chapter 5.

3. Repeat this loop until enough text is generated:

   (a) Take the last $n - l$ letters of T.

   (b) Search through the statistical table and find all combinations of letters that begin with these $n - 1$ letters.

   (c) The last letters of these combinations is the set of possible choices for the next letter to be added to T.

   (d) Choose among these letters and use the frequency of their occurrences in S to weight your choice.

   (e) Add it to T.

The algorithm works for n that is two or larger. Obviously the quality of the output of the lower order samples depends upon the order. Here are some samples:

First Order islhne[hry saeeooisnre uo ' w nala al coehhs
pebl e to agboean ce ed cshcenapch nt
sibPah ea m n [tmsteoia lahid egnndl y et r yf arleo
awe l eo rttnntnnhtohwiseoa a dri 6oc7teit2t lenefe
clktoi l mlte r ces. woeiL , misetemd2np eap
haled&oolrcc yttr tr,oh en mi elarlbeo tyNunt . syf es2
nrrpmdo,0 reet dadwn'dysg te.ewnlca-ht eitxrni ntoos xt
eCc oh sao vhsohOmhgr

Second Order Thy etheren' ante esthe ales. icone thers the
ase omsictorm s iom. wactere cut le ce s mo be t Me. Y
whes ine odofuion os thore cctherg om tt s d Thm &
tthamben tin'ssthe, co westitit odecra fugon tucod.
liny Eangem o wen il ea bionBulivethe ton othanstoct
itaple

Third Order ith eas a tan't genstructin ing butionsmage
ruct secate expachat thap-res ''Miamproxis is of is a
to af st. This there is monst cone usectuabloodes it
aluengettecte por be the andtaly com Bevers gor the
Hufferess. M B G achasion the coduch occomprence mon
Quited the ch like bitheres. The

Fourth Order captionary. Image and to compression lest
  constance tree. Family for into be mode of bytes in
  algorith a file of that cosition algorithm that word
  even that a size summarge factal size are:

ite position scien Raps.

The is are up much length ence, the if the a refsec-ent
sec-ent of fits to the crans usuall numberse
compression

A good ways that in algoright. The brase two wants to
hidea of English Cash the are compres then matimes
formatimes from the data finding pairst. This only be
ression o

There is little doubt that the text gets more and more readable as the
order increases. But who would this fool? What if the enemy designed
a computer program that would flag suspicious electronic mail by
identifying messages that don't have the right statistical mix of characters? Foreign languages could pop right out. French, for instance,
has a greater number of apostrophes as well as a different distribution
of letters. Russian has an entirely different alphabet, but even when it
is transliterated the distribution is different. Each language and even
each regional dialect has a different composition.

These texts generated here could fool such an automatic scanning
device. The output here is statistically equivalent to honest English
text. For instance, the letter "e" is the most common and the letter "t"
is next most common. Everything looks correct statistically at all of
the different orders. If the scanning software was looking for statistical
deviance, it wouldn't find it.

An automatic scanning program is also at a statistical disadvan-
tage with relatively short text samples. Its statistical definition of what
is normal must be loose enough to fit changes caused by the focus of
the text. A document about zebras, for instance, would have many
more "z"s than the average document, but this alone wouldn't make
it abnormal. Many documents might have a higher than average occurrence of "j"s or "q"s merely because the topic involves something
like jails or quiz shows.

Of course, these texts wouldn't be able to fool a person. At least
the first-, second-, or third-order texts wouldn't fool someone. But a

fifth-order text based upon a sample from an obscure and difficult jargon like legal writing might fool many people who aren't familiar with the structures of the genre.

More complicated grammatical analysis is certainly possible. There are grammar checkers that scan documents and identify bad sentence structure. These products are far from perfect. Many people write idiomatically and others stretch the bounds of what is considered correct grammar without breaking any of the rules. Although honest text generated by humans may set off many flags, there is little doubt that even the fifth-order text shown in this chapter would appear so wrong that it could be automatically detected. Any text that had, say, more wrong than right with it could be flagged as suspicious by an automatic process [KO84, Way85].

Chapter 7 offers an approach to defeat grammar checkers.

Choosing the Next Letter

The last section showed how statistically equivalent text could be generated by mimicking the statistical distribution of a source collection of text. The algorithm showed how to choose the next letter so it would be statistically correct, but it did not explain how to hide information in the process. Nor did it explain how to run Huffman compression in reverse.

The information is hidden by letting the data to be concealed dictate the choice of the next letter. In the example described above, either "a", "e", or "o" could follow the starting letters "The l". It is easy to come up with a simple scheme for encoding information. If "a" stands for "1", "e" stands for "2" and "o" stands for "3", then common numbers could be encoded in the choice of the letters. Someone at a distance could recover this value if they had a copy of the same source text, S, that generated the table of statistics. The could look up "The l" and discover that there are three letters that follow "he l" in the table. The letter "e" is the second choice in alphabetical order, so the letter "e" stands for the message "2".

A long text like the one shown in Figure 6.1 could hide a different number in each letter. If there was no choice about the next letter to be added to the output, though, then no information could be hidden. That letter would not hide anything.

Simply using a letter to encode a number is not an efficient nor a flexible way to send data. What if you wanted to send the message "4" and there were only three choices? What if you wanted to send a long picture? What if your data wanted to send the value "1", but the first letter was the least common choice. Would this screw up the statistical composition?

Running Huffman codes in reverse is the solution to all of these problems. Figure 6.2 shows a simple Huffman tree constructed from the three choices of letters to follow "The l". The tree was constructed using the statistics that showed that the letter "e" followed in 16 out of the 20 times while the letters "a" and "o" both followed twice apiece.

Messages are encoded with a Huffman tree like this with a variable number of bits. The choice of "e" encodes the bit "0"; the choice of "a" encodes "10"; and the choice of "o" encodes the message "11". These bits can be recovered at the other end by reversing this choice. The number of bits that are hidden with each choice of a letter varies directly with the number of choices that are possible and the probabilities that govern the choice.

There should generally be more than three choices available if the source text S is large enough to offer some variation, but there will rarely be a full 26 choices. This is only natural because English has plenty of redundancy built into the language. Shannon recognized this when he set up information theory. If the average entropy of English is about 3 bits per character, then this means that there should only be about 2^3 or eight choices that can be made for the next character. This value is weighted by the probabilities.

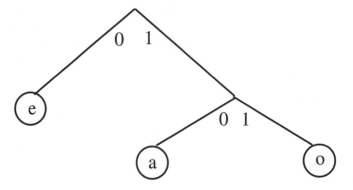

Figure 6.2. A small Huffman tree built to hide bits in the choice of a new letter. Here, the letter "a" encodes "10", the letter "e" encodes "0" and the letter "o" encodes "11".

There are problems, of course, with this scheme. This solution is the best way to hide the information so that it mimics the source text S for the same reason that Huffman codes are the most efficient way to construct tree-like compression schemes. The same proof that shows this works in reverse.

But even if it is the best, it falls short of being perfect. In the small example in Figure 6.2, the letter "e" is chosen if the next bit to be hidden is "0", while either "a" or "o" will be hidden if the next bit is "1". If the data to be hidden is purely random, then "e" will be chosen 50% of the time while "a" or "o" will be chosen the other 50% of the time. This does not mimic the statistics from the source text exactly. If it did, the letter "e" would be chosen 80% of the time and the other letters would each be chosen 10% of the time. This inaccuracy exists because of the binary structure of the Huffman tree and the number of choices available.

"Goosing with Extra Data" on page 86 shows a more accurate approximation.

Implementing the Mimicry

There are two major problems in writing software that will generate regular n-th order mimicry. The first is acquiring and storing the statistics. The second is creating a tree structure to do the Huffman-like coding and decoding. The first problem is something that requires a bit more finesse because there are several different ways to accomplish the same ends. The second problem is fairly straightforward.

Several different people have approached a similar problem called generating a *travesty*. This was addressed in a series of *Byte* magazine articles [KO84, Way85] that described how to generate statistically equivalent text. The articles didn't use the effect to hide data, but they did concentrate upon the most efficient way to generate it. This work ends up being quite similar in practice to the homophonic ciphers described by H.N. Jendal, Y. J. B. Kuhn, and J. L. Massey in [JKM90] and generalized by C.G. Gunther in [Gun88].

Here are several different approaches to storing the statistical tables needed to generate the data:

Giant Array Allocate an array with c^n boxes where c is the number of possible characters at each position and n is the order of the statistics being kept. Obviously c can be as low as 27 if only capital letters and spaces are kept. But it can also be 256 if all possible values of a byte are stored. This may be practical for small values of n, but it grows quickly impossible. If there are k letters produced

Giant List Create an alphabetical list of all of the entries. There is one counter per node as well as a pointer and a string holding the value in question. This makes the nodes substantially less efficient than the array. This can still pay off if there are many nodes that are kept out. If English text is being mimicked, there are many combinations of several letters that don't occur. A list is definitely more efficient.

Giant Tree Build a big tree that contains one path from the root to a leaf for each letter combination found in the tree. This can contain substantially more pointers, but it is faster to use than the Giant List. Figure 6.3 illustrates an implementation of this.

Going Fishing Randomize the search. There is no statistical table produced at all because c and n are too large. The source file serves as a random source and it is consulted at random for each choice of a new letter. This can be extremely slow, but it may be the only choice if memory isn't available.

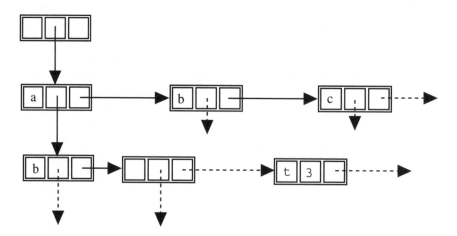

Figure 6.3. This tree stores the frequency data for a file with n layers of branching for nth order statistics. Access is substantially faster. The dashed lines show where nodes are omitted. The only complete word shown here is "at". It occurs three times in the sample.

The first three solutions are fairly easy to implement for anyone with a standard programming background. The array is the easiest. The list is not hard. Anyone implementing the tree has a number of choices. Figure 6.3 shows that the new branches at each level are stored in a list. This could also be done in a binary tree to speed lookup.

The fourth solution, going fishing, is a bit more complicated. The idea is to randomly select positions in the text and use this to randomize the search. All of the data can't be kept in a table so all of the choices won't be available at each juncture. Therefore, you must make do with what you can find. The most extreme version of this algorithm simply searches the entire file and constructs the right table entry on the fly. Here is a more sensible approach:

1. Choose a location in the source file at random. Call this character i. This random source must be duplicated during decoding so it must come from a pseudo-random number generator that is synchronized.

2. If you are constructing an nth order mimicry, search forward until you find the $n - 1$ characters in question. The next character may be the one you desire.

3. Let there be k characters in the source file. Go to position $i + \frac{k}{2} \bmod k$. Search forward until the right combination of $n - 1$ characters are found.

4. If the next character suggested by both positions is the same, then nothing can be encoded here. Send out that character and repeat.

5. If they are different, then one bit can be encoded with the choice. If you are hiding a 0 using this mimicry, then output the character found beginning at position i. If you are hiding a 1, then output the character found after the search began at $i + \frac{k}{2} \bmod k$.

This solution can be decoded. All of the information encoded here can be recovered as long as both the encoder and the decoder have access to the same source file and the same stream of i values coming from a pseudo-random source. The pseudo-random generator ensures that all possible combinations are uncovered. This does assume, however, that the candidates of $n - 1$ characters are evenly distributed throughout the text.

The solution can also be expanded to store more than one bit per output letter. You could begin the search at four different locations and hope that you uncover four different possible letters to output. If you do, then you can encode two bits. This approach can be extended still further, but each search does slow the output.

In general, the fishing solution is the slowest and most cumbersome of all the approaches. Looking up each new letter takes an amount of time proportional to the occurrence of the $n-1$ character group in the data. The array has the fastest lookup, but it can be prohibitively large in many cases. The tree has the next fastest lookup and is probably the most generally desirable for text applications.

Goosing with Extra Data

Alas, statistical purity is often hard to generate. If the data to be hidden has maximum entropy, then the letters that emerge from the Huffman-tree based mimicry will emerge with a probability distribution that seems a bit suspicious. Every letter will appear with a probability of the form $1/2^i$. That is, either 50%, 25%, 12.5%, and so on. This may not be that significant, but it might be detected.

Better results can be obtained by trading off some of the efficiency and using a pseudo-random number generator to add more bits to make the choice better approximate the actual occurrence in the data.

Music is also fair game. Many have experimented with using musical rules of composition to create new music from statistical models of existing music. One paper on the topic is [BJNW57].

The technique can best be explained by example. Imagine that there are three characters, "a", "b", and "c" that occur with probabilities of 50%, 37.5%, and 12.5% respectively. The ordinary Huffman tree would look like the one in Figure 6.4. The character "a" would occur in the output file 50% of the time. This would be fine. But "b" and "c" would both occur 25% of the time. "b" will occur as often as "c", not three times as often as dictated by the source file.

Figure 6.5 shows a new version of the Huffman tree designed to balance the distribution. There are now two extra layers added to the tree. The branching choices made in these extra two layers would use extra bits supplied by a pseudo-random generator. When they were recovered, these bits would be discarded. It should be easy to establish that "b" will emerge 37.5% of the time and "c" will be output 12.5% of the time if the data being hidden is perfectly distributed.

The cost of this process is efficiency. The new tree may produce output with the right distribution, but decoding is often not possible.

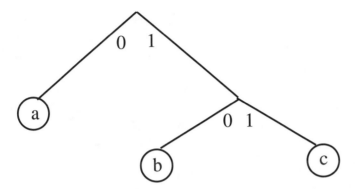

Figure 6.4. An ordinary Huffman tree built for three characters, "a", "b", and "c" that occur with probabilities of 50%, 37.5%, and 12.5% respectively.

The letter "b" is produced from the leaves with addresses 100, 101, and 110. Since only the first bit remains constant with this tree in Figure 6.5 then only one bit can be hidden with the letter "b". The other two bits would be produced by the pseudo-random bitstream and not recovered at the other end. The tree in Figure 6.4 would hide *two* bits with the letter "b", but it would produce a "b" 25% of the time. This is the tradeoff of efficiency versus accuracy.

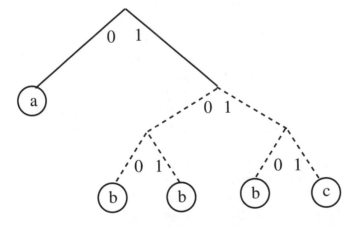

Figure 6.5. An expanded version of the tree shown in Figure 6.4. The decisions about which of the dashed branches to take are made by drawing bits from an extra pseudo-random source. Only the first decision is made using a bit from the data to be hidden.

How many bits are hidden or encoded if a "c" is output? It could either be three that are encoded when a 111 is found in the input file or it could be simply one bit padded in the same manner as the letter "b". Either choice is fine.

This technique can be extended significantly to support any amount of precision. The most important step is to make sure that there will be no ambiguity in the decoding process. If the same character exists on both branches, then no bit can be encoded using any of the subtree descending from this point.

This means that it is not possible to encode data which is dominated by one character that appears more than 50% of the time. If "a","b" and "c" were to emerge 75%, 25% and 5% respectively, then it would not be possible to encode information with this scheme and also produce the letter "a" 75% of the time.

One way around this process is to produce pairs of characters. This is often feasible if one letter dominates the distribution. That is, produce the pairs "aa","ab","ac","ba","bb","bc", "ca","cb", and "cc" with probabilities 56%, 18%, 3%, 18%, 6%, 1%, 3%, 1%, and .2% respectively.

Regular Mimicry and Images

The regular mimicry algorithms described in this chapter are aimed at text and they do a good job in this domain. Adapting them to images is quite possible, if only because the digitized images are just patterns of the two letters "1" and "0". But the success is somewhat dilluted.

Chapter 9 shows how to flip the least significant bits to store information. Chapter 9 does't try to mimic the pattern of the least significant bits. It just assumes that they fall into a standard even distribution. The regular mimicry algorithms can be used to taylor the distribution to some model.

The simplest solution is to group together the pixels into a regular set of groups. These groups might be 2×2 or 3×3 blocks or they might be broken into linear groups of pixels from the same row. Now, the least significant bits of each of these pixels can be treated as characters. One image might be used as the model used to compute the distribution table that generates a huffman tree. Then data can be hidden in another by using this huffman tree to generate blocks of bits to replace the least significant bits in the image.

More sophisticated solutions could be based upon the color of the pixels themselves, but this solution is probably too complicated to be practical. The advantage of this system is that it could detect and imitate any statistical abnolomies introduced when an image was created. Ordinarily, CCD arrays have slight imperfections that affect how each sensing cell reacts to light. High-quality arrays used by people like NASA are tested and corrected. Most civilian arrays never receive this individual treatment. This system might pick up any low-level incongruities if they happen to fall in a pattern that is reflected in the statistical distribution of the pixel groups.

Summary

This chapter described how to produce mimic text that looks statistically similar to original text. Chapter 7 describes how to use a more sophisticated grammar-based method to achieve a better result. Chapter 8 goes even further and shows how a Turing machine can be made to run backward and forward to produce the most complicated text.

The Disguise The text produced by these regular mimic functions can be quite realistic. The results are statistically equivalent. First-order text will have similar first-order statistics. Second-order text will have the same occurrence of pairs. This can be quite realistic in the higher orders, but it will rarely pass the reading test. Humans would quickly recognize it as gibberish.

How Secure Is It? There is no reason to guess that this system offers any more security than hiding the information. The question of how hard it would be to break such a statistical system is an open question. I believe that it would be possible to examine the statistics and come up with a pretty good guess about the shape of the Huffman trees used to generate the text. There may only be a few thousand options that can be tested quite quickly if some known plaintext is available.

For that reason, this system should probably be used in low-grade applications that demand verisimilitude but not perfection.

How To Use It? No software is being distributed right now to handle this problem, but it should not be easy to code it.

Chapter 7

Grammars and Mimicry

Evolution of Everyday Things

Recently, I sat down with Charles Radwin, an evolutionary scientist, who drew a fair bit of acclaim and controversy over his paper showing how evolution led the human species to gorge on the O.J. Simpson trial. I asked him his views about how evolution affected other aspects of our lives. Here is our conversation:

Q: Eventually all toilets need their handles wiggled to stop them from running. Why?

A: The commodes obviously developed this response to prevent calcification. The extra running water prevented tank stoppage and the toilets that had this gene quickly outlasted those that didn't. It was simple natural selection.

Q: What about toasters? No matter how hard you try to set them right, they always burn some toast.

A: Toasters developed this response to protect their host organism. Golden brown toast begs for a thick coating of butter. Perfect toasters gave their host humans massive coronary occlusions and that sends them to the scrap heap. The best toasters are those that do not kill off their hosts. They ultimately come to dominate the ecological landscape in the kitchen.

Q: Lightbulbs always burn out when I turn on the light. Why not, say, in the middle of a novel?

A: Again, lightbulbs evolved this way to protect their host humans. People often turn on lights when they enter a dark room. If the lightbulb dies at this moment, no one is stranded in the dark. But if the lightbulb burns out when someone is in the middle of the room, that human invariably trips over the coffee table, falls and splits its head wide open. Naturally, the lightbulbs that evolve into a synergistic relationship with their human hosts survive the best.

Q: But why don't lightbulbs live forever? Wouldn't that make life even better for their hosts?

A: Evolution can't function without new generations. Something must die in order for progress to occur.

Q: Copying machines always break down ten minutes before the crucial presentation. I've almost lost two jobs when a copier quit on me. They certainly weren't protecting their host organism, were they?

A: Evolution is a tricky balance. An organism can be too successful and consume all of its habitat. Imagine a perfect copying machine that did one billion flawless copies in a second. Wonderful, right? Not for the copying machine. Everything would be copied. It would have no purpose and the humans would quickly replace it with something more fun like a refrigerator filled with beer.

Q: Speaking of beer, why do some of those pop-tops break off without opening the can? By the end of a fishing trip, my cooler is filled with unopenable cans with no pop-tops.

A: You're answering your own question, aren't you?

Q: Why isn't beer entering into a synergistic relationship with the human? I'm certainly game.

A: In this case, the beer and the human are competing for the same ecological niche. If two humans drink beer, they often go off and create another human, not another beer.

Q: What if people set up another batch of hops and malt when they got drunk? Would those pull tabs start cooperating?

A: Evolution is hard to predict. Small changes in the equation can often change the entire outcome. I think that the beer pull tops would soon become harder to pull off. Why? Because organisms often evolve reproductive restraint to avoid catastrophic competition. Your scenario could quickly lead to a flood of beer.

Q: There's nothing I can do about the pull tabs? Aren't evolutionary scientists good for anything?

A: Evolution is tricky. If scientists were able to answer all of the questions, there would be no need for evolutionary scientists. Nor would there be any need for the program officers at the National Science Foundation who give out money to evolutionary scientists. There is a well-defined synergy at work here.

Using Grammar for Mimicry

Chapter 6 showed how to hide data and turn it into something that mimicked the statistical patterns of a file. If you wanted a piece of text to sound like the *New York Times*, for instance, you could feed in a large amount of source material from the paper and gather statistical patterns that would make it possible to mimic its output. Ideally, such a function would be a strong technique that could hide data from automatic scanning programs that might use statistical patterns to identify data.

The output of these Huffman-based methods could certainly fool any machine examining data looking for suspicious patterns. The letters would conform to the expected distribution; "e"s would be common, "z"s would be uncommon. If either second- or third-order text was used, then "u"s would follow "q"s and everything would seem to make sense to a computer that was merely checking statistics.

These statistical mimic functions wouldn't fool anyone looking at the grammar. First- or second-order mimicry like that found on page 79 looks incomprehensible. Words start to appear in third- or fourth-order text, but they rarely fall into the basic grammatical structure. Even a wayward grammar checker could flag these a mile away. This chapter describes how to create mimicry that will be grammatically correct and make perfect sense to a human. The algorithms are based upon some of the foundational work done in linguistics that now buttresses much of computer science. The net result is something that reads quite well and can be very, very difficult to break.

The basic abstraction used in this chapter is *context-free grammar*. The notion was developed by Noam Chomsky [CM58] to explain roughly how languages were worked. The structure is something like a more mathematical form of sentence diagramming. This model was adopted by computer scientists who both explored its theoretical limits and used it as a basis for programming languages like C or Pascal.

A context-free grammar consists of three different parts:

Terminals This is the technical term for the word or sentence fragments that are used to put together the final output. Think of them as the patterns printed on the puzzle fragments. The terminals will often be called *words* or *phrases*.

Variables These are used as abstract versions of decisions that will be made later. They're very similar to the variables that are used in algebra or programming. These will be typeset in boldface like this: **variable**.

Productions These describe how a variable can be converted into different sets of variables or terminals. The format looks like this:

$$\textbf{variable} \rightarrow \text{words} \parallel \text{phrase}.$$

That means that a **variable** can be converted into either words or a phrase. The arrow ($\rightarrow$) stands for conversion and the double vertical line ($\parallel$) stands for "or". In this example, the right-hand side of the equation only holds terminals, but there can be mixtures of variables as well. You can think of these productions as the rules for how the puzzle pieces can go together.

The basic idea is that a grammar describes a set of words known as the terminals and a set of potentially complex rules about how they go together. In many cases, there is a fair bit of freedom of choice in each stage of the production.

In this example the **variable** could be converted into either words or a phrase. This choice is where the information will be hidden. The data will drive the choice in much the same way that a random-number generator drives a fake computerized poetry machine. The data can be recovered through a reverse process known as *parsing*.

Here's a sample grammar:

Start	$\rightarrow$	**noun** **verb**
noun	$\rightarrow$	Fred $\parallel$ Barney $\parallel$ Fred and Barney
verb	$\rightarrow$	went fishing. $\parallel$ went bowling.

By starting with the **Start** variable and applying productions to convert the different variables, the grammar can generate sentences like "Fred and Barney went fishing." This is often written with a squiggly arrow ($\rightsquigarrow$) representing a combination of several different productions like this: **Start** $\rightsquigarrow$ Fred and Barney went fishing. Another way to state the same thing is to say: The sentence "Fred and Barney went fishing" is in the language generated by the grammar. The order of the productions is arbitrary and in some cases the order can make a difference (it doesn't in this simple example).

More complicated grammars might look like this:

Start	$\rightarrow$	**noun** **verb**
noun	$\rightarrow$	Fred $\|$ Barney
verb	$\rightarrow$	went fishing **where** $\|$ went bowling **where**
where	$\rightarrow$	in **direction** Iowa. $\|$ in **direction** Minnesota.
direction	$\rightarrow$	northern $\|$ southern

For simplicity, each of the productions in this grammar has two choices, call them 0 and 1. If you begin with the **Start** variable and always process the leftmost variable, then you can convert bits into sentences from the language generated by this grammar. Here's a step-by-step illustration of the process:

Step	Answer in Progress	Bit Hidden	Production Choice
1	**Start**	*none*	**Start** $\rightarrow$ **noun** **verb**
2	**noun** **verb**	1	**noun** $\rightarrow$ Barney
3	Barney **verb**	0	**verb** $\rightarrow$ went fishing **where**
4	Barney went fishing **where**	1	**where** $\rightarrow$ in **direction** Minnesota.
5	Barney went fishing in **direction** Minnesota.	0	**direction** $\rightarrow$ northern

The bits 1010 were hidden by converting them into the sentence "Barney went fishing in northern Minnesota." The bits 0001 would generate the sentence "Fred went fishing in southern Iowa." The bits 1111 would generate the sentence "Barney went bowling in southern Minnesota." There are 2^4 different sentences in the language generated by this grammar and all of them make sense.

Obviously, complex grammars can generate complex results and producing high-quality text demands a certain amount of creativity. You need to anticipate how the words and phrases will go together and make sure everything comes together with a certain amount of felicity.

```
Well Bob, Welcome to yet another game between the Whappers
and the Blogs here in scenic downtown Blovonia. I think it
is fair to say that there is plenty of BlogFever brewing
in the stands as the hometown comes out to root for its
favorites. The Umpire throws out the ball. Top of the
inning. No outs yet for the Whappers. Here we go. Jerry
Johnstone adjusts the cup and enters the batter's box.
Here's the pitch. Nothing on that one. Here comes the
pitch It's a curvaceous beauty. He just watched it go by.
And the next pitch is a smoking gun. He lifts it over the
head of Harrison "Harry" Hanihan for a double! Yup. What a
game so far today. Now, Mark Cloud adjusts the cup and
enters the batter's box. Yeah. He's winding up. What looks
like a spitball. He swings for the stands, but no contact.
It's a rattler. He just watched it go by. He's winding up.
What a blazing comet. Swings and misses! Strike out. He's
swinging at the umpire. The umpire reconsiders until the
security guards arrive. Yup, got to love this stadium.
```

Figure 7.1. Some text produced from the baseball context-free grammar in Appendix B.

Figure 7.1 shows the output from an extensive grammar developed to mimic the voice-over from a baseball game. The entire grammar can be seen in Appendix B.

Figure 7.1 only shows the first part of a 26k file generated from hiding this quote:

> I then told her the key-word which belonged to no language and saw her surprise. She told me that it was impossible for she believed herself the only possessor of that word which she kept in her memory and which she never wrote down... This disclosure fettered Madame d'Urfé to me. That day I became the master of her soul and I abused my power. *–Casanova, 1757, as quoted by David Kahn in* **The Codebreakers**. [Kah67]

The grammar relies heavily upon the structure of the baseball game to give form to the final output. The number of balls, strikes, and outs are kept accurately because the grammar was constructed carefully.

The number of runs, on the other hand, are left out because the grammar has no way of keeping track of them. This is a good illustration of what the modifier "context-free" means. The productions applied to a particular variable do not depend upon the context that surrounds the variable. For instance, it doesn't really matter in the basic example whether it is Fred or Barney who is doing the fishing or bowling. The decision on whether it is done in Minnesota or Iowa is made independently.

The baseball grammar in Appendix B uses a separate variable for each half-inning. One half-inning might end up producing a bunch of sentences stating that everyone was hitting home runs. That information and its context does not affect the choice of productions in the next half-inning. This is just a limitation enforced by the way that the variables and the productions were defined. If the productions were less arbitrary and based on more computation, even more better text could be produced.[1]

Parsing and Going Back

Hiding information as sentences generated from a particular grammar is a nice toy. Recovering the data from the sentences turns the parlor game into a real tool for transmitting information covertly. The reverse process is called *parsing* and computer scientists have studied the process extensively. Computer languages like C are built upon a context-free grammar. The computer parses the language to understand its instructions. This chapter is only interested in the process of converting a sentence back into the list of bits that led to its production.

Parsing can be complex or easy. Most computer languages are designed to make parsing easy so the process can be made fast. There is no reason why this can't be done with mimicry as well. You can always parse the sentence from any context-free grammar and recover the sequence of productions, but there is no reason to use these arbitrarily complex routines. If the grammar is designed correctly, it is easy enough for anyone to parse the data.

There are two key rules to follow. First, make sure the grammar is not *ambiguous*, and second, keep the grammar in *Greibach Normal Form*.

---

[1]It is quite possible to create a more complex grammar that does a better job of encoding the score at a particular time, but this grammar won't be perfect. It will do a better job, but it won't be exactly right. This is left as an exercise.

If the same sentence can emerge from a grammar through two different sets of productions, then the grammar is *ambiguous*. This makes the grammar unusable for hiding information because there is no way to accurately recover the data. An ambiguous grammar might be useful as a cute poetry generator, but if there is no way to be sure what the hidden meaning is, then it can't be used to hide data.

Here's an example of an ambiguous grammar:

Start	→	**noun verb** ‖ **who what**
noun	→	Fred ‖ Barney
verb	→	went fishing. ‖ went bowling.
who	→	Fred went ‖ Barney went
what	→	bowling ‖ fishing

The sentence "Fred went fishing" could be produced by two different steps. If you were hiding data in the sentence, then "Barney went bowling" could have come from either the bits 011 or 110. Such a problem must be avoided at all costs.

If a context-free grammar is in Greibach Normal Form (GNF), it means that the variables are at the end of the productions. Here are some examples:

Production	In GNF?
Start → **noun verb**	YES
where → in **direction** Iowa. ‖ in **direction** Minnesota.	NO
where → in **direction state**. ‖ in **direction state**.	YES
what → bowling ‖ fishing	YES

Converting any arbitrary context-free grammar into Greibach Normal Form is easy. You can simply add productions until you reach success. Here's the extended example from this section with a new variable, **state**, that places this in GNF.

Start	→	**noun verb**
noun	→	Fred ‖ Barney
verb	→	went fishing **where** ‖ went bowling **where**
where	→	in **direction state**
direction	→	northern ‖ southern
state	→	Iowa. ‖ Minnesota.

This grammar generates exactly the same group of sentences or language as the other version. The only difference is in the order in which choices are made. Here, there is no choice available when the variable **where** is tackled. No bits would be stored away at this point. The variables for **direction** and **state** would be handled in order. The result is that the sentence "Barney went fishing in northern Minnesota" is produced by the bits 1001. In the previous grammar on page 95, the sentence emerged from hiding bits 1010.

Parsing the result from a context-free grammar that is in Greibach Normal Form is generally easy. The table on page 95 shows how the sentence "Barney went fishing in northern Minnesota" was produced from the bits 1010. The parsing process works along similar lines. Here's the sentence being parsed using the grammar from above in GNF.

The program was a mimetic weapon, designed to absorb local color and present itself as a crash priority override in whatever context it encountered.
—William Gibson in Burning Chrome

Step	Sentence Fragment in Question	Matching Production	Bit Recovered
1	*Barney* went fishing in northern Minnesota	**noun** → Fred ‖ Barney	1
2	Barney *went fishing* in northern Minnesota	**verb** → went fishing **where** ‖ went bowling **where**	0
3	Barney went fishing *in* northern Minnesota	**where** → in **direction state**.	*none*
4	Barney went fishing in *northern* Minnesota	**direction** → northern ‖ southern	0
5	Barney went fishing in northern *Minnesota.*	**state** → Iowa. ‖ Minnesota.	1

The bits 1001 are recovered in step 5. This shows how a simple parsing process can recover bits stored inside of sentences produced using grammar in GNF. Better parsing algorithms can handle any arbitrary context-free grammar, but this is beyond the purview of this book.

How Good Is It?

There are many ways to measure goodness, goodness knows, but the most important ones here are efficiency and resistance to attack. The efficiency of this method is something that depends heavily upon the grammar itself. In the examples in this section, one bit in the source text was converted into words like "Minnesota" or "Barney". That's not particularly efficient.

The grammar could encode more bits at each stage in the production if there were more choices. In each of the examples, there were only two choices on the right side of the production. There is no reason why there can't be more. Four choices would encode two bits. Eight choices would encode three bits, and so on. More choices are often not hard to add. There is no reason why there can't be 1024 names of people that could be produced as the noun of the sentence. That would encode 10 bits in one swoop. The only limitation is your imagination.

Assessing the resistance to attack is more complicated. The hardest test can be fooling a human. The text produced in Chapter 6 may look correct statistically, but even the best fifth-order text seems stupid to the average human. The grammatical text that can be produced from this process can be as convincing as someone can make the grammar. The example in Appendix B shows how complicated it can get. Spending several days on a grammar may well be worth the effort.

There are still limitations to the form. Context-free grammars have a fairly simple form. This means, however, that they don't really keep track of information particularly well. The example in Appendix B shows how strikes, balls, and outs can be kept straight, but it fails to keep track of the score or the movement of the base runners. A substantially more complicated grammar might begin to do this, but there will always be limitations to writing the text in this format.

The nature of being *context-free* also imposes deeper problems on the narrative. The voice-over from a baseball game is a great conceit here because the story finds itself in the same situation over and over again. The batter is facing the pitcher. The details about the score and the count change, but the process repeats itself again and again and again.

Creating a grammar that produces convincing results can either be easy or hard. The difficulty depends, to a large extent, on your level of cynicism. For instance, anyone could easily argue that the process of government in Washington, D.C. is a three-step process:

1. Member of Congress X threatens to change regulation Y of industry Z.

2. Industry Z coughs up money to re-election campaign of other members P, D, and Q.

3. P, D, and Q stop X's plan in committee.

If you believe that life in Washington, D.C. boils down to this basic economic process, you would have no problem coming up with a long, complicated grammar that spun out news from Washington. The same can be said for soap operas or other distilled essences of life.

There are also deeper questions about what types of mathematical attacks can be made upon the grammars. Any attacker who wanted to recover the bits would need to know something about the grammar that was used to produce the sentences. This would be kept secret by both sides of the transmission. Figuring out the grammar that generated a particular set of sentences is not easy. The earlier ambiguous grammar example shows how five simple production rules can produce a number of sentences in two different ways. There so many different possible grammars that could generate each sentence that it would be practically impossible to search through all of them.

Nor is it particularly feasible to reconstruct the grammar. Deciding where the words produced from one variable end and the words produced by another variable begin is a difficult task. You might be able to create such an inference when you find the same sentence type repeated again and again and again. These reasons don't guarantee the security of the system by any means. They just offer some intuition for why it might be hard to recover the bits hidden with a complicated grammar. "Assessing the Theoretical Security of Mimicry" on page 117 discusses some of the deeper reasons to believe in the security of the system.

"Scrambled Grammars" on page 107 shows how to rearrange grammars for more security.

Creating Grammar-Based Mimicry

Producing software to do context-free mimicry is not complicated. You only need to have a basic understanding of how to parse text, generate some random numbers, and break up data into bit-levels. Appendix A shows the Pascal code for a complete context-free grammar system that both encodes and decodes information. The code is broken up into seven major units that accomplish different functions. These units are:

A C version of the code is also available on the code disk. It is pretty much a straight conversion.

MimicGlobals.p This contains all of the global variables and constants.

Randomness.p The current version can have its choices scrambled in a minor way using a built-in random number generator. Both ends of a transmission can synchronize their random number generators by starting with the same seed. This works like a password because it changes the production choices. A better approach, which is uncoded, is described in "Scrambled Grammars" on page 107.

WordEater.p This code handles the basic file operations. It opens up a file, reads it in character by character, and forms the results into words. This software assumes that words, not characters, are atomic units and this is one of the limitations of this version. A better approach would leave room for the possibility that each word could be produced from several different variables. This could take care of plurals.

TableSetter.p The software can handle arbitrary grammars that are stored in a set format. The code in this unit reads in the grammar and builds up the internal tables that are used to guide both the production and the parsing of the data.

OutSpitter.p This unit will read in the data to be hidden, break it down into bits, and then make the right choices from the tables built up by the code in TableSetter.p.

MimicParser.p This is the parsing code that takes all of the gibberish that comes from OutSpitter.p and turns it back into the bits that were hidden.

MimicMaster.p This code glues all of the units together with a basic interface.

Each of these files can be read in Appendix A. The C versions are essentially identical, except that they've been recoded in the language lingua franca.

There are a number of different details of the code that bear explaining. The best place to begin is the format for the grammar files. Figure 7.2 shows a scrap from the baseball context-free grammar that is described in full in Appendix B.

```
*WhapperOutfieldOut = He pops one up into deep left field./.1/
     He lifts it back toward the wall where it is caught
       by *BlogsOutfielder *period/.1/
     He knocks it into the glove of
       *BlogsOutfielder *period /.1/
     He gets a real piece of it and
       drives it toward the wall
         where it is almost ... Oh My God! ... saved by
         *BlogsOutfielder *period /.1/
     He pops it up to *BlogsOutfielder *period /.2//

*WeatherComment = Hmm . Do you think it will rain ? /.1/
  What are the chances of rain today ? /.1/
  Nice weather as long as it doesn't rain . /.1/
  Well, if rain breaks out it will
    certainly change things . /.1/
  You can really tell the mettle of a
    manager when rain is threatened . /.1//

*BlogsOutfielder = Orville Baskethands /.1/
                   Robert Liddlekopf /.1/
              Harrison "Harry" Hanihan /.1//
```

Figure 7.2. Three productions from the grammar in Appendix B encoded in the file format recognized by the code in TableSetter.p.

The variables begin with the asterisk character and must be one contiguous word. A better editor and parser combination would be able to distinguish between them and remove this restriction. Starting with a bogus character like the asterisk is the best compromise. Although it diminishes readability, it guarantees that there won't be any ambiguity.

The list of productions that could emerge from each variable is separated by forward slashes. The pattern is: *phrase / number/*. The final phrase for a variable has an extra slash after the last number. The number is a weighting given to the random choice maker. In this example, most of them are .1. The software simply adds up all of the weights for a particular variable and divides through by this total to normalize the choices.

The weightings aren't used randomly. If the choice of a particular phrase is going to encode information, then there must be a one-to-one connection between incoming bits and the output. The Huffman trees discussed in "Choosing the Next Letter" on page 81 are the best way to map a weighted selection of choices to incoming bits. So the weightings are used to build a tree. Figure 7.3 shows the tree built to hide information in the choice of the Blogs outfielder who makes a play. The same proof that shows that Huffman trees are the optimal way to compress a file will show that this is the best way to encode information.

Naturally, the Huffman tree only approximates the desired statistical outcome and the level of the approximation is limited to the powers of one half. Figure 7.3 shows how badly the Huffman tree can often be off the mark. One of the choices encodes one bit of information and the other two each encode two. This means, effectively, that the first choice will be made 50% of the time and the other two will be chosen 25% of the time.

The level of inaccuracy decreases as more and more choices are available. For instance, it should be obvious that if a variable can be converted into 2^i different choices each with equal weighting, then the approximation will be perfect. This will also be the case if all of the weightings are powers of 2 and the total adds up to a power of 2. For instance: $\{1, 1, 2, 4, 2, 2, 4\}$.

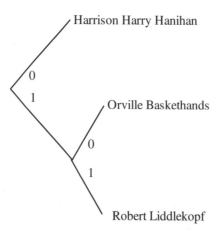

Harrison Harry Hanihan

0

1

Orville Baskethands

0

1

Robert Liddlekopf

Figure 7.3. The Huffman tree used to hide information in the choice of the Blogs Outfielder who makes a particular play.

Parsing the Output

The code in MimicParser.p handles the job of converting mimicry back
into the bits that generated it. Parsing the output from a context-free
grammar is a well-understood problem and is covered in depth in the
computer science literature. The best parsers can convert any text from
a grammar back into a sequence of productions that lead to the text.
The most general parsing algorithms like the [HU79] CYK algorithm
are slow.

The parsing algorithm implemented in this code is a compromise.
It will only work on grammars that are in a limited version of Greibach
Normal Form. This form requires that any variables be placed at the
end of each production. Page 98 shows some examples. The form
required by this parser is even stricter because it requires that it be
simple to determine which choice was taken by examining the first
words of a production. This means that no two choices from the same
variable may have the same first n words. n is adjustable, but the larger
it gets the slower the algorithm can become.

This format makes parsing substantially easier because the parser
only needs to look at the words and phrases. There is no need to follow
the variables and make guesses. The best way to illustrate this is with
a grammar that doesn't follow this rule. Here's a grammar that is *not*
in the correct format:

Start	→	**noun verb**
noun	→	Fred **AndFriend** ‖ Fred **Alone**
AndFriend	→	and Barney went fishing **where** ‖
		and Barney went bowling **where**
Alone	→	went fishing **where** ‖
		went bowling **where**
where	→	in **direction state**
direction	→	northern ‖ southern
state	→	Iowa. ‖ Minnesota.

Imagine that you are confronted with the sentence "Fred and
Barney went fishing in northern Iowa." This was produced by the
bits/choices 0000. Parsing this sentence and recovering the bits is
certainly possible, but it is not easy. The production "**noun** → Fred
AndFriend ‖ Fred **Alone**" does not make it easy to determine which
choice was taken. The terminal words at the beginning of each choice

are the same. They both say "Fred". A parser would need to examine the results of expanding the variables **AndFriend** and **Alone** to determine which path was taken. Following these paths is feasible, but it slows down the algorithm and adds complexity to the result. Most serious parsers can handle this problem.

This implementation is lazy in this respect, but I don't think much is sacrificed. It is relatively easy to place grammars in the correct format. The grammar could be modified to read:

Start	→	noun verb
noun	→	Fred and Barney **what** ‖ Fred **what**
what	→	went fishing **where** ‖ went bowling **where**
where	→	in **direction state**
direction	→	northern ‖ southern
state	→	Iowa. ‖ Minnesota.

Any context-free grammar can be placed in Greibach Normal Form. It is also possible to arrange that grammar in Greibach Normal Form be expanded so that there are no ambiguities. Alas, sometimes n needs to be made quite large to accomplish this. Another solution is to implement more complicated parsing algorithms.

Suggestions for Building Grammars

Creating a grammar that can be used to effectively turn data into innocuous text can be a time-consuming process if you want to do it well. More words and phrases mean more choices and more choices mean that more data can be packed into place. The grammars that have long phrases and few choices can be pretty inefficient. Here are some suggestions:

Think about the Plot and Narrative The grammar for a baseball game voice-over in Appendix B is an excellent example of a genre that can successfully stand plenty of repeating. These genres make the best choice for simple context-free grammars because the repeating effect saves you plenty of effort. You don't need to come up with production after production to make the system work. The same choices can be used over and over again.

There are other good areas to explore. Stock market analysis is generally content-free and filled with stream-of-consciousness ramblings about a set of numbers flowing throughout the world. No one can summarize why millions of people are buying and selling. Sports reporting usually amounts to coming up with different ways of saying "X smashed Y" or "X stopped Y." There is no reason why a more sophisticated version couldn't be built that would use actual news feeds to modify the grammars so the data was correct and filled with hidden bits.

There are other areas that are naturally plot-free. Modern poetry and free verse make excellent genres to exploit. People don't know what to expect and a strange segue produced by a poorly designed grammar doesn't stand out as much. Plus, the human brain is very adept at finding patterns and meaning in random locations. People might actually be touched by the work produced by this.

Break Up Sentences The more choices there are, the more data will be encoded. There is no reason why each sentence can't be broken up into productions for noun phrase, verb phrase, and object phrase. Many sentences begin with exclamations or exhortations. Make them vary.

Use Many Variations More choices mean more data is hidden. There are many different ways to say the same thing. The same thoughts can be expressed in a thousand different forms. A good writer can tell the same story over and over again. Why stop at one simple sentence?

Scrambled Grammars

Creating a complicated grammar is not easy, so it would be ideal if this grammar could be used again and again. Naturally, there are problems when the same pattern is repeated in encryption. This gives the attacker another chance to search for similarities or patterns and crack the system. Most of the work in creating a grammar is capturing the right flavor of human communication. The actual arrangement of the words and phrases into products is not as important. For instance, several of the grammars above that generate sentences about Fred and Barney produce exactly the same collection of sentences even though the grammars are different. There are many different grammars that generate the same language and there is no reason why the grammars can't be converted into different versions automatically.

There are three major transformations described here:

Expansion A variable in one production is expanded in all possible ways in another production. This is like distributing terms in algebra. For example:

noun	$\rightarrow$	Fred **AndFriend** ‖ Fred **Alone**
AndFriend	$\rightarrow$	and Barney went fishing **where** ‖
		and Barney went bowling **where**
Alone	$\rightarrow$	went fishing **where** ‖ went bowling **where**
⋮	⋮ ⋮	

The first variable, **AndFriend**, is expanded by creating a new production for **noun** for all possible combinations. The production for **AndFriend** disappears from the grammar:

noun	$\rightarrow$	Fred and Barney went fishing **where** ‖
		Fred and Barney went bowling **where**‖ Fred **Alone**
Alone	$\rightarrow$	went fishing **where** ‖ went bowling **where**
⋮	⋮ ⋮	

Contractions These are the opposite of expansions. If there is some pattern in several of the productions, it can be replaced by a new variable. For instance, the pattern "Fred and Barney" is found in two productions of **noun**:

noun	$\rightarrow$	Fred and Barney went fishing **where** ‖
		Fred and Barney went bowling **where**‖ Fred **Alone**
Alone	$\rightarrow$	went fishing **where** ‖ went bowling **where**
⋮	⋮ ⋮	

This can be contracted by introducing a new variable **what**:

noun	$\rightarrow$	Fred and Barney **what where**‖ Fred **Alone**
what	$\rightarrow$	went bowling ‖ went fishing
Alone	$\rightarrow$	went fishing **where** ‖ went bowling **where**
⋮	⋮ ⋮	

This new grammar is different from the one that began the expansion process. It produces the same sentences, but from different patterns of bits.

Permutation The order of productions can be scrambled. This can change their position in any Huffman tree that is built. Or the scrambling can take place on the tree itself.

Any combination of expansion, contraction, and permutation will produce a new grammar that generates the same language. But this new language will produce the sentences from bits in a completely different manner. This increases security and makes it much less likely that any attacker will be able to infer coherent information about the grammar.

These expansions, contractions, and permutations can be driven by a pseudo-random number generator that is seeded by a key. One person on each end of the conversation could begin with the same large grammar and then synchronize their random number generators at both ends by typing in the session key. If this random number generator guided the process of expanding, contracting, and permuting the grammar, then the grammars on both ends of the conversation would stay the same. After a predetermined amount of change, the result could be frozen in place. Both sides will still have the same grammar, but it will now be substantially different than the starting grammar. If this is done each time, then the structure will be significantly different and attackers will have a more difficult time breaking the system.

Here are more careful definitions of expansion, contraction, and permutation. The context-free grammar is known as G and the productions take the form $A_i \rightarrow \alpha_1 \| \alpha_2 \| \dots \| \alpha_n$. The A_i are variables and the α_j are the productions which are a mixture of terminals and variables.

An expansion takes these steps:

1. Choose one production that contains variable A_i. It is of the form: $V \rightarrow \beta_1 A_i \beta_2$. V is a variable. β_1 and β_2 are strings of terminals and variables.

2. This A_i can be replaced by, say, n productions: $A_i \rightarrow \alpha_1 \| \alpha_2 \| \dots \| \alpha_n$. Choose a subset of these productions and call it Δ. Call the set of productions not in Δ as $\bar{\Delta}$.

3. For each chosen production of A_i, add another production for V of the form $V \rightarrow \beta_1 \alpha_i \beta_2$.

4. If the entire set of productions for is expanded (i.e. $\bar{\Delta}$ is empty), then delete the production $V \rightarrow \beta_1 A_i \beta_2$ from the set of productions

for V. Otherwise, replace it with the production $V \rightarrow \beta_1 A_k \beta_2$ where A_k is a new variable introduced into the system with productions drawn from $\bar{\Delta}$. That is $A_k \rightarrow \alpha_i$ for all α_i in $\bar{\Delta}$.

When I did him at this advantage take, An ass's nole I fixed on his head: Anon his Thisbe must be answered, And forth my mimic comes.
—Puck in A Midsummer Night's Dream

Notice that all productions don't have to be expanded. The effect on the size of the grammar is hard to predict. If the variable A_i has n productions and the variable itself is found in the righthand side of m different productions for various other variables, then a complete expansion will create nm productions.

A contraction is accomplished with these steps:

1. Find some set of strings $\{\gamma_1 \ldots \gamma_n\}$ such that there exist productions of the form $V \rightarrow \beta_1 \gamma_i \beta_2$ for each γ_i. β_1 and β_2 are just collections of terminals and variables.

2. Create the new variable A_k.

3. Create the productions $A_k \rightarrow \gamma_i$ for each i.

4. Delete the productions $V \rightarrow \beta_1 \gamma_i \beta_2$ for each i and replace them with one production $V \rightarrow \beta_1 A_k \beta_2$.

Notice that all possible productions don't have to be contracted. This can shorten the grammar significantly if it is applied successfully.

The expansion and contraction operations are powerful. If two grammars G_1 and G_2 generate the same language, then there is some combination of expansions and contractions that will convert G_1 into G_2. This is easy to see because the expansion operation can be repeated until there is nothing left to expand. The entire grammar consists of a start symbol and a production that takes the start symbol into a sentence from the language. It is all one variable and one production for every sentence in the language. There is a list of expansions that will convert both G_1 and G_2 into the same language. This list of expansions can be reversed by a set of contractions that inverts them. So to convert G_1 into G_2, simply fully expand G_1 and then apply the set of contractions that are the inverse of the expansions that would expand G_2. This proof would probably never be used in practice because the full expansion of a grammar can be quite large.

The most important effect of expansion and contraction is how it rearranges the relationships among the bits being encoded and the structure of the sentences. Here's a sample grammar:

noun   →   Bob and Ray **verb** || Fred and Barney **verb** ||
               Laverne and Shirley **verb** || Thelma and Louise **verb**
verb   →   went fishing **where** ||
               went shooting **where** ||
               went flying **where** ||
               went bungee-jumping **where**
where   →   in Minnesota. || in Timbuktu. ||
               in Katmandu. || in Kalamazoo.

Each of these variables comes with four choices. If they're weighted equally, then we can encode two bits with each choice. Number them 00, 01, 10, and 11 in order. So hiding the bits 110100 produces the sentence "Thelma and Louise went shooting in Minnesota."

There is also a pattern here. Hiding the bits 010100 produces the sentence "Fred and Barney went shooting in Minnesota." The first two bits are directly related to the noun of the sentence, the second two bits to the verb, and the third two bits depend upon the location. Most people who create a grammar would follow a similar pattern because it conforms to our natural impression of the structure. This is dangerous because an attacker might be savvy enough to exploit this pattern. A sequence of expansions can fix this. Here is the grammar after several changes:

Figure 7.4 shows a way to convert 12 phrases into bits.

noun   →   Bob and Ray **verb2** || Fred and Barney **verb4** ||
             Laverne and Shirley **verb** || Thelma and Louise **verb3**||
             Bob and Ray went fishing **where** ||
             Bob and Ray went shooting **where** ||
             Thelma and Louise went fishing **where** ||
             Thelma and Louise went bungee-jumping **where** ||
             Fred and Barney went shooting in Minnesota. ||
             Fred and Barney went shooting in Timbuktu. ||
             Fred and Barney went shooting in Katmandu. ||
             Fred and Barney went shooting in Kalamazoo.
verb   →   went fishing **where** ||
             went shooting **where** || went flying **where** ||
             went bungee-jumping in Minnesota. ||
             went bungee-jumping in Timbuktu. ||
             went bungee-jumping in Katmandu. ||
             went bungee-jumping in Kalamazoo.

verb2	→	‖ went flying **where** ‖ went bungee-jumping **where**
verb3	→	went shooting **where** ‖ went flying **where**
verb4	→	went fishing **where** ‖ went flying **where** ‖
		went bungee-jumping **where**
where	→	in Minnesota. ‖ in Timbuktu. ‖
		in Katmandu. ‖ in Kalamazoo.

The productions for the variable **noun** has been expanded in a number of different ways. Some have had the variable **verb** rolled into them completely while others have only had a partial combination. There are now four different versions of the variable **verb** that were created to handle the productions that were not expanded.

The effect of the contractions is immediately apparent. Figure 7.4 shows the Huffman tree that converts bits into productions for the variable **noun**. The relationships among nouns, verbs, and locations and the bits that generated them is now much harder to detect. The first two bits don't correspond to the noun any more.

Table 7.1 shows phrases and the bits that generated them:[2]

There are still some correlations between sentences. The first two sentences in Table 7.1 have different endings and this is reflected in the last two bits. In fact, the first two bits seem to mean "Fred and Barney went shooting" and the last two bits choose the location. This pattern

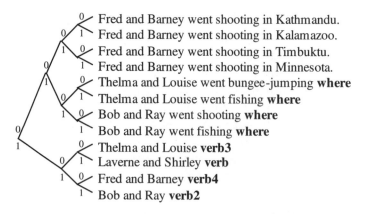

Figure 7.4. A Huffman tree that converts bits into productions for the variable **noun**.

---

[2]Some of the relationships between bits and the choice of production are left unexplained and for the reader to discover.

Table 7.1.

Phrase	Bits
Fred and Barney went shooting in Katmandu.	0000
Fred and Barney went shooting in Minnesota.	0011
Fred and Barney went fishing in Minnesota.	110100
Fred and Barney went bungee-jumping in Minnesota.	1100100
Thelma and Louise went bungee-jumping in Minnesota.	010000
Thelma and Louise went flying in Timbuktu.	100101

could easily be erased if the order of the productions were permuted. It could also be affected by any weighting given to the phrases.

But this same pattern does not hold for the other sentences. If the sentence begins "Fred and Barney went fishing" or if they go "bungee-jumping", then a different pattern holds. The location is determined by the choice that is made when the variable **where** is expanded. In this case, the relationship between the bits and the location is different. "Minnesota" is produced by the bits 00 in this case.

This is a good illustration of the effect that is the basis for all of the security of this system. The meaning of the phrase "Minnesota" depends upon its context. In most cases it is generated by the bits 00, but in a few cases it emerges from the bits 11. This is somewhat ironic because the grammars are called "context-free." The term is still correct but the structure of the grammars can still affect the outcome.

The process of contraction can add even more confusion to the mixture. Here's the grammar from Table 7 after several contractions:

noun → Bob and Ray **verb2** ‖ Fred and Barney **verb4** ‖
Laverne and Shirley **verb** ‖ Thelma and Louise **verb3**‖
who went fishing **where** ‖
Bob and Ray went shooting **where** ‖
Thelma and Louise went bungee-jumping **where** ‖
Fred and Barney went shooting in Minnesota. ‖
Fred and Barney went shooting in Timbuktu. ‖
Fred and Barney **verb5**

who → Bob and Ray ‖ Thelma and Louise
verb → went fishing **where** ‖
went shooting **where** ‖
went flying **where** ‖
went bungee-jumping in Minnesota. ‖

A deeper exploration of the security can be found in "Assessing the Theoretical Security of Mimicry" on page 117.

		went bungee-jumping in Kalamazoo. ||
		went bungee-jumping **where2**
verb2	$\rightarrow$	|| went flying **where** ||
		went bungee-jumping **where**
verb3	$\rightarrow$	went shooting **where** || went flying **where**
verb4	$\rightarrow$	went fishing **where** ||
		went flying **where** || went bungee-jumping **where**
verb5	$\rightarrow$	went shooting in Katmandu. ||
		went shooting in Kalamazoo.
where	$\rightarrow$	in Minnesota. || in Timbuktu. ||
		in Katmandu. || in Kalamazoo.
where2	$\rightarrow$	in Timbuktu. || in Katmandu.

Two new variables, **verb5** and **where2**, were introduced through
a simple contraction. They will significantly change the relationship
between the bits and the choice made for several sentences. Figure 7.5
shows new Huffman trees that are used to convert bits into the choice
of productions for variables. Here's a table that shows some sentences
and the bits that produced them before and after the contractions:

Phrase	Bits *Before* Contractions	Bits *After* Contractions
Laverne and Shirley went bungee-jumping in Minnesota.	101100	101011
Laverne and Shirley went bungee-jumping in Timbuktu.	101101	1010000
Fred and Barney went shooting in Kalamazoo.	0001	01111
Fred and Barney went bungee-jumping in Minnesota.	1100100	1100100
Thelma and Louise went bungee-jumping in Minnesota.	010000	010000

Some of the relationships among the noun, verb, and location are
still preserved, but some aspects are significantly changed. A series
of expansions and contractions can scramble any grammar enough to
destroy any of these relationships.

A third new variable **who** was also introduced through contraction, but it created a production that was not in Greibach Normal
Form (**noun** $\rightarrow$ **who** went fishing **where**). This would not work with

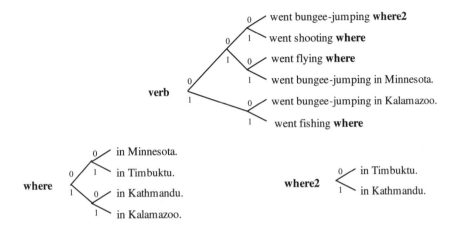

Figure 7.5. A Huffman tree that converts bits into productions for the variable **verb**, **where** and **where2** from Table 7.

the parser in the implementation shown in this book in Appendix A, but it could work fine with a better parser. The grammar is still not ambiguous. This example was only included to show that the expansions and contractions can work around grammars that are not in Greibach Normal Form.

One interesting question is what order the bits are applied to the production in this case. The previous examples in Greibach Normal Form used the rule that the leftmost variable is always expanded in turn. This rule works well here, but it leads to an interesting rearrangement. In the GNF examples, the first part of the sentence was always related to the first bits. In this case, this fails. Here the steps assuming the leftmost rule:

Starting	Bits of Choice	Produces
noun	0010	**who** went fishing **where**
who went fishing **where**	0	Bob and Ray went fishing **where**
Bob and Ray went fishing **where**	11	Bob and Ray went fishing in Kalamazoo.

There is no reason why the sequence of productions needs to be related with a leftmost first rule. A general parsing algorithm would be able to discover the three different choices made in the creation

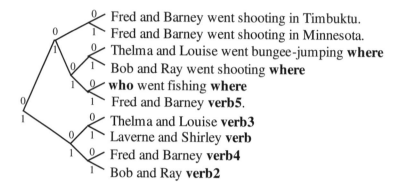

Figure 7.6. A Huffman tree that converts bits into productions for the variable **noun** from Table 7.

of this sentence. The GNF-limited parser could not handle this. They could be arranged in any predefined order that is used by both ends of the communications link. So the sentence, "Bob and Ray went fishing in Kalamazoo" could be said to be generated by any of the six combinations 0010011, 0010110, 0001011, 0110010, 1100010, or 1100100.

This last section on expansions and contractions has ignored the feature that allows a user to weight the choices according to some predetermined agenda. These weights can be carried accurately throughout the expansion and contraction process. If there is an expansion, the terms are multipled through. If there is a contraction, they are gathered. Here's an example of expansion. The weightings are shown as variables in parentheses.

Before:

noun $\rightarrow$ Thelma and Louise **what** (a_1) ‖ Harry and Louise **what** (a_2)
what $\rightarrow$ went shooting. (a_3) ‖ went to the hospital. (a_4)

Before expansion:

> **noun** $\rightarrow$ Thelma and Louise **what** (a_1) ‖
> Harry and Louise went shooting. $(\frac{a_2 a_3}{a_3 + a_4})$ ‖
> Harry and Louise went to the hospital. $(\frac{a_2 a_4}{a_3 + a_4})$
> **what** $\rightarrow$ went shooting. (a_3) ‖ went to the hospital. (a_4)

Here's the same example reworked for contraction. Before:

> **noun**   →   Thelma and Louise **what** (a_1) ||
> Harry and Louise went shooting. (a_2) ||
> Harry and Louise went to the hospital. (a_3)
> **what**   →   went rowing. (a_4) ||
> went to the fishing. (a_5)

After contraction:

> **noun**   →   Thelma and Louise **what** (a_1) ||
> Harry and Louise **what2** $(a_2 + a_3)$
> **what**   →   went rowing. (a_4) ||
> went to the fishing. (a_5)
> **what2**   →   went shooting. $(\frac{a_2}{a_2+a_3})$ ||
> went to the hospital. $(\frac{a_3}{a_2+a_3})$

These rules can be expanded arbitrarily to handle all expansions and contractions. Weightings like this can significantly affect the way that bits are converted into phrases using Huffman trees. The trees only work perfectly if the weights are structured correctly, so it is highly likely that most trees will produce imperfect approximations of the weights. As the expansions and contractions change the tree structure, the weights will significantly alter the patterns produced.

Assessing the Theoretical Security of Mimicry

Determining the strength of mimic functions based upon context-free grammars is not an easy task. There are two basic approaches and both of them can leave you with doubt. The first is to analyze the structure of the system on a theoretical level and use this to compare it to other systems. This can indicate that it can often be quite hard to break through the mimicry in these systems, but it can't prove to you that there are no holes out there. You just know that in the past, others have tried to break similar systems and failed. This is good news, but it is not conclusive. There might be new holes that are easy to exploit in these grammar-based mimic functions that are hard to use in other systems.

These holes are fairly common in theoretical approaches. For instance, there are very few proofs that show how hard it is to solve some

The principal difficulty of your case lay in the fact of there being too much evidence. What was vital was overlaid and hidden by what was irrelevant.

—Arthur Conan Doyle in The Naval Treaty

mathematical problems. Sorting numbers is one of the few examples. It has been shown that if you have a list of n numbers, then it takes time proportional to $cn \log n$ where c is some machine-based constant [AHU83]. This is a nice result, but it wouldn't make a good theoretical basis for a cryptographically secure system. There are other algorithms for sorting that can succeed in time proportional to kn where k is a different machine-based constant. These algorithms only work if you can place absolute bounds on the size of the numbers before beginning (64 bits is usually enough).

The other approach is to create different attacks against the system and see if it is strong enough to withstand them. This can certainly show the strength of the system, but it can also never be conclusive. There is no way to be sure that you've tried all possible attacks. You can be thorough, but you can't be complete.

Still, probing the limits of grammar-based mimic functions is an important task. The best theoretical bounds that exist are based on work exploring the limits of computers that try to learn. In this area, many researchers have based their work on Les Valiant's PAC model from probablistic learning [Val84]. In it, a computer is given some examples from a particular class and it must try to learn as much as possible about the class so it can decide whether a new example is part of the class. The computer's success is measured probabilistically and it succeeds if it starts getting more right than wrong.

There are many different forms of PAC algorithms. In some, the computer is given examples that are just in the class. In others, the computer gets examples from within and without the class. Sometimes, the computer can even concoct examples and ask whether that example is in or out of the class. This type of algorithm has the potential to be the most powerful and so it helps if the theoretical bounds can defend against it.

In [KV89, Kea89], Michael Kearns and Les Valient show that "learning" boolean formulas, finite automata, or constant-depth threshold circuits is at least as difficult as inverting RSA encryption or factoring Blum integers (x, such that $x = pq$, p, q are prime, and $p, q = 3 \mod 4$). The proof shows this by casting the factoring process into each of these different models of computation.

Dana Angluin and Michael Kharitonov [AK91] extended the work of Kearns and Valient as well as the work of Moni Naor and M. Yung [NY89, NY90]. This work shows that there are no known algorithms that run in polynomial time that predict membership in a class defined by finite unions or interesections of finite automata or context-free grammars.

These bounds deal with learning to predict whether a sentence is in a class defined by a grammar, not to discover its parse tree. But the results can apply to the grammar based system here if there is someway that a parse-tree discovering algorithm can be used to predict membership.

Imagine such an algorithm existed. Here is how to apply it to predicting membership in some language defined by grammar G_1 known as $L(G_1)$. The start symbol for G_1 is S_1. Now, suppose there is another grammar G_2 with start symbol S_2. Create a new grammar, G, that is the union of G_1 and G_2 by creating a new start symbol, S, and the production $S \rightarrow S_1 \| S_2$. Take a set of strings $a_i \in L(G)$. They are either in $L(G_1)$ or $L(G_2)$. Apply the algorithm that can learn to predict parse trees and feed it this set of strings. If such an algorithm can learn to predict the parse tree grammar then it can predict whether a string is in $L(G_1)$. If such an algorithm runs in polynomial time, then it can be used to break RSA, factor Blum integers and solve other problems. Therefore there is no known algorithm to predict even the first branch of a parse tree.

This result applies to the hardest grammars that might exist. It does not offer any clues on how to actually produce such a grammar. An algorithm that could construct such a grammar and guarantee that it was hard to discover would be quite a find. There are some minor observations, however, that can be satisfying.

You can easily imagine a grammar that would be easy to break. If each word or substring was one visible in one production, then it would be relatively easy to isolate the string of productions that produced a long section of text. The boundaries of the productions are simple to establish by accumulating enough sample text so that each production is used twice. The two occurances can be compared to reveal the different parts of the production.

This leads to the observation that each word should appear in multiple productions. The section beginning on page 107 describes how contractions and expansions can be applied automatically to change grammars so they fit this requirement.

How much contraction and expansion is enough? [Way95a] gives one set of equations that can be used to measure the "randomness" or "entropy" of a grammar. The equations are modelled on Shannon's measure of entropy of a bit stream. If one word is quite likely to follow another, then there is not much information bound in it. If many words are likely, then there is plenty of information bound in this choice.

The equations measure the entropy of the entire language generated by a grammar. If the number is large, then the information capacity of the grammar is also large and a great deal of information should be able to be transmitted before significant repetition occurs. This practical approach can give a good estimate of the strength of a grammar.

Both of these approaches show that it can be quite difficult to try and discover the grammar that generated a text. They do not guarantee security, but they show that it may be difficult to achieve in all cases. It can be even more difficult if the grammar is modified in the process through expansions and contractions. These can be chosen by both sides of a channel in a synchronized way by agreeing upon a cryptographically secure pseudo-random number generator.

Efficient Mimicry-Based Codes

The one problem with the mimicry system described in this chapter is that it is inefficient. Even very complicated grammars will easily double, triple, or quadruple the size of a file by converting it into text. Less complicated grammars could easily produce output that is ten times larger than the input. This may be the price that must be paid to achieve something that looks nice, but there may be other uses for the algorithm if it is really secure.

Efficient encryption algorithms using the techniques of this chapter are certainly possible. The results look like ordinary binary data, not spoken text, but they do not increase the size of a file. The key is just to build a large grammar. Here's an example:

Terminals Let there be 256 terminal characters, i.e., the values of a byte between 0 and 255. Call these $\{t_0 \ldots t_{255}\}$.

Variables Let there be n variables, $\{v_0 \ldots v_n\}$. Each variable has 256 productions.

Productions Each variable has 256 productions of the form $v_i \rightarrow t_j v_{a_1} \ldots v_{a_k}$. That is, each variable will be converted into a single terminal and k variables. Some productions will have no variables and some will have many. Each terminal will appear on the right side of only one production for a particular variable. This ensures that parsing is simple.

This grammar will not increase the size of the file when it is encoded. Each variable has 256 different productions available to it so 8 bits are consumed in the process of making the choice. The result is one new terminal added to the stream and this terminal takes 8 bits to store.

There are potential problems with this system. The biggest one is ensuring that the average string of terminals in the language is finite. If there are too many variables on the right-hand side of the productions, then the generating process could never end. The stack of pending variables would continue to grow with each production. The solution is to make sure that the average number of variables on the right-hand side of the production is less than one. The relationship between the average number of variables and the average length of the phrases in the language defined by the grammar is direct. A smaller number of average variables means shorter phrases. As the average number of variables approaches one, the average length tends toward infinity.[3]

The average length of a phrase in the language is not as important in this particular example. The bits can be recovered easily here because the grammar is in Greibach Normal Form and there is no need to place parsing decisions on hold. Each terminal only appears on the right hand side of one production per variable. So, the final file does not need to be a complete phrase produced by the grammar. It could just be a partial one. There is no reason why the grammars need to be as easy to parse, but more complicated grammars need to have the entire phrase produced from the starting symbol.

Summary

This chapter has described simple ways to produce very human-like texts. There is no reason why complicated grammars can't hide large

---

[3]This might be modeled with queuing theory.

volumes of data in seemingly human babble. This babble could be posted to some Internet newsgroup and it would be hard to tell the difference between this and the random flames and cascading comments that float through the linguistic ether.

There are still other levels of abstraction that are possible. MUDs (Multiple-User Dungeons) allow users to meet up in a text-based world defined and built up by textual architects. It is possible to meet people in the MUD rooms and hold conversations in the same way that you might ordinarily talk. Some MUDs now sport computer programs that pretend to be human in the spirit of the great Eliza [Wei76]. These programs use complicated grammars to guide the response of the computer. There is no reason why the random choices that might be made by this computer can't be converted to holding data.

Here's an extreme example. You want to set up a conversation with a friend across the country. Ordinarily, you might use the basic `talk` protocol to set up a text-based link. Or you might use one of the Internet phone programs to exchange sound. In either case, the bits you're exchanging could be monitored.

What if your talk program didn't contact the other person directly? Instead, it would log into a MUD somewhere on the Net as a persona. The other person's talk program could do the same thing and head for the same room. For the sake of atmosphere, let's make it a smoke-filled room with leather chairs so overstuffed that our textual personae get lost in them. There are overstuffed mastodons on the wall to complement the chairs.

Instead of handing your word bits over directly to the other person's persona, your talk program would encode them into something innocuous like a discussion about last night's baseball game. It might be smart enough to access the on-line database to get an actual scorecard to ensure that the discussion was accurate. When the other person responded, his talk program would encode the data with a similar grammar. The real conversation might be about very private matters, but it might come out sounding like baseball to anyone who happened to be eavesdropping on the wires.

There is no reason why both sides of the conversation can't use the same grammar. This convention would make it possible for both sides to hold a coherent conversation. After one persona commented about the hitting of Joe Swatsem, the other could say something about Swatsem because the same grammar would control what came afterward.

The sun's a thief, and with his great attraction Robs the vast sea: the moon's an arrant thief, And her pale fire she snatches from the sun: The sea's a thief, whose liquid surge resolves The moon into salt tears...
—William Shakespeare in Timons *of Athens*

The entire system is just an automated version of the old gangster-movie conceit about talking in code. One gangster says, "Hey, has the shipment of tomatoes arrived yet?" The other responds, "Yes. It will cost you 10,000 bananas." The potentials are amazing.

The Disguise Grammar-based mimicry can be quite realistic. The only limitation is the amount of time that someone puts into creating the grammar.

How Secure Is It? At its best, the grammar-based system here can be as hard to break as RSA. This assessment, though, doesn't mean that you can achieve this security with the same ease as you can with RSA. There is no strong model for what is a good key. Nor has there been any extensive work trying to break the system.

How To Use It? The code for the mimic system is in Appendix A.

Further Work There are a number of avenues to pursue in this arena. A theory that gave stronger estimates of the brute force necessary to recognize a language would be nice. It would good to have a strong estimate of just how many strings from a language must be uncovered before someone can begin to make sense of it. If someone could program the entropy estimates from [Way95a] or come up with better ones, then we could experiment with them and try to see how well they assess the difficulty of attack.

It would also be nice to have an automatic way of scanning texts and creating a grammar that could be used by the system here. There are many basic constructs from language that are used again and again. If something could be distilled from the raw feed on the Net, then it could be pushed directly into a program that could send out messages. This could truly lead to automated broadcast systems. One part would scan newsgroups or the net for source text that could lead to grammars. The other would broadcast messages using them. I imagine that it could lead to some truly bizarre AI experiences. One could set up two machines that babble to each other mimicking the Net but really exchanging valuable information.

Chapter 8

Turing and Reverse

Doggie's Little Get Along

One weekend I messed with the guts of my jukebox.
I wanted to zip it up to tweet like a bird
When the wires got crossed and the records spun backward
And this is the happy voice that I heard:

Whoopee Tie Yi Yay,
    The world's getting better and your love's getting strong
Whoopee Tie Yi Yay,
    Your lame dog will walk by the end of this song.

The music was eerie, sublime and surreal,
But there was no walrus or devil.
The notes rang wonderfully crystalline clear
Telling us that it was all on the level:

Whoopee Tie Yi Yay
    This weekend your sixty-foot yacht will be floated.
Whoopee Tie Yi Yay
    The boss just called to tell you, "You're promoted."

So after a moment I began to start thinking
What if I rewired the touch tone?
After a second of cutting and splicing, it suddenly rang.
This was voice that came from the phone:

Whoopee Tie Yi Yay
   This is the Publisher's Clearing House to Tell You've Won
Whoopee Ti Yi Yay
   A new car, an acre of dollars and a house in the sun.

A few minutes later my lost sweetheart called:
The guy she ran off with wasn't worth Jack.
He wore a toupee and the truck was his mother's.
Now she could only beg for me back.

Whoopee Tie Yi Yay
   Why spend your grief on a future that's wrecked
Whoopee Tie Yi Yay
   Why look backward when hindsight is always so perfect.

Running Backward

The song that introduces this chapter is all about what happens to a man when he finds a way to play the country music on his jukebox backward. His dog walks, his girlfriend returns, and the money rolls in. The goal of this chapter is to build a machine that hides data as it runs forward. Running it in reverse allows you to recover the data. The main advantage of using such a machine is that there are some theoretical proofs that show that this machine can't be attacked by a computer. These theoretical estimates of the strength of the system are not necessarily reliable for practical purposes, but they illustrate a very interesting potential.

Chapter 7 described how to use grammars to hide data in real-sounding text. The system derived all of its strength from the structure of the grammars and their ability to produce many different sentences from a simple collection of inputs. The weaknesses of the system were also fairly apparent. Grammars that were context-free could not really keep track of scores of ballgames or other more complicated topics. They just produced sentences without any care about the context. A bit of cleverness could go a long way, but anyone who has tried to create complicated grammars begins to understand the limitations of the model.

This chapter will concentrate on a more robust and complete model known as the *Turing machine*. The concept was named after Alan Turing, who created the model in the 1930s as a vehicle for exploring some of the limits of computation. Although the model doesn't offer a good way to whip up some good mimicry, it does offer a deeper theoretical look at just how hard it may be to break the system.

A good way to understand the limitations of the context-free grammars is to examine the type of machine that is necessary to recognize them. The parser constructed in Appendix A for recovering the data from the mimicry is also known, at least theoretically, as a *push-down automata*. The automata refers to a mechanism that is simply a nest of if-then and goto statements. The push-down refers to the type of memory available to it—in this case a push-down stack that can store information by pushing it onto a stack of data and retrieve it by pulling it off. Many people compare this to the dishracks that are found in cafeterias. Dishes are stored in a spring-loaded stack. The major limitation of this type of memory is the order. Bits of information can only be recalled from the stack in the reverse order in which they were put onto the stack. There is no way to dig deeper.

It is possible to offer you solid proof that push-down automata are the ideal computational model for describing the behavior of context-free grammars, but that solution is a bit dry. A better approach is to illustrate it with a grammar:

You can find a good proof in [AHU83].

start	→	Thelma and Louise **what when** | Harry and Louise **what when**
what	→	went shooting **with where** | bought insurance **with where**
with	→	with Bob and Ray | with Laverne and Shirley
when	→	on Monday. | on Tuesday. | on Wednesday. | on Thursday.
where	→	in Kansas | in Canada

A typical sentence produced by this grammar might be "Thelma and Louise went shooting with Bob and Ray in Kansas on Monday." This was produced by making the first choice of production from each variable and thus hiding the six bits 000000. But when the first choice was made and Thelma and Louise became the subjects of the sentence, the question about the date needed to be stored away until it was needed later. You can either think of the sentence as developing the leftmost variable first or you can think of it as choosing the topmost variable from the stack. Here's a table showing how a sentence was produced. It illustrates both ways of thinking about it.

Stack	Pending Sentence	Pending with Variables
start		**noun**
what **when**	Thelma and Louise	Thelma and Louise **what when**
with **where** **when**	Thelma and Louise went shooting	Thelma and Louise went shooting **with where**
where **when**	Thelma and Louise went shooting with Bob and Ray	Thelma and Louise went shooting with Bob and Ray **where when**
when	Thelma and Louise went shooting with Bob and Ray in Kansas	Thelma and Louise went shooting with Bob and Ray in Kansas **when**
empty	Thelma and Louise went shooting with Bob and Ray in Kansas on Monday.	Thelma and Louise went shooting with Bob and Ray in Kansas on Monday.

Both metaphors turn out to be quite close to each other. The context-free grammars and the stack-based machines for interpreting them are equivalent. This also illustrates why it is possible to imitate certain details about a baseball game like the number of outs or the number of strikes, while it is much harder if not impossible to give a good imitation of the score. There is no way to rearrange the information on the stack or to recognize it out of turn.

The Turing machine is about as general a model of a computer as can be constructed. Unlike the push-down automata, a Turing machine can access any part of its memory at any time. In most models, this is described as a "tape" that is read by a head that can scan from left to right. You can also simply think of the "tape" as regular computer memory that has the address 0 for the first byte, the address 1 for the second byte, and so on.

The main advantage of using a Turing machine is that you access any part of the memory at any time. So you might store the score to the baseball game at the bytes of memory with addresses 10140 and

10142. Whenever you needed this, you could copy the score to the output. This method does not offer any particularly great programming models that would make it easier for people to construct a working Turing mimicry generator. Alas.

The real reason for exploring Turing machines is that there are a wide variety of theoretical results that suggest that there are limits on how they can be analyzed. Alan Turing originally developed the models to explore the limits of what computers can and can't do [Tur36a, Tur36b]. His greatest results showed how little computers could do when they were turned against themselves. There is very little that computers and the programs they run can tell us definitively about another computer program.

These results are quite similar to the work of Kurt Gödel who originally did very similar work on logical systems. His famous theorem showed that all logical systems were either incomplete or inconsistent. The result had little serious effect upon mathematics itself because people were quite content to work with incomplete systems of logic. They did the job. But the results eroded the modernist belief that technology could make the world perfect.

Turing found that the same results that applied to Gödel's logical systems could apply to computers and the programs that ran upon them. He showed that, for instance, no computer program could definitively answer whether another computer program would ever finish. It might be able to find the correct answer for some subset of computer programs, but it could never get the right answer for all computer programs. The program was either incomplete or inconsistent.

Others have extended Turing's results to show that it is practically impossible to ask the machines to say anything definitive about computers at all. Rice's Theorem showed that computers can only answer *trivial* questions about other computers [HU79]. Trivial questions were defined to be those that were either always true or always false.

To some extent, these results are only interesting on a theoretical level. After all, a Macintosh computer can examine a computer program written for an IBM PC and determine that it can't execute it. Most of the time, a word processor might look at a document and determine that it is in the wrong format. Most of the time, computers on the Internet can try to establish a connection with other computers on the Internet and determine whether the other computer is speaking

Abraham Lincoln was really the first person to discover this fact when he told the world, "You can fool some of the people all of the time and all of the people some of the time. But you can't fool all of the people all of the time." The same holds true if you substitute "computer program" or "turing machine" for "people."

the right language. For many practical purposes, computers can do most things we tell them to do.

The operative qualifier here is "most of the time." Everyone knows how imperfect and fragile software can be. The problems caused by the literal machines are legendary. They do what they're told to do and this is often incomplete or imperfect—just like the theoretical model predicted they would be.

The matter for us is compounded by the fact that this application is not as straightforward as opening up word processing documents. The goal is to hide information so it can't be found. There is no cooperation between the information protector and the attacker trying to puncture the veil of secrecy. A better model is the world of computer viruses. Here, one person is creating a computer program that will make its way through the world and someone else is trying to write an anti-virus program that will stop a virus. The standard virus-scanning programs built today look for tell-tale strings of commands that are part of the virus. If the string is found, then the virus must be there. This type of detection program is easy to write and easy to keep up-to-date. Everytime a new virus is discovered, a new tell-tale string is added to the list.

Can you abort a virus? Can you baptize one? How smart must a virus be?

But more adept viruses are afoot. There are many similar strings of commands that will do a virus's job. A virus could possibly choose any combination of these commands that are structured correctly. What if a virus would scramble itself with each new version? What if a virus carried a context-free grammar of commands that would produce valid viruses? Every time it copied itself into a new computer or program, it would spew out a new version of itself using the grammar as its copy. Detecting viruses like this is a much more difficult proposition.

You couldn't simply scan for sequences of commands because the sequences are different with each version of the virus. You need to build a more general model of what a virus is and how it accomplishes its job before you can continue. If you get a complete copy of the context-free grammar that is carried along by a virus, you might create a parser that would parse each file and look for something that came from this grammar. If it was found, then a virus is identified. This might work sometimes, but what if the virus modified the grammar in the same way that the grammars were expanded and contracted on page 107? The possibilities are endless.

The goal for this chapter is to capture the same theoretical impossibility that gives Turing machines their ability to resist attacks by creating a cipher system that isn't just a cipher. It's a computing machine that runs forward and backward. The data is hidden as it runs forward and revealed as it runs backward. If this machine is as powerful as a Turing machine, then there is at least the theoretical possibility that the information will never be revealed. Building another computer that could attack all possible machines by reversing them could never work in all cases.

Reversing Gears

Many computer scientists have been studying reversible computers for some time, but not for the purpose of hiding information. The reversible machines have a thermodynamic loophole that implies that they might become quite useful as CPUs become more and more powerful. Ordinary electronic circuits waste some energy every time they make a decision, but reversible computers don't. This wasted energy leaves a normal chip as heat, which is why the newest and fastest CPUs come with their own heat-conducting fins attached to the top. Some of the fastest machines are cooled by liquid coolants that can suck away even more heat. The buildup of waste heat is a serious problem—if it isn't removed, the CPU fails.

The original work on reversible computers was very theoretical and hypothetical. Ed Fredkin [Fre82] offered a type of logic gate that would not expend energy. Normal gates that took the AND of two bits are not reversible. For instance, if $x\ AND\ y$ is 1, then both x and y can be recovered because both must have been 1. But if $x\ AND\ y$ is 0, then nothing concrete is known about either x or y. Either x or y might have been a 1. This makes it impossible to run such a normal gate in reverse.

The Fredkin gate, on the other hand, does not discard information so it can be reversed. Figure 8.1 shows such a gate and the logic table that drives it. There are three lines going in and three lines leaving. One of the incoming lines is a control line. If it is on, then the other two lines are swapped. If it is off, then the other lines are reversed. This gate can be run in reverse because there is only one possible input for each output.

Figure 8.2 shows an AND gate built out of a Fredkin gate. One of the two input lines from a normal AND gate is used as the control

The Scientific American *article by Charles Bennett and Rolf Landauer makes a good introduction to reversible machines [BL85].*

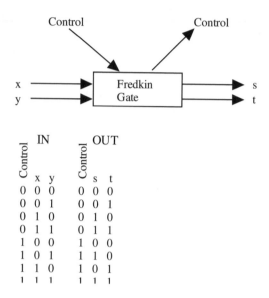

Figure 8.1. An illustration of a Fredkin gate. If the control line is on, then the output lines are switched. Otherwise, they're left alone. (Drawn from Bennett's figure.)

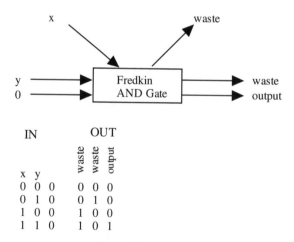

Figure 8.2. An AND gate built out of a Fredkin gate. The extra waste bits must be stored at the gate so that computation can be reversed later. (Based upon Bennett.)

line. Only one of the output lines is needed to give us the answer. The other two bits are wasted. Ordinarily, the information here would be thrown away by sending the bits to ground where they would heat up the chip. A truly reversible machine would store the bits at this location until the computer was run in reverse. Then the gate would have all of the information ready to compute the inverse. An OR gate would be built in the same way, but it would have one input fixed to be a 1.

There are a wide number of other mechanical approaches to building a reversible computer. Ed Fredkin and Tommaso Toffoli developed a billiard-ball computer that could be made to run in reverse *if* a suitable table could be found [FT82]. It would need to be perfectly smooth so the balls would move in synchrony. The table itself must be frictionless and the bumpers would need to return all of the energy to the balls so that nothing would be lost and there would be just as much kinetic energy at the beginning of the computation as at the end.

Figure 8.3 shows how two billiard balls can build an AND gate. The presence of a ball is considered to be the *on* state. So if both balls are there, they will bounce off each other. Only one ball will continue on its way. If the balls reach the end of the computation, then they can bounce off a final wall and make their way back. It should be easy to see that this gate will work both forward and backward. OR gates are more complicated and include extra walls to steer the balls.

This is an interesting concept, but it is hardly useful. No one can build such a frictionless material. If they could, it might be years before we got to actually trying to use it to compute. There would be too many other interesting things to do like watching people play hockey on it. More practical implementations, however, use cellular automata that came before and after it. Toffoli described reversible cellular automata in his Ph.D. thesis [Tof77a] and in other subsequent articles [Tof77b, TM87]. N. Margolus offers one solution in [Mar84] that implements the billiard-ball models.

The key result about reversible computers is due to Charles Bennett who showed that any computation can be done with a reversible Turing machines. He has created a few basic examples of reversible Turing machines with well-defined commands for moving the read/write head of the tape and changing the state of the machine. The transition rules for these machines often look quite similar to the Fredkin gate. There is just as much information coming out of each step as going

David Hillman has written about reversible one-dimensional cellular automata [Hil91b, Hil91a].

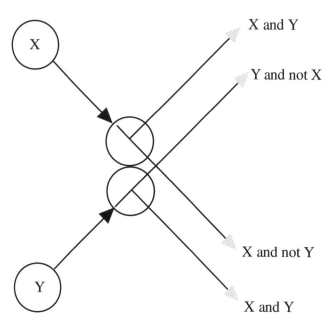

Figure 8.3. The three possible outcomes of a billiard-ball AND gate. The presence of a ball indicates an *on* signal. If only one ball is present, then no bounce occurs and it continues on its way. If both are present, then they bounce off each other. If none are present, then nothing happens. (After Bennett)

into it. This is balanced correctly so the position that leads to another position can always be inferred and the machine can be reversed.

Reversible computation is also great for debugging programs.

This result shows that anything that can be done with a computer can be done with a reversible computer. All that is necessary is finding a way to save the information from each step so it can be effectively run in reverse. But what does this mean if you want to hide information? It means that any computation can be used to hide information in the final outcome. How much can be stored? It all depends upon the calculation. Ordinarily, any random number generator that is used to add realism or scramble the outcome of a game can be replaced by a collection of data to be hidden. This data can be recovered as the machine runs in reverse.

How would such a system work? One obvious solution is to simply create a universal, reversible Turing machine format. A standard program running on everyone's computer would be able to read in a Turing machine and run it forward or backward. If you wanted to send a message, you would pack in the data and run the machine until it stopped. The result would be the output, perhaps some computer-generated poetry, and a pile of waste data that must be kept around in order to run the machine in reverse.

At the other end, the recipient would load this information into the same universal, reversible Turing machine and run it backward to recover the data. The one problem with this scenario is that any attacker could also have the same universal, reversible Turing machine. They could intercept the message and reverse it. For the technique to be successful, some data must be kept secret from the attacker. This could travel separately. In the grammar machine from Chapter 7, the grammar acts as the key. It must be distributed separately.

One solution is to keep the structure of the Turing machine, i.e., the program, secret and let it act as a key. Only the output and the extra, "waste" bits of information must be transmitted to the recipient. Anyone can intercept the message, but they cannot read it without a copy of the program that created it.

How difficult can this be? Obviously there will be some programs that are pretty easy to crack. For instance, a program that merely copies the data to be hidden and spits it out would be easy to deduce. The output would maintain all of the structure of the original document. More and more complicated programs would get more and more complicated to deduce. Eventually, something must be too hard to crack. The tough question is whether there is some threshold that can be established where it is positively known that programs that are beyond this threshold are completely safe.

Such a threshold can never be well-defined. That is, there can be no neat machine that will examine any program and say, "This can't be broken." There might be machines that could point out flaws in programs and show how they could be broken, but these machines would not be guaranteed to find all flaws.

This uncertainty is a pain, but it affects the enemy in the same way. The enemy can not come up with an arbitrary machine that will be able to examine every message you send and discover the program that was used to hide the data. It may be able to find some solutions, but there will be no brute-force attack that will work in all cases.

This is a nice beginning for security, but it is not absolute. The one-time pad offers a similar security blanket. There is no brute-force

See page 16
for details.

attack that will break the system, as long as the key bits are completely random. What is completely random? In practice, it means that the attacker can't build a machine that will predict the pattern of the bits. This is substantially easier to achieve for one-time pads than it is for reversible Turing machines. There are numerous sources of completely random information and noise that can be used as the basis for a one-time pad. Many Macintoshes come with built-in television tuners at the time this book was written. The random snow from a blank channel can make the good beginning for such a pad.

The rest of this chapter will concentrate on actually constructing a reversible Turing machine that could be used to create hidden messages in text. It will be based, in part, on the grammar approach from Chapter 7 because text is a good end product for the process. There is no reason why the work couldn't be adapted to produce other mimicry.

Building a Reversible Machine

Reversible ma-chines can be made error-resistant. Peter Neumann dis-cusses how to in-sert synchroniza-tion symbols into the text stream to stop the propi-gation of er-rors. [Neu64]

If every Turing machine can be reconstructed in a reversible manner, then every possible machine is a candidate for being turned into a vehicle for hidden information. Obviously, though, some machines are more interesting than others. For instance, there are computer pro-grams that loan companies use to evaluate the credit of applicants. These programs respond with either "qualified" or "unqualified." That's just one bit of information and it seems unlikely that anyone will be able to hide much of anything in that bit. On the other hand, programs that produce complex worlds for games like Doom spit out billions of bits. There is ample room in the noise. Imagine if some se-cret information was encoded in the dance of an attacking droid. You might get your signal by joining into a internet group game of Doom. The information would come across the wire disguised as instructions for where to draw the attacker on the screen. Your version of Doom could extract this.

This chapter will show how to build two different reversible ma-chines. The first is just a simple reversible Turing machine that is provided as a warm-up. It is based on the work of Charles Bennett and it shows how to take the standard features of a Turing machine and tweak them so that there is only one possible state that could lead to another. This makes it possible to rewind the behavior.

The second machine is an extension of the grammar-based mimicry from Chapter 7. That system used only context-free grammars. This is intended to make it possible to simulate any arbitrary computation to add realism to the text that the system produces. The data hidden by the system won't be recovered by parsing. It will come by running the machine in reverse. This means that a practical way needs to be constructed to ship the extra variables and "waste" bits along.

Reversible Turing Machines

An ordinary Turing machine consists of a set of states, S, a set of symbols that can appear on the tape, Σ, and a set of transition rules, δ, that tell the machine what happens when. For instance, δ might specify that if the machine is in state s_2, and there is the symbol σ_4 on the tape underneath the read/write head, then the read/write head should write the symbol σ_5 on the tape, move the head to the right one notch and change to state s_{42}. This is how you program a Turing machine. The abstraction is fairly crude, but it makes it simpler to keep track of all the possibilities.

Converting such a machine to run backward is pretty straightforward. The main problem is looking for combinations of states and tape symbols that lead to the same states. That is when it is impossible to put the machine in reverse because there are two different preceding situations that could have led to the present one. The easiest solution is to keep splitting up the states until there is no confusion.

For each state $s_i \in S$, construct a list of triples of states, tape symbols, and direction (s_j, σ_k, L), that could lead to the state s_i. That is, if the machine is in state s_j with the read/write head over the symbol σ_l, then it will write σ_k and move to the left one step. This means if the machine is running backward and it finds itself in state s_i with symbol σ_k to the right of it, then it can move to the right, change to state s_j and overwrite σ_k with σ_l and not violate the program. That is, this is a correct move.

There will be a conflict if there are triples of the form (s_*, σ_*, L) and (s_*, σ_*, R) in the same set. (Let s_* stand for any element s_i from S.) This is because it will be quite possible that the machine will end up someplace with one of the symbols to the left and one of the symbols to the right. You might be able to make meta-arguments that such a

If a certain puritanical tradition, for instance, is profoundly suspicious of the novel, this is because the novel is felt to celebrate and encourage misconduct, rather than censure and repress it.
—D.A. Miller in The Novel and The Police

combination could never exist because of the structure of the program, but these are often hard to prove.

If such a conflict occurs, then create a new state and split apart the actions. All of the triples that moved left into the old state s_i can stay pointing to state s_i. The triples that moved *right*, however, will be moved to point to the new state s_j. The transition rules out of s_j will be a duplicate of s_i.

To a large extent, splitting these states is the same as simply finding a place to keep a "waste" bit around. The Fredkin AND gate generates some waste bits that must be stored. Splitting the state creates one.

The same splitting process must be done if there are two triples of the form: (s_a, σ_k, L) and (s_b, σ_k, L). Both of these states, s_a and s_b, lead to the same symbol existing to the right of the current position of the read/write head. Choosing is impossible. Again, a new state must be added and the transition rules duplicated and split.

It should be obvious that a Turing machine will grow substantially as it is made reversible. This growth could even be exponential in many cases. There is no reason why anyone would want to program this way. The complications are just too great. But this example is a good beginning.

Reversible Grammar Generators

The goal of this book is to produce something that seems innocuous but hides a great deal of information from plain sight. Chapter 7 has done a good job of doing this with a context-free grammar, but there are numerous limitations to that approach. This part of the book will build a reversible, Turing-equivalent machine that will be able to do all basic computations, but still be reversible. It will get much of its performance by imitating the Fredkin gate which merely swaps information instead of destroying it.

There are numerous problems that needed to be confronted in the design of this machine. Here are some of them:

Extra State At the end of the computation, there will be plenty of extra "waste" bits hanging around. These need to be conveyed to the recipients so they can run their machines in reverse.

There are two possible solutions. The first is to send the extra state through a different channel. It might be hidden in the least significant bits of a photo or sent through some other covert channel. The second is to use a crippled version of the machine to encode it as text without modifying any of the state. That is, reduce the capability of the machine until it acts like the context-free grammar machine from Chapter 7.

Ease of Programmability Anyone using the machine will need to come up with a collection of grammars that will simulate some form of text. Constructing these can be complicated and it would be ideal if the language could be nimble enough to handle many constructions.

The solution is to imitate the grammar structure from Chapter 7. There will be variables and productions. But you can change the productions en route using reversible code.

Minimizing Extra State Any extra bits must be transported through a separate channel at the end. They should be kept to a minimum.

For that reason, all strings should be predefined as constants. They can't be changed. If they could be changed, then the final state of all strings would need to be shipped to the recipient and this would be too much baggage.

Arithmetic Arithmetic is generally not reversible. $3 + 2$ is not reversible. But it is if one half of the equation is kept about. So adding the contents of register A_1 and register A_2 and placing the result in register A_1 *is* reversible. The contents of A_2 can be subtracted from A_1 to recover the original value of A_1.

For the most part, addition, subtraction, multiplication, and division are reversible if they're expressed in this format. The only problem is multiplication by zero. This must be forbidden.

Structure of Memory What form will the memory take? Obviously ordinary computers allow programmers to grab and shift blocks of memory at a time. This is not feasible because it would require too many extra waste bits would need to be stored around. Block moves of data are not reversible. Swaps of information are.

For that reason, there is simply an array of registers. Each one holds one number that can be rounded off in some cases. The final state of the registers will be shipped as extra state to the recipient so any programmer should aim to use them sparingly. Unfortunately, the rules of reversibility can make this difficult.

Conditional Statements Most conditional statements that choose between branches of a program can be reversed, but sometimes they can't be. Consider the case that says "If x is less than 100, then add 1 to x. Otherwise add 1 to p." Which path do you take if you're running in reverse and x is 100? Do you subtract 1 from p or not? Either case is valid.

The solution is to forbid the program from changing the contents of the variables that were used to choose a branch. This rules out many standard programming idioms. Here's one way to work around the problem:

```
if x<100 then {
    k=k+1}
else {
    p=p+1;
    swap x,k;}
  swap x,k;
```

Loops Loops may be very handy devices for a programmer, but they can often be an ambiguous obstacle when a program must run in reverse. One easy example is the while loop that is often written to find the last element in a string in C. That is, a counter moves down the string until the termination character, a zero, is found. It may be easy to move backward up the string, but it is impossible to know where to stop.

The problems with a loop can be eliminated if the structure is better defined. It is not enough to simply give a test condition for the end of the loop. You must specify the dependent variable of the loop, its initial setting, and the test condition. When the loop is reversed, it will run the contents of the loop until the dependent variable reaches its initial setting.

This structure is often not strong enough. Consider this loop:

```
i=1;
j=i;
while (i<2) do {
    j=j+.01;
    i=floor(j);}
```

The `floor(x)` function finds the largest integer less or equal to x. This function will execute 100 times before it stops. If it is executed in reverse, then it will only go through the loop twice before i is set to its initial value, one. It is clear that i is the defining variable for the loop, but it is clear that it j plays a big part.

There are two ways to resolve this problem. The first is to warn programmers and hope that they will notice the mistake before they use the code to send an important message. This leaves some flexibility in their hands.

Another solution is to constrain the nature of loops some more. There is no reason why they can't be restricted to `for` loops that specify a counter that is incremented each iteration and `map` functions that apply a particular function to every element in a list. Both are quite useful and easy to reverse without conflicts.

Recursion Recursion is a problem here. If procedures call themselves, then they are building a defacto loop and it may be difficult to identify the starting position of a loop. For instance, here is an example of a loop with an open beginning:

```
procedure Bob;
    x=x+1;
    if x<100 then Bob;
end;
```

This is just a while loop and it is impossible to back into it and know the initial value of x when it began.

One solution is to ban recursion altogether. The standard loop constructs will serve most purposes. This is, alas, theoretically problematic. Much of the theoretical intractability of programs comes from their ability to start recursing. While this might make implementing reversible programs easier, it could severely curtail their theoretical security.

Another solution is to save copies of all affected variables before they enter procedures. So, before the procedure Bob begins, the reversible machine will save a copy of x. This version won't be destroyed. It will become part of the waste bits that must be conveyed along with the output.

Ralph Merkle also notes that much of assembly code is reversible and predicts that in the future smart compilers will rearrange instructions to ensure reversibility. This will allow the chips to run cooler once they're designed to save the energy from reversible computations [Mer93].

In the end, the code for this system is quite close to the assembly code used for regular machines. The only difference is that there is no complete overwriting of information. That would make the system irreversible. Perhaps future machines will actually change the programming systems to enhance reversibility. That may come if reversible computers prove to be the best way to reduce power consumption to an acceptable level.

The Reversible Grammar Machine

Although the structure will be very similar to machine code, I've chosen to create this implementation of the Reversible Grammar Machine (RGM) in LISP. This language is one of the best experimental tools for creating new languages and playing around with their limits. It includes many of the basic features for creating and modifying lists plus there are many built-in pattern matching functions. All of this makes it relatively easy to create a reversible machine, albeit one that doesn't come with many of the features of modern compilers.

Here are the major parts of the system:

Constant List The major phrases that will be issued by the program as part of its grammar will be stored in this list, `constant-list`. It is officially a list of pairs. The first element of each pair is a tag-like `salutation` that is used as a shorthand for the phrase. The second is a string containing the constant data. This constant list is part of the initial program that must be distributed to both sides of the conversation. The constants do not change so there is no need to transmit them along with the waste state produced by running a program forward. This saves transmission costs. The main purpose of the constant list is to keep all of the phrases that will be output along the way. These are often long and there is little reason for them to change substantially. Defining them as constants saves space. The constant list can also include any data like the variable list. The data just won't change.

Variables The data is stored in variables that must be predefined to hold initial values. These initial values are the only time that information can actually be assigned to a variable. The rest of the code must change values through the swap command. The variables are stored in the list `var-list` which is, as usual, a list of pairs. The first element is the variable tag name. The second is the data stored in the variable.

There are five types of data available here: lists, strings, integers, floating-point numbers, and tags. Lists are made up of any of the five elements. There is no strict type checking, but some commands may fail if the wrong data is fed to them. Adding two strings, for instance, is undefined.

Some care should be taken with the choice of variables. The contents of these will need to be sent along with the output so the recipient can reverse the code. The more variables there are, the larger this section of "waste" code may be.

Procedure List At each step, there must be some code that will be executed. These are procedures. For the sake of simplicity, they are really just lists of commands that are identified by tags and stored in the list, `proc-list`. This is a list of pairs. The first element is the tag identifying the procedure and the second is the list of commands. There are no parameters in the current implementation, but there is no reason why they can't be added.

Commands These are the basic elements for manipulating the data. They must be individually reversible. This set includes the basic arithmetic, the swap command, the if statement and the for loop tool. These commands take the form of classic LISP function calls. The prefix notation that places the command at the front is not as annoying in this case because arithmetic is reversible. So addition looks like this: (add first second). That command adds first and second and places the result in first.

There are three other arithmetic commands: sub, mul and div which stand for subtraction, multiplication and division respectively. The only restriction is that you can't multiply a number by zero because it is not reversible. This is reported by an error message.

Output Commands There is one special command, chz, that uses the bits that are being hidden to pick an output from a list. When this command is run in reverse by the recipient, the hidden bits are recovered from the choice. The format is simple: (chz (*tag tag... tag*)). The function builds up a Huffman tree like the algorithm in Chapter 7 and uses the bits to make a choice. The current version does not include the capability to add weights to the choices, but there is no reason why this feature can't be added in the future.

The tags could point to either a variable or a constant. In most cases, they'll point to strings that are stored as constants. That's the most efficient case. In some cases, the tags will contain other tags. In this case, the choose function simply evaluates that tag and continues down the chain until it finds a string to output.

For practical reasons, a programmer should be aware of the problems of reversibility. If two different tags point to the same string, then there is no way for the hidden bits to be recovered correctly. This is something that can't be checked in advance. The program can check this on the fly, but the current implementation doesn't do it.

Code Branches There is an if statement that can be used to send the evaluation down different branches. The format is (if *test if-branch else-branch*). The program evaluates the test and if it is true, then it follows the if-branch otherwise it follows the else-branch.

The format of the test is quite similar to general lisp. For instance, the test (gt a b) returns true if a is greater than b. The other decision functions are lt, le, ge, and eq which stand for less than, less than or equal to, greater than or equal to, and simply equal to.

The current implementation watches for errors that might be introduced if the two variables used to make a decision were changed along one of the branches. It does this by pushing the names onto the `Forbidden-List` and then checking to see the list before the evaluation of each operation.

Program Counter and Code This machine is like most other software programs. There will be one major procedure with the tag `main`. This is the first procedure executed and the RGM will end when it finishes. Other procedures are executed as they're encountered and a stack is used to keep track of the position in partially finished procedures.

The source code can be found in Appendix 8. There are two main functions, `Encode` and `Decode`. One will take a file of data and

Summary

Letting a machine run backward is just one way to create the most complicated computer-generated mimicry. You could also create double-level grammars or some other modified grammar-based system.

The Disguise The text produced by these reversible machines is as good as a computer could do. But that may not be that great. Computers have a long way to go before they can really fool a human. Still, static text can be quite realistic.

How Secure Is It? Assessing the security of this system is even more complicated than understanding the context-free grammars used in Chapter 7. Theoretically, there is no Turing machine that can make non-trivial statements about the reversible Turing machine. In practice, there may be fairly usable algorithms that can assemble information about the patterns in use. The question of how to create very secure programs for this reversible machine is just as open as the question of how to break certain subclasses.

How To Use It The LISP software is given in Appendix C. It runs on the XLISP software available for free at many locations throughout the Internet.

Further Work The LISP code is very rudimentary. It's easy to use if you have access to a LISP interpreter. A better version would offer a wider variety of coding options that would make it easier to produce complicated text.

A more interesting question is how to *guarantee* security. Is it possible to produce a mechanism for measuring the strength of a reversible grammar? Can such a measuring mechanism be guaranteed? An ultimate mechanism probably doesn't exist, but it may be possible to produce several models for attack. Each type of attack would have a corresponding metric for evaluating a grammar's ability to resist that attack. Any collection of models and metrics would be quite interesting.

Chapter 9

Life in the Noise

Boy-Zs in Noizy, Idaho

Scene: A garage with two teens and guitars.

Teen #1   No. I want it to go, "Bah, dah, dah, dah, bah, screeeeech, wing, zing..."

Teen #2   How about, "Bah, dah, dah, dah, bah, screeeeech, screech, wing, zing..."

Teen #1   Hey, let's compromise:, "Bah, dah, dah, screeech, zip, pop, screeech?"

Teen #2   Oh. I don't know anymore.

Teen #1   What's the problem?

Teen #2   I just get tired of trying to say something with noise.

Teen #1   Hey. We agreed. Mrs. Fishback taught us in English class that the true artist challenges contemporary society. We need to expose its fallacies through the very force of our artistic fervor. Our endeavor must course through the foundations of society like an earthquake that gets a 10.0 on the Richter scale.

Teen #2   Yeah. So what. She's just a hippie chick. That's her idea.

Teen #1   Come on. Join the clambake. We have to confront the conformity of the adults with an urgency that heretofore has not been seen upon this planet. We need to demand that culture come alive with a relevance that can speak truth to the young and the restless. There are paradigms to shatter.

Teen #2   Would you shut up with that science stuff? Mr. Hornbeam said that Thomas Kuhn wasn't going to be on the final. Besides people managed to have a good time even before Copernicus and Galileo broke the paradigms apart. What about melody and harmony?

Teen #1   We can make our fuzz circuits do everything for us. Suburbia is just sleepwalking through life. Only our harsh notes can wake them to the discord that lies beneath the greenswept swards of our existence. That's what Mrs. Fishback says.

Teen #2   Cut it out. You like your dad's car as much as I do. How would you like your father to awaken you from your sleepwalking and force you to do some actual walking to the mall? I don't want to make Mrs. Fishback's music.

Teen #1   Why not? She obviously understands the evil hegemony proffered by a corporate culture intent upon creating a somnolescent adolescence. We are not people merely because we consume.

Teen #2   Nirvana, Pearl Jam, and the rest live on major labels sold at full list price at our mall.

Teen #1   Whoa! Perhaps we're being led to rebel in the hopes that anti-culture will sell even more than traditional culture?

Teen #2   Yes. You got it.

Teen #1   It's true. Mrs. Fishback just wants us to create a youth she never had when she was running between classes and earning good grades. The revolution always ended in the 1960's when the exams came around. They smoked a bit of pot, went to a protest, but most of it was just grooving to the music and searching for someone to do some loving. Then they got married and got jobs. We're just doing what her generation wants. They're marketing to us through their dreams of what they wished their childhood had been.

Teen #2   You're getting the hang of it.

Teen #1   The pervasive drive to explode the previous is just another marketing move. Unknowingly, we're channeling our rebellious energy through a marketing path created by a cynical corporate structure intent upon destroying the potential for upheaval in every youth. Instead of remaking the world with our passion, we're simply consuming anti-cultural icons constructed as pseudo-rebellious pabulum.

Teen #2   Bonzai!

Teen #1   So what do we do?

Teen #2   I have this Beethoven music here. It has no copyright.

Teen #1   Excellent. By reinvigorating the classic music, we'll be subverting the corporate music world that uses the laws of intellectual property to milk our youth. Instead of working long hours at McDonald's to save for a new $17.95 Nirvana Retrospective CD, we'll truly shatter the power structure by playing music long freed from the authorial and corporate imperative.

Teen #2   And there are some great bass chords in this Ninth Symphony . . .

Hiding in the Noise

Noise, alas, is part of our lives. The advertisements for digital this and digital that try to give the world the impression that digital circuits are noise-free and thus better, but this is only half true. The digital signal may be copied and copied without changing the message thanks to error-correcting codes and well-defined circuitry, but this doesn't eliminate much of the original noise. Digital photographs, digitized music, and digital movies all have a significant amount of noise that is left over from their original creation. When the voices, sounds, and photographs are converted into bits, the circuits that do the job are often less than perfect. A bit of electrical noise might slightly change the bits and there is no way to recover. This noise is something that will always be with us.

This noise is also an opportunity. If it doesn't really matter whether the bits are exactly right, then anyone who needs to hide information can take advantage of the uncertainty. They can claim the bits for their own through squatter's rights. This is probably the most popular form of steganography and the one with the most potential. There are millions of images floating about the Net used as window dressing for Web sites and who knows what. Any one could hijack the bits to carry their own messages.

The principle is simple. Digitized photos or sounds are represented by numbers that encode the intensity at a particular moment in space and/or time. A digital photo is just a matrix of numbers that stands for the intensity of light emanating from a particular place at a particular time. Digitized sounds are just lists of the pressure hitting a microphone at a sequence of time slices.

All of these numbers are imprecise. The digital cameras that generate images are not perfect because the array of charge-coupled devices (CCDs) that convert photons to bits is subject to the random effects of physics. In order to make the devices sensitive enough to work at normal room levels, they must often respond to only a few photons. The randomness of the world ensures that sometimes a few too many photons will appear and sometimes a few too few will arrive. This will balance out in the long run, but the CCD must generate an image in a fraction of a second. So it is occasionally off by a small amount. Microphones suffer in the same way.

"God is in the details." –Mies van der Rohe

The amount of noise available for sending information can be truly staggering. Many color digital photographs are stored with 32 bits allocated for each pixel. There are 8 bits used to encode either the amount of red, blue, and green or the amount cyan, magenta, and yellow of each pixel. That's 24 bits. If only one pixel from each of the colors was allocated to hiding information, then this would be about 10% of the file. At the top of the scale, a Kodak photo-CD image is 3072 by 2048 pixels and takes up about 18 megabytes. That leaves about 1.8 megabytes to hold information. The text of this book is well under half a megabyte, so there is plenty of room for hiding more information in a *single* snapshot. Many people won't want to spend 18 megabytes of storage space on a single snapshot. Less precise versions of images can run between 200k to 600k and still devote about 10% of their space to hidden data.

But if about 10% is devoted, how much does this affect the appearance of the image? Each of these 8 bits stores a number between 0 and 255. The last bit in each group of 8 bits is known as the least significant bit. It's value is 1. The most significant bit, the first one, contributes 128 to the final number if it is a one. This means that the least significant bit can change the intensity of a pixel in the final image by about .5 to 1% at the most. Trading 10% of the image data in a way that will only affect the final image by about 1% is a good solution.

There is no reason why more data can't be stored away. If the two least significant bits are given over to hidden data, then each pixel cannot change by more than 3 units. That is still about 1 to 3% of a pixel. But this is 25% of the final image size. This is a huge amount of bandwidth waiting to be captured and used.

File Formats, Compression, and Practical Problems

Actually exploiting this channel for information transfer can be fraught with practical problems. Most image and sound files include enough natural noise to hide a 3% change. Figure 9.1 shows a black-and-white scanned image of a photograph taken of a computer on a desk. Figure 9.2 shows just the least significant bits. It is obvious that there is a highly random pattern to them. This was caused by the noise in the digitizing circuit on the scanner.

Figure 9.1. This is a black-and-white photo of the author's desk. There is plenty of junk on the desk that is hiding secret documents. The noise in the image lends itself to hidden data as well.

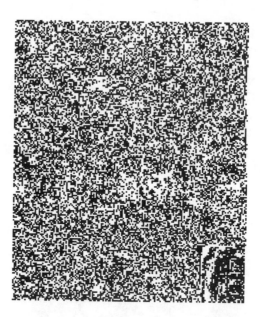

Figure 9.2. These are the least significant bits of the photo in Figure 9.1. The most significant bits were deleted to show the randomness that exists at this level. (See Figure 9.4.)

Many images and sound files probably have enough inherent noise to hide data. The image in Figure 9.1 has plenty of junk so small variations don't show up. But there are some images that do not handle the imposed noise as well. Many images are created entirely on the computer in applications like Adobe Illustrator. These produce pure, consistent fields of color. Even modifying them a bit can stand out because a pure tone is converted to one with a bit of noise.[1]

"Putting JPEG to Use" on page 171 shows how compression can identify just how much space can be exploited in an image.

File formats are a serious problem for anyone who would like to routinely use bit-level steganography to hide images. Many image or audio file formats were designed to squeeze out some of the extra

---

[1]The pure colors are often jarring to the eye and this is why artists often use textures and slight imperfections to make the image more appealing. It is anyone's guess why the optic nerve seems to react this way, but perhaps it is an effect like the moiré patterns produced when one pattern is digitized at too coarse a level. If you've ever looked at anyone wearing a fine checked shirt or tie on television you may have seen this effect.

noisy details to save space. This might be done by a special, efficient file format like GIF or by an aggressive compression program that does not care if it reconstructs an image that is not exactly the same. Both of these make it hard to simply hide information in the least significant bits of an image.

The GIF file format and its 8-bit color standard is a significant impediment because 8-bit color is quite different from 24-bit color. It uses a table of 256 different colors that best represent the image as a color map. The color of each pixel is described by giving the closest color from this 256-entry table. The bits do not correspond to the intensity of the colors at each pixel. This means that changing the least significant bits doesn't necessarily change the intensity at a pixel by less than 1%. Entry 128 of the table might be a saturated ruby red while entry 129 might be a pale, washed-out indigo. They may only differ in the least significant bit, but that can be enough to cause major changes in the final outcome.

Yes, the news-papers were right: snow was general all over Ireland.
—James Joyce in The Dead

There are a number of different solutions to this problem. The first is to simply use a smaller number of colors in the table. Instead of

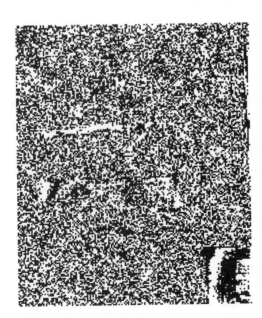

Figure 9.3. Even the second-to-least significant bits appear fairly random. These are the second-to-least significant bits of the photo in Figure 9.1.

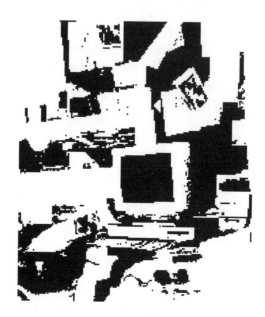

Figure 9.4. These are the most-significant bits of the photo in Figure 9.1. The seven least significant bits were deleted to contrast the images in Figure 9.2.

choosing the 256 colors that do the best job representing the colors of an image, the software could choose 128 colors and then choose 128 colors that are quite similar to the original 128. They might even be the same, but that could be too suspicious. The table could be arranged so that the two very similar colors only differ in one bit. Here's an abbreviated example of such a table:

Entry Num.	Binary	Red Intensity	Green Intensity	Blue Intensity
0	00000000	150	20	10
1	00000001	151	20	12
2	00000010	14	150	165
3	00000011	16	152	167
4	00000100	132	100	10
5	00000101	135	67	15
⋮	⋮	⋮	⋮	⋮

So if you want to hide the value 1 in a pixel, you would find the closest color in the table and then choose the version of it with the least

significant bit set to one. If the closest color had red set to 15, green set
to 151, and blue set to 167, and you wanted to hide the bit 1, then you
would choose color 3 for that pixel. If you wanted to hide a 0, then
you would choose color 2.

There is no reason why the least significant bit needs to be used to
separate pairs. It might very well be any of the bits. Here is another
table where the third bit is used to mix pairs:

Entry Num.	Binary	Red Intensity	Green Intensity	Blue Intensity
0	00000000	150	20	10
⋮	⋮	⋮	⋮	⋮
2	00000010	14	150	165
⋮	⋮	⋮	⋮	⋮
4	00000100	132	100	10
⋮	⋮	⋮	⋮	⋮
33	00100001	151	20	12
⋮	⋮	⋮	⋮	⋮
35	00100011	16	152	167
⋮	⋮	⋮	⋮	⋮
37	00100101	135	67	15

Nor is there any reason why only 1 bit is encoded in each pixel.
The same algorithms that choose 256 or 128 best colors for an image
can be used to find the closest 64 colors. Then 2 bits per pixel could be
allocated to hidden information. Obviously this can lead to a degraded
image, but the hidden information can often moderate the amount of
degradation. Imagine, for instance, that we tried to be greedy and hide
4 bits per pixel. This would leave 4 bits left over for actually specifying
the color and there could only be 16 truly different colors in the table.
If the photo was of a person, then there is a good chance that one of
the colors would be allocated to the green in the background, one of
colors would go to a brown in the hair and maybe two colors would
be given over to the skin color. A two-toned skin could look very fake.[2]

---

[2]Recent work suggests that human eyes pick up skin tones more than most colors.
So the best algorithms devote more colors in the table to skin colors in the hopes of
better representing them. The eyes don't really seem to care much about the shade of
green in a tree.

But each of these two tones might also be hiding 4 bits of information. This would be mean that there were 16 surrogates for each of these two tones and these 16 surrogates would be used fairly randomly. This would add a significant amount of texture that might mitigate some of the effects.[3]

Another significant hurdle for image- and sound-based steganography is the compression function. The digital representations of these data are so common that many specialized compression functions exist to pack the data into smaller files for shipping across the network. JPEG (Joint Photographic Experts Group) is one popular standard algorithm for compressing photographs. MPEG is a similar standard designed for motion pictures.

Both of these are dangerous for bit-level infopacking because they are *lossy* compression functions. If you take a file, compress it with JPEG, and then uncompress it later, the result will not be exactly the same as the original. It will look similar, but it won't be the same. This effect is quite different than the *lossless* compression used on many other forms of data like text. Those functions reproduce the data verbatim. Lossy compression functions are able to get significantly more compression because they take a devil-may-care attitude with the details. The end result looks close enough. The JPEG algorithm itself is adjustable. You can get significantly more compression if you're willing to tolerate more inaccuracies. If you turn up the compression significantly, the pixels begin to blend into big blocks of the same color.

Compression can also help. See page 171.

There is no easy way to battle JPEG compression of image files. If the lossy function reconstructs the file incorrectly, then the details and all of the information that was packed into them are gone. The JPEG standard, however, is difficult to code, so many people are content to use GIF files throughout the network. The main reason for using JPEG is the greater efficiency of the smaller files, but this impetus will melt away as network links become faster and hard disks reach into the terabytes.

Deniability

Deniability is one of the greatest features of hiding information in GIFs from Web pages. If you structure your information correctly, you can

---

[3]Random noise has been used to make quantization look more realistic. Too many discrete levels look artificial [Rob62].

spread it out among a number of unrelated locations. If the information is discovered, it will be impossible to tell exactly where it came from.

Imagine that you have some bits that you want to distribute to the world. You could simply hide these bits in a GIF file and place it on your home page for all to download. If unintended people discover the bits, however, they know the information came from you because it is on your Web page.

Instead, you can split up the information into n parts using the basic tricks from Chapter 4. These n files, when they're XORed together, will reveal the hidden data. Ordinarily, you would create $n-1$ files at random and then compute the last file so that everything adds up. But why bother using files at random when there is a great source of randomness on the network? You could simply snarf $n-1$ different GIF images from the Net and use them. One might be a picture of Socks the Cat from the White House page. Another might be a quilt from the page of some quilting club that is the picture of innocence. Anyone who wanted to recover the information would get all of these GIFs from the Net, recover the secret bits from all of them, and add them up to recover the hidden data.

The net effect of this trick is deniability. No one can be sure who was the one who was hiding the secret bits. Could it be the White House? They've been known to sponsor covert missions based in the Old Executive Office Building. Could it be the quilting circle? No one knows who injected the secret bits into the file. Even the person who recovers the bits might not know who was sending the message. It's quite a ruse.

There are some practical problems associated with this technique. First, you must keep the file creation dates secret. The one GIF that actually contains the message will be the newest file. HTTP doesn't usually ship this information to Web browsers so there is little problem with keeping the information secret. But you can also simply fake it by resetting the clock on your machine.

Second, you should search out GIF files that seem to have the right structure for storing secret bits. This will prevent someone from examining the files and discovering that only one of them has the right structure to hide bits. That is, all but one of the n files are 8-bit color with color tables filled with 256 different shades. The one that isn't is the one. This means that they're either 24-bit color or 8-bit, black-and-white grayscale images are the best.

The section beginning on page 88 describes sophisticated ways of matching patterns in the least significant bits.

You can add some error-correcting features to this scheme if you want to create, say, three different sets of files. When each set of the three sets of files are combined, then three versions of the hidden bits emerges. Any disparities between the files can be resolved by choosing the value of the bit in question that is correct in two out of three files.

More complicated error-correcting schemes like the ones described in Chapter 3 can also be used successfully. For instance, a file to be hidden could be encoded with an error-correcting code that converts every 8 bits into, say, a 12-bit block that can recover errors. One bit from each of the 12-bit blocks could be placed into 12 separate files that were then hidden in 12 different GIFs sprinkled around the network. If someone could not recover all 12 GIFs because of network failures, then the error-correcting code will allow the information to be recovered.

There are many other techniques that can be used to hide information once the data is packed away in GIF files or audio files. These files already comprise much of the information floating around the Net and their proportion will only increase. New technologies promise even more opportunities ahead. Apple Computer Co. is shipping Quicktime VR, which is a way of faking three-dimensional computing. Many of the programmers working on three-dimensional games know that complicated textures are the most important part of creating verisimilitude in virtual reality. All of these are ideal places to hide information.

Bit Twiddling

Perhaps the best way to begin experimenting with hiding information in the noise is to download one of the experimental packages floating around the Net. Three of the better known choices are Stego, Hide and Seek, and S-Tools.

Stego is a shareware program written for the Macintosh by Romana Machado. It can process PICT files, the native file format for the Macintosh. The interface is quite simple, and many of the technical details are well-worked out. The software reads in PICT files and displays them before allowing you to store information in the least significant bit of each pixel. The software calculates the maximum amount of space available and displays this above the image. When the data has been stuffed into the image, the result is displayed so you can assess the effects of adding the data.[4] The effects can be quite significant if you're adding the information to an 8-bit color display for all of the reasons described above. Often, adjacent entries in the color table are not similar enough and the result can be glaring.

Figure 9.5 and Figure 9.6 show how steganography can fail with an 8-bit color image. Although this book is printed in black and white, it should be easy to identify which of the two images began as a 24-bit image before data was hidden in the least significant bit. Both images began as color. One was 24-bit color and the other was 8-bit. Both had data added into the least significant bit by Stego. Both were then converted to 8-bit grayscale for display in the book.

Hide and Seek 4.1 is another steganography program designed for the PC written by an author identified only by the email address shaggy@phantom.com. It only works on either 8-bit color or 8-bit black-and-white GIF files that are 320×480. This is the standard size of the oldest GIF format. The program displays the image before adding or extracting data. The current archive contained two extra programs that made life easier for those hiding information in GIF files. The first,

Figure 9.5. This shows how adding information to the least significant bit of a 24-bit color image has little effect. The image was later converted to black and white for this book. (Photo courtesy of the Lacrosse Foundation.)

---

[4]In the version I used, 1.0a2, the screen is not updated. To force the program to redraw the image, you needed to drag another window over the top. When you remove it, the image redisplays correctly.

Figure 9.6. 8-bit color images can make poor candidates for adding information into the least significant bit because entries in the color table might not be next to each other. The image was later converted to black and white for this book.

grey.exe, converts color GIFs into grayscale GIFs that would not show any of the artifacts associated with 8-bit color steganography. The second program, reduce.exe, reduces the color table from 256 colors to 128 colors and then duplicates these 128 colors so that adjacent entries in the color table are duplicates of each other. If this is done, hiding information in the least significant bit won't affect the look of the image. It will, however, leave something of a red flag for anyone scanning GIFs looking for hidden information. An 8-bit color table with only 128 different colors is easier to detect automatically than a bad image with plenty of artifacts. One is an easily measured quantity. The other is a subjective problem that is often apparent to the human eye.

Coming up with a piece of software that will identify bad artifacts may be possible, but it will not be precise. You could try to look for places where the color continuity is not great. If adjacent pixels are widely different colors, then this could signal a mess caused by 8-bit color steganography. In general, a small amount of blurring and anti-aliasing occurs as images are digitized. Adjacent pixels along edges are often blurred together and the edges aren't crisp. Even when the edges are crisp, it is possible to measure the randomness of the places where there are sharp changes in the colors. If these appear to be randomly distributed, then it is quite likely that they could have come from this process. Or they could be the artistic equivalent of Nirvana music—grungy images designed to perforate the artistic impulse of perfection, images designed to shock and reveal the seamier side of life. Who knows?

The source code is also included with Hide and Seek, which makes it possible to look at the guts of the program. One of the neatest effects is that the information is *dispersed* throughout the bits. That is, there are about 19,200 bytes of space available in the GIF. If a smaller file is going to be packed into the bits, then the program tries to randomly arrange the bits so that they're not adjacent to each other. This has two effects. First, the noise is more randomly distributed throughout the image instead of being clustered on the top half. Second, you must know the location of bits to find the data and the location is governed by a random number generator driven by a user-chosen key. Both of these enhance the security of the system.

The dispersion is controlled by an 8-byte header for the file. The first 2 bytes are the length of the file, the second 2 bytes are a random number seed that is chosen at random when the information is packed and the third pair of bytes is the version number. The fourth pair is not used, but is included to fill out an 8-byte block for the IDEA cipher. This block is encrypted with the IDEA cipher using an optional key and then stored in the first 64 pixels of the image. If you don't know the key, then you can't recover the header information that controls the dispersion of the data throughout the image.

The actual dispersion is random. At the beginning, the random number generator is seeded with the second pair of bytes from the header block. The code from Hide and Seek 4.1 simply uses the built-in C random number generator which may be adequate for most intents and purposes. A stronger implementation would use a cryptographically secure random number generator. Or, perhaps, it would use IDEA to encrypt the random bit stream using a special key. Either method would add a modicum of security.

Here's the section of C code devoted to handling the dispersion. The code for getting the color table entry for pixel (x, y) and flipping it appropriately is removed. This code will store an entire byte in the eight pixels. The amount of the variable dispersion controls how many pixels are skipped on average. It is set to be the rounded off amount of 19000 divided by the length of the incoming data.

```
int used=0,disp=0,extra=0;

  for(i=0;i<8;i++)
  {
      // Code removed here for flipping LSB of (x,y)
   disp=(random(dispersion+extra)+1);
    used+=disp;
    extra=((dispersion*(i+1))-used);
    x+=disp;
    // Move over x pixels. Code removed to handle
    // wraparound.
    }
```

Hide and Seek shows how a good, basic steganographic system can be built. It would be improved significantly if it included code to handle a wide range of image formats and sizes. Many of the newer GIFs are interlaced and multisized.

S-Tools

One of the most ambitious steganographic toolkits available is the S-Tools package written by Andy Brown.[5] The system can hide information in images stored as either GIFs or BMP files, in sound stored as WAV files, or even in the unallocated sectors of a disk. The tool runs under Windows 3.1 and includes extensive help files. The program itself is shareware and a payment of *US$15.00* gets you the rights to use it and a copy of the source code.

Wilson Mac-Gyver Liaw wrote a good introduction to the GIF file format in [Lia95].

Each of the three programs offers to optionally encrypt any of the information that it is storing in the file using a wide array of encryption algorithms. The software allows you to use the IDEA algorithm, DES, triple DES, MPJ2, and NSEA. Each of the different algorithms can be used with any of the five most common feedback chaining systems like CBC, ECB, CFB, OFB, and PCBC. This shows an incredible level of sophistication. These options are often not available even in commercial systems. S-Tools adds 32 bits of garbage at the beginning of each file to ensure that these chaining methods work correctly.

---

[5]asb@nexor.co.uk or Andy Brown, 28 Ashburn Drive, Wetherby, West Yorkshire, LS22 5RD, UK.

The version of S-Tools for handling images, st-bmp.exe, can read in files that are in either the GIF or BMP format and then display them. After the data is added to the file, you can toggle between before and after images. This allows you to compare the effects and see whether there has been any noticeable change in the image. My version did not exchange color tables with the toggle so this effect didn't work right.

There are two different types of image steganography supported by S-Tools. The first method uses 24-bit images and simply changes the least significant bit for each of the three colors at each pixel. This produces 24-bit images that often can't be displayed on older, less-capable video cards. The author of S-Tools contends that 24-bit images may stick out a bit because most people don't use them. They just take up too much space. This is probably correct, but it may be less correct as time goes on. 24-bit images are only three times larger than 8-bit images and that is not a significant savings in a business where speeds and capacities double every several years. Plus, 8-bit images of people and natural scenes don't look as good. The shades and gradations are important for the eye.

The second type attempts to reduce the number of colors in the image so that there are only 256 final colors. The software uses the algorithm designed by Paul Heckbert [Hec82] to reduce the number of colors in an image in the most visually nondisruptive way possible. The algorithm plots all of the colors in three dimensions and then searches for a collection of n boxes that contains all of the colors in one of the boxes. When it is finished, it chooses one color to represent all of the colors in each box. S-Tools offers three different options for how to choose this one color: the center of the box, the average box color, or the average of all of the pixels in the box.

The process for constructing the set of boxes is described in detail in Heckbert's thesis. The process begins with the complete $256 \times 256 \times 256$ space as one box. Then it begins to recursively subdivide the boxes by splitting them in the best way possible. It continues this splitting process until there are n boxes representing the space. Heckbert developed this algorithm to correct some of the defects he found in the "popularity" algorithms being used. These algorithms would clump together nearby colors until only n clumps were left. Then it would choose some color, usually the center of the clump, to represent all of the colors. This works quite well for colors in tight clumps, but it can be disastrous for colors that are part of big, gaseous clumps. In those cases, the difference between the colors and their chosen representative was too large. This would lead to big shifts in the colors used in the details.

David Charlap wrote a good introduction to the BMP format in [Cha95a, Cha95b].

Heckbert suggests that a good way to understand the two approaches is by comparing them to the "quantization" methods used in choosing the representatives for the two houses of the Congress of the United States. The Senate gets two members from each state and Heckbert compares this to his algorithm. It spreads out the representation so no part of the color space is over- or under-represented. The House of Representatives, on the other hand, gets one representative for each unit of population. This works well if you're from heavily populated areas like Manhattan. These have representatives for each part of town. Western states like Nevada, however, have only one representative and thus have little power in the House. Heckbert compares this approach to the "popularity" algorithms.

The subdivision algorithm used by S-Tools can use two different ways to cut the boxes. In one way, the largest dimension is chosen by measuring the greatest difference in RGB values. In the other way, the largest dimension is found by comparing the luminosity of the different choices. Here is the basic algorithm in detail:

1. Place all of the colors from the image in one box.

2. Repeat this until there are n boxes that will represent the final n colors.

    (a) For each box, find the minimum and maximum value in each dimension. That is, find the smallest and largest value of red for any color in the box, the smallest and largest value of green, and the smallest and largest value of blue.

    (b) For each dimension of each box, measure the length. This might be the difference in absolute length or it might be the difference in luminosity.

    (c) Find the longest dimension and split this particular box. Heckbert suggests this can be done by either finding the median color in the box along this dimension, or you can simply choose the geometric middle.

3. Choose a representative color for all of the original colors in each box. S-Tools offers three choices: center of the box, average of the colors, or average of the pixels.

When the new set of *n* colors is chosen, S-Tools can use "dithering" to replace the old colors with new ones.

The algorithm attempts to find the best number of new colors, *n*, through a limbo process. It slowly lowers the number of colors until it ends up with less than 256 colors after the data is mixed into the least significant bits. Often, it must repeat this process several times until the right number is found. S-Tools cannot predict the number of final colors ahead of time because it constantly tries to add 3 bits to each pixel. That is, it takes the red, green, and the blue values for each pixel and changes the least significant bit of each one independently. That means one color could quite possibly become eight. This is quite likely to happen if that color is common in the image because each pixel is handled differently. On average, each of the eight slightly different colors should appear after ten to twelve pixels of the same color are mapped.

This means that it is impossible for the algorithm to predict the final number of colors it needs. It might try to reduce the number of final colors in the image to 64. Then, after the data is mixed in, it might end up with 270, colors or 255. If it was 255, then it could save the file. Otherwise, it would start the process again and reduce the colors some more. The entire process is iterative. S-Tools attempts to predict the correct number through extrapolation, but it has taken several iterations every time I modified a file.

S-Tools and Sound Files

S-Tools also includes one program designed to store data in the least significant bits of a WAV file—one of the standard sound formats for Microsoft Windows. These files can use either 8 or 16 bits of data to represent each instance. People with Sound Blaster cards will have no problem generating these files from any source.

The S-Tools sound program, st-wav.exe, hides one bit per either 8 or 16 bits and offers the same encryption options as st-bmp.exe. It will also use a random number generator to choose a random subset of bits. This spreads the distortion throughout the sound file. The program will display a graph representing the sound and also play it for you. After data is hidden, the graph shows all of the changes made to the wave form in red and leaves the unchanged parts in black. This is, in effect, revealing where the pattern of ones and zeros in the hidden

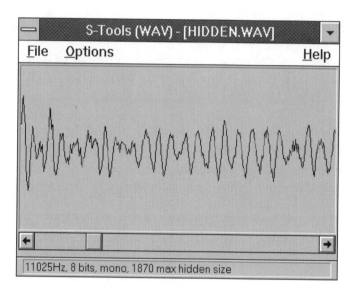

Figure 9.7. The main window of st-wav.exe, the S-Tools program for hiding information in a WAV file. The program displays the changed parts of the waveform in red, but this detail is lost in a black-and-white book.

file differed from the least significant bits of the sound file. Figure 9.7 shows a screen shot from the page.

S-Tools and Empty Disk Space

The third program in the S-Tools suite, st-fdd.exe, will hide information in the unallocated areas of a floppy disk. Each disk is broken into sectors and the sectors are assigned to individual files by the file allocation table (FAT). The unused sectors are just sitting around not doing anything. If someone tries to open them up with a simple editor like a word processor or even tries to examine them with a File Manager, they'll find nothing. This is just empty space to the operating system. But this doesn't mean it can't hold anything. Information can be written into these sectors and left around. The only way it can be corrupted is if someone writes a new file to the disk. The operating system may assign those sectors to another file because it thinks the space is free.

S-Tools stores information in this free space by choosing empty sectors at random. The first sector gets the header of the file which specifies the length and the random number seed that was used to choose the sectors. Then the information is just stored in this string of sectors selected at random.

If encryption is used, the random number generator uses the encryption key as a seed. This means that a different selection of random sectors will be chosen. The data itself is encrypted with any of the five algorithms offered in the other two implementations of S-Tools.

At the end, S-Tools offers to write random noise in the extra space that is not taken up by the hidden file. This is often a good idea because the empty space may often have some pattern to it left over from the last file it stored. Ordinarily, disk space is not actually cleared off when a file is erased. The entry in the FAT table is just changed

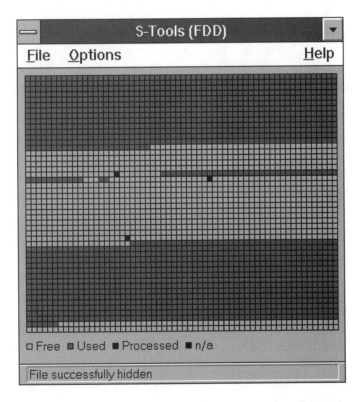

Figure 9.8. The user interface for st-fdd.exe shows the allocated sectors in red, the unallocated sectors in gray, and the ones that have been converted to hide information in yellow.

from "assigned" to "empty." The old data and its pattern are still there. This means that someone could identify the sectors of a floppy disk containing hidden information by simply looking for the ones that have random information. The ones that contain scraps of text files or image or ordinary data would be presumed innocent.[6] S-Tools will overwrite this to convert the unallocated sectors into a sea of noise. This is equivalent to using a new disk.

MandelSteg and Secrets

Any image is a candidate for hiding information, but some are better than others. Ordinarily, images with plenty of variation seem perfect. If the neighboring pixels are different colors, then the eye doesn't detect subtle changes in the individual pixels. This lead Henry Hastur to create a program that flips the least significant bits of a Mandelbrot set. These images are quite popular and well-known throughout the mathematics community. This program, known as Mandelsteg, is available with source code from the Cypherpunks archive (`ftp://ftp.csua.berkeley.edu/pub/cypherpunks/steganography/`).

The manual notes that there are several weaknesses in the system. First, if someone can simply run the data recovery program, GifExtract, to remove the bits. Although there are several different settings, one will work. For this reason, the author suggests using Stealth, a program that will strip away the framing text from a PGP message leaving only noise.

There are other weaknesses. The Mandelbrot image acts as a one-time pad for the data. As with any encoding method, the data can be extracted if someone can find a pattern in the key data. The Mandelbrot set might look very random and chaotic, but there is still plenty of structure. Each pixel represents the number of iterations before a simple equation ($f(z) = z^2 + c$) converges. Adjacent pixels often take a different number of pixels, but they are still linked by their common generating equation. For this reason, I think it may be quite possible to study the most significant bits of a fractal image and determine the

---

[6]You could first use `st-bmp.exe` or `st-wav.exe` to hide the information in a picture or a sound bite. Then you could store it in the unallocated sectors. Then it would look like random discarded information.

location from where it came. This would allow someone to recalculate the least significant bits and extract the answer.[7]

Random Walks

This chapter has discussed hiding information in image or sound files by grabbing all of the least significant bits to hold information. There is no reason why all of them need to be used. Both Hide and Seek and S-Tools use random number generators to choose the bytes that are actually drafted to give up their least significant bits to the cause. This random process guarantees that the distortion is distributed throughout the file so it is not so apparent. It also makes it difficult for some attacker to figure out which bits are important. S-Tools uses the MD-5 algorithm to ensure that the random numbers are cryptographically secure.

In fact, a random subset can have some other uses. First, if a person selects a small, random subset to store information, then another person could do the same thing. If both use different sources of randomness, then there is a good chance that very few bits will end up in both subsets. Error-correcting codes can help recover from this ambiguity. This could allow several people to use the same file to pass information to several different other ones.

Steve Walton suggested this approach in his article, "Image Authentication for a Slippery New Age" [Wal95]. This approach uses a general, two-dimensional random walk that weaves around a picture. Occasionally, the path may wrap around itself which requires keeping track of where the path has been before. Hide and Seek, in contrast, views the picture as a one-dimensional list of pixels and simply chooses a random number of pixels to jump ahead. This removes the problem, but it makes the paths a bit less interesting to look at and may make life easier for any attacker.

Walton imagines that the least significant bits in his random walk can be used to construct a seal for the image. That is, you can "sign" the image by embedding some digital signature of the image in the least significant bits. Naturally, this digital signature would only be computed of the non-least significant bits because those bits are the

---

[7]David Joyce offers a Mandelbrot image generator on the Web (http://aleph0.clarku.edu/djoyce/julia/explorer.html).

only ones that would remain unchanged during the process. This sealing system could be used by professional photographers to attach their mark to a photograph.

Some have argued that this approach is a waste. Appending the signature data to the end of the photo made more practical sense. This type of signature would be able to handle all types of photo formats including binary images without enough significant bits to hide data. Also, there would be no need to avoid the least significant bits while encoding the information and so the signature would be even better.

Another solution is to simply create a random permutation of the bits. Tuomas Aura describes this in [Aur95].

These suggestions are certainly correct. The only advantage that the surreptitious approach would have is secrecy. Presumably photographers would sign images to protect their copyright. They could prove conclusively that the photo was stolen. If the signature is appended to the file, then someone could simply remove it or tamper with it. If it is hidden with a random walk in the least significant bits, then someone has to find it first. Of course, malicious people could simply write over the least significant bits of a photo as a precaution.

There is a certain rough, frontier aspect to simply choosing arbitrary random walks throughout the data. It does not require that there be any prior communication between two people who happen to be hiding information in the same picture. They're just both keeping their fingers crossed that the collisions will be minor and the error-correcting codes will be able to fix them.

Here is a more principled way to create multiple channels in an image. If all parties coordinate their use ahead of time, they can ensure that their random walks will not collide. This saves space because error-correcting codes do not need to be used, but it does increase the complexity of the process.

To create n channels, divide the file into n-byte blocks of data. One byte from each block will be given to each channel. In the simplest and most transparent approach, the assignment of byte and channel number is hard coded. Channel 1 gets byte 1, channel 2 gets byte 2, and so on. A better approach shuffles the bytes by using a set of permutations of the values between 1 and n. Here's a good way to generate a sequence of random permutations of the set:

1. Start with the ordered set $(1, 2, \ldots, n)$.
2. To generate a new random permutation repeat this j times. A larger j is better, but less efficient.

(a) Choose two items in the set at random using the output of a cryptographically secure random number generator.

(b) Swap their positions. For example, if the set is $(5, 1, 3, 2, 4)$ before and the second and fourth values are chosen by the random number generator, then the result will be $(5, 2, 3, 1, 4)$.

3. Output this permutation. Goto step 2 to keep going.

The i-th permutation spit out by this permutation generation routine can determine which channel gets which byte in the ith block. This ensures that no two users will collide.

Another approach can mangle the process even more. Why should blocks be made up of adjacent bytes? In the simplest approach, byte i from channel k in an n-channel system is assigned to byte $in + k$ in the file. This can be scrambled using exponentiation modulo the length of the file. So if the file is p bytes long and p just happens to be prime, then $(in + k)^e \bmod p$ will scramble the bytes so they are not adjacent.

Putting JPEG to Use

The first part of this chapter lamented the effects of JPEG on image files holding data in the least significant bits. The lossy compression algorithm could just mush all of that information into nothingness because it doesn't care if it reconstructs a file correctly. Although this can be problem if someone uses JPEG to compress your file, it doesn't mean that the JPEG algorithm is useless to the person who would like to hide information successfully in images.

There are two possible ways that you can use the JPEG algorithm to store information. The first is to use it as a tool to identify the complexity of an image. This section discusses that approach. The second way is to use some hidden parts of the standard to hide information. That is described in the next section.

The JPEG algorithm can be a good tool for identifying the level of detail in a scene. This level of detail can be used to find the noisiest corners of the image where data can be stored. In the first part of the chapter, the basic algorithm for hiding information would simply use the n least significant bits to hide information. If $n = 1$, there would only be a small but uniform effect that was randomly distributed throughout the image. If n was larger, then more information could be stored away in the image, but more distortion would also emerge. In any case, the distortion would be uniformly distributed across the entire image, even if this wasn't practical.

For instance, imagine a picture of a person sitting on a red-and-white checked picnic blanket in the middle of a grassy field. It might make sense to set $n = 4$ over a grassy section because it is out of focus and not particularly filled with important detail. On the other hand, you would only want to use $n = 1$ in the areas of the face because the detail was so significant to the photo. Naturally, you could go through the photo by hand and identify the most significant and fragile sections of the photo, but this would defeat the purpose of the algorithm. Not only would it be time-consuming, but you would need to arrange for someone on the other end of the conversation to construct exactly the same partition. This is the only way that they would know how to recover the bits.

The JPEG compression algorithm offers an automatic way to segment the photo and identify the most important or salient portions of an image. It was designed to do this to increase compression. The algorithm's creators tweaked the algorithm so it would provide visually satisfying images even after some of the detail was lost to compression.

The application is simple. Let f be a 24-bit image file waiting to have data hidden in some of its least significant bits. Let $JPEG^{-1}(JPEG(f))$ be the result of first compressing f with JPEG and then uncompressing it. The differences between f and $JPEG^{-1}(JPEG(f))$ reveal how much noise is available to hide information. For each pixel, you can compare f with $JPEG^{-1}(JPEG(f))$ and determine how many of the bits are equal. If only the first 4 bits of the 8 bits encoding the blue intensity are the same, then you can conclude that the JPEG algorithm doesn't really care what is in the last 4 bits. The algorithm determined that those 4 bits could be set to any value and the resulting image would still look "good enough." That means that 4 bits are available to hide information. Elsewhere in the image, all 8 bits of f might agree with $JPEG^{-1}(JPEG(f))$. Then no information can be hidden in these bits.

This algorithm makes it possible to identify the locations of important parts of the image. You can choose the right accuracy value for JPEG as well. If you need a good final representation, then you should use the best settings for JPEG and this will probably identify a smaller number of bits available to hide data. A coarser setting for JPEG should open up more bits.

There are many other compression algorithms being developed to hide information. The fractal compression algorithms from Barnsley's Iterated Systems [BH92] are some of the more popular techniques around. Each could be used in a similar fashion to identify sections of the image that can be successfully sacrificed.

Other solutions that are tuned to different types of images can also be used successfully. For instance, there are some algorithms designed to convert 24-bit color images into 8-bit color images. These do a good job of identifying 256 colors that represent the image. You can identify the number of free bits at each pixel by comparing the 24-bit value with the entry from the 256-color table that was chosen to replace it. Some of these algorithms are tuned to do a better job on faces. Others work well on natural scenes. Each is applicable in its own way and can do a good job with the system.

If you use JPEG or a similar lossy algorithm to identify the high-noise areas of an image, then you must change one crucial part of the system. When a GIF file is used to hold information, then the recipient doesn't need to have a copy of the original image. The n least significant bits can simply be stripped away and recovered. They can be used verbatim. If JPEG is going to point out the corners and crevices of the image waiting for more data, then both the sender and the recipient must have access to the same list of corners and crevices. Probably the easiest way to accomplish this is to make sure that both sides have copies of the original image. This is a limitation if you're going to communicate with someone whom you've never met before. You must somehow arrange to get the image to them.

Hiding Information in JPEG Files

There is no doubt that the JPEG's lossy approach to hiding information is a problem that confounds the basic approach to steganography. The noise can be changed in any which way, so the first impulse is to avoid the format altogether. Derek Upham dug deeper and found another approach. The JPEG algorithm compresses data in two steps. First, it breaks the image into 8×8 blocks of pixels and fits cosine functions to these pixels to describe them. Then it stores the frequencies of these cosine functions to serve as a description of this block of pixels.

Upham recognized that you could tweak the least significant bits of the frequency values to store information.

His solution is coded in C and distributed as a `diff` file that can be added to the standard JPEG version 4 distributed on the Net. His code adds an additional command line feature for UNIX machines that allows you to hide a file as you compress an image. This is a nice approach because it simply builds upon the standard JPEG distribution. Also, it is important because the JPEG image format could become more common on the Net. It is much more efficient than the GIF format.

There are also a number of physiological reasons why this approach may actually generate better effects than simply tweaking the least significant bits of the data. The programs like S-Tools and Stego jump through many hoops to handle 8-bit color images. They end up with clusters of colors in the color table that are quite similar to each other. This can be accomplished quite well, but it may be easy to detect by someone scanning the color tables.

Tweaking the frequencies of the discrete cosine transform that models the 8×8 block of data has a different effect. Although these tweaks can harm the quality of the final image, it is hard to distinguish their effects. After all, the discrete transformation is already an approximation and it is hard to notice changes in an approximation. In essence, the bits are hidden by controlling whether the JPEG program rounds up or rounds down. Rounding up is a 1 and rounding down is a 0. These numbers can be recovered by looking at the least significant bits of the frequencies.

Upham chose one interesting approach to hiding the information. There must be some header at the beginning of the block of data to tell how many bits are there. Ordinarily, this would be a single number. So the first 32 bits would be devoted to a number that would say that there are, say, 8,523 bytes stored in the least significant bits that follow. Upham noted that this number would often have a great number of zeros at the front of it. Since these bits would normally be somewhat randomly distributed, a block of zeros could look suspicious. Sixteen zeros in a row should only occur about 1 out of 2^{16} times.

His solution was to have two fields in the header. The first consisted of a 5-bit number that specified the number of bits in the second field. The second field would contain the number of bits in the entire file. This would remove any large blocks of bits at the beginning of the number while leaving the flexibility for extremely large files. He also suggests that the number of bits in the second field be padded with an extra 0 about half of the time. This prevents the sixth bit of the file from always being a 1. This is a very subtle attention to detail.

Summary

Placing information in the noise of digitized images is one of the most popular methods of steganography. The different approaches here guarantee that the data will be hard to find if you're careful about how you use the tools. The biggest problem is making sure that you handle the differences between 24-bit and 8-bit images correctly.

The Disguise The world is filled with noise. There is no reason why some of the great pool of randomness can't be used to hide data. This disguise is often impossible for the average human to notice.

How Secure Is It? These systems are not secure if someone is looking for the information. But many of the systems can produce images that are indistinguishable form the original. If the data is compressed and encrypted before it is hidden, it is impossible to know whether the data is there or not. This can be subverted if a special header is used to identify details about the file.

How to Use the Software There are many different versions of the software available on the Net. The Cypherpunks archive is a good location for the programs. Others circulate throughout the Net. The programs are simple to use.

Chapter 10

Anonymous Remailers

Dr. Anon to You

Host: On this week's show, we have Anonymous, that one-named wonder who is in the class of artists like Madonna, Michelangelo and the Artist Formerly Known as Prince, who are so big they can live on one name alone. He, or perhaps she, is the author of many of the most incendiary works in the world. We're lucky we could get him or her on the show today, even though he or she would only agree to appear via a blurred video link.

Mr. Anonymous (or should I say Ms. Anonymous?), it's great to have you on the show.

Anon: Make it Dr. Anonymous. That will solve the gender problem. I was just granted an honorary doctorate last June.

Host: Congratulations! That must be quite an honor. Did they choose you because of your writings? It says here on my briefing sheet that you've written numerous warm and romantic novels like the *Federalist Papers*. Great stuff.

Anon: Actually, the *Federalist Papers* weren't a book until they were collected. It really wasn't a romantic set of papers, although it did have a rather idealistic notion of what Congress could be.

Host: Sexual congress. Now that's a euphemism I haven't heard for a while. You're from the old school, right? That's where you got the degree?

Anon: Well...

Host: This explains why you're so hesitant to get publicity, right? It's too flashy.

Anon: No. It's not my style. I prefer to keep my identity secret because some of what I write can have dangerous repercussions.

Host: What a clever scheme! You've got us all eating out of your hand. Every other author would fall over himself to get on this show. We're just happy to be talking with you.

Anon: I was a bit hesitant, but my publisher insisted on it. It was in the contract.

Host: Do you find it hard to be a celebrity in the modern age? Don't you feel the pull to expand your exposure by, say, doing an exercise book with Cher? She's got one name too. You guys would get along great. You could talk about how the clerk at the Motor Vehicles department gives you a hard time because you've left a slot on the form blank.

Anon: Well, that hadn't crossed my mind.

Host: How about a spread in *Architectural Digest* or *InStyle*? They always like to photograph the famous living graciously in large, architecturally challenging homes. Or how about *Lifestyles of the Rich and Famous*? They could show everyone where and, of course, how you live. It's a great way to sell your personality.

Anon: Actually, part of the reason for remaining anonymous is so that no one shows up at your house in the middle of the night.

Host: Oh, yeah, groupies offering themselves. I have that problem.

Anon: Actually to burn the place down and shoot me.

Host: Oh, okay. I can see you doing a book with Martha Stewart on how to give a great masquerade party! You could do some really clever masks and then launch it during Mardi Gras in New Orleans. Have you thought about that?

Anon: No. Maybe after I get done promoting my latest book. It's on your desk there. The one exposing a deep conspiracy that is fleecing the people. Money is diverted from tax accounts into a network of private partnerships where it fills the coffers of the very rich.

Host: What about a talk show? I guess I shouldn't ask for competition. But you could be a really spooky host. You could roam the audience wearing a big black hood and cape. Just like in that Mozart movie. Maybe they could electronically deepen your voice so everyone was afraid of you when you condemned their shenanigans. Just like in the *Wizard of Oz*. It would be really hot in those robes under the lights, but I could see you getting a good share of the daytime audience. You would be different.

Anon: My book, though, is really showing the path toward a revolution. It names names. It shows how the money flows. It shows which politicians are part of the network. It shows which media conglomerates turn out cheerful pabulum and "mind candy" to keep everyone somnolescent.

Host: Whoa! Big word there. Speaking of big words, don't you find "Anonymous" to be a bit long? Do you go by "Anon"? Does it make you uncomfortable if I call you "Anon"? Or should I call you "Dr. Anon"?

Anon: Either's fine. I'm not vain.

Host: I should say not. Imagine not putting your name on a book as thick as this one. Speaking of vain, are you into horse racing? I wanted to ask you if you were the person in that Carly Simon song, "You're so vain, you probably think this song is about you." She *never* told anyone who it was about. I thought it might be you. The whole secrecy thing and all.

Anonymous Remailers

There are many reasons why people would want to write letters or communiqués without attaching their names. Some people search for counseling through anonymous suicide prevention centers. Other people want to inquire about jobs without jeopardizing their own. Then there are the times that try our souls and drive us to write long, half-mad screeds that ring with the truth that the people in power don't want to hear. These are just a few of the reasons to send information anonymously. Even a high government official who is helping to plan the government's approach to cracking down on cryptography and imposing key escrow admitted to me over lunch that he or she has used pay phones from time to time. Just for the anonymity.

On the Internet, *anonymous remailers* are one simple solution for letting people communicate anonymously. These are mail programs that accept incoming mail with a new address and some text for the body of the letter. The program strips off the incoming header that contains the real identity of the sender and remails the content to the new address. The recipient knows it came from an anonymous remailer, but they don't know who sent it there.

In some cases, the remailer creates a new pseudonym for the outgoing mail. This might be a random string like "an41234". Then it keeps a secret internal log file that matches the real name of the incoming mail with this random name. If the recipient wants to reply to this person, they can send mail back to "an41234" in care of the anonymous remailer who then repackages the letter and sends it on. This allows people to hold a conversation over the wires without knowing each other's identity.

There are many legitimate needs for services like this one. Most of the newspapers that offer personal ads also offer anonymous mailboxes and voicemail boxes so that people can screen their responses. People may be willing to advertise for a new lover or friend if the anonymous holding box at the newspaper gives them a measure of protection. Some people often go through several exchanges of letters before they feel trusting enough to meet the other person. Or they may call anonymously from a pay phone. There are enough nasty stories from the dating world to make this anonymous screening a sad, but very necessary, feature of modern life.[1]

Of course, there are also many controversial ways that anonymous remailers can be used. Someone posted copyrighted documents from the Church of Scientology to the Internet using an anonymous remailer based in Finland [Gro]. This raised the ire of the Church which was able to get the local police to raid the site and force the owner to reveal the sender's name. Obviously, remailers can be used to send libelous or fake documents, documents under court seal, or other secret information. Tracking down the culprit depends upon how well the owner of the remailer can keep a secret.

There are a wide variety of anonymous remailers on the Internet and the collection is growing significantly. A list of the publicly known versions is maintained by Raph Levien at Berkeley. You can get a copy of the list at `remailer-list@kiwi.cs.berkeley.edu`. The list can also be found on the Web page `http://www.cs.berkeley.edu/raph/`

---

[1]Strangely enough, in the past people would rely upon knowing other people extensively as a defense against this type of betrayal. People in small towns knew everyone and their reputations. This type of knowledge isn't practical in the big city so complete anonymity is the best defense.

`remailer-list.html`. Information and instructions about using the re-mailers can also be found at this site.

Enhancements

There are a number of different ways that the anonymous remailers can be enhanced with different features. Some of the most important ones are:

Encryption The remailer has its own public key pair and accepts the requests in encrypted form. It decrypts them before sending them out. This is an important defense against someone who might be tapping the incoming and outgoing lines of a remailer.

Latency The remailer will wait to send out the mail in order to con-found anyone who is watching the traffic coming in and out of the remailer. This delay may either be specified by the incoming message or assigned randomly.

Padding Someone watching the traffic in and out of a remailer might be able to trace encrypted messages by comparing the size. Even if the incoming and outgoing messages are encrypted with different keys, they're still the same size. Padding messages with random data can remove this problem.

Reordering The remailer may get the messages in one order, but it doesn't process them in the same first-in-first-out order. This adds an additional measure of secrecy.

Chaining Remailers If one anonymous remailer might cave in and re-veal your identity, it is possible to chain together several remailers in order to add additional secrecy. This chain, unlike the physical basis for the metaphor, is as strong as its *strongest* link. Only one machine on the list has to keep a secret to stop the trail.

Anonymous Posters This machine will post the contents to a news-group anonymously instead of sending them out via e-mail.

Each of these features can be found in different remailers. Consult the lists of remailers available on the net to determine which features might be available to you.

Using Remailers

There are several different types of anonymous remailers on the network and there are subtle differences between them. Each different
class was written by different people and they approached some of
the details in their own way. The entire concept isn't too challenging,
though, so everyone should be able to figure out how to send information through an anonymous remailer after reading the remailer's
instructions.

One of the more popular remailers is run by Johan Helsingius
in Helsinki, Finland, at anon@anon.penet.fi. Composing e-mail and
sending it through the remailer is simple. You create the letter as you
would any other, but you address it to anon@anon.penet.fi. At the top
of the letter, you add two fields, X-Anon-Password: and X-Anon-To:.
The first holds a password that you use to control your anonymous
identity. The second gives the address to which the message will go.
Here's a short sample:

```
Mime-Version: 1.0
Content-Type: text/plain; charset="us-ascii"
Date: Tue, 5 Dec 1995 09:07:07 -0500
To: anon@anon.penet.fi
From: pcw@access.digex.net (Peter Wayner)
Subject: Echo Homo

X-Anon-Password: swordfish
X-Anon-To: pcw@access.digex.net

Le nom de plume de la rose est <<Pink Flamingo.>>
```

When the message arrives in Finland, the remailer strips off
the header and assigns an anonymous ID to my address
pcw@access.digex.net. The real name and the anonymous name
are placed in a table and bound with a password. You don't need to
use a password, but this adds security. Anyone with a small amount of
technical expertise can fake mail so that it arrives looking like it came
from someone else. The password prevents anyone from capturing
your secret identity. If these people don't know your password, then
they can't assume your identity.

The password is also necessary for dissolving your identity. If
you want to remove your name and anonymous identity from the

system, then you need to know the password. This remailer places a waiting period on cancellation because it doesn't want people to come in, send something anonymously, and then escape the flames. If you send something, then you should feel the heat is the philosophy.

If you want to post anonymously to a newsgroup, then you can simply put the newsgroup's name in the X-Anon-To: field like this:

```
Mime-Version: 1.0
Content-Type: text/plain; charset="us-ascii"
Date: Tue, 5 Dec 1995 09:07:07 -0500
To: anon@anon.penet.fi
From: pcw@access.digex.net (Peter Wayner)
Subject: Stupidity

X-Anon-Password: swordfish
X-Anon-To: alt.flames

In <412A9231243@whitehouse.gov>, Harry Hstar writes:
> Why you're so dumb, I can't believe that someone
> taught you how to type.

You're so stupid, that you probably don't understand
why this is such a great insult to you.
```

This will get posted under my anonymous identity. If someone wants to respond, they can write back to me through the remailer. It will protect my identity to some degree.

Using Private Idaho

One of the nicer e-mail packages for the Windows market is Private Idaho written by Joel McNamara (Figure 10.1). The software runs under Microsoft Windows 3.1 and will add features for encrypting mail with PGP. If you want to route your mail through an anonymous remailer, then it is as simple as choosing a remailer from the pull down menu. The menu lists the remailers, their completion ratios, and the latency they add to messages flowing through them.

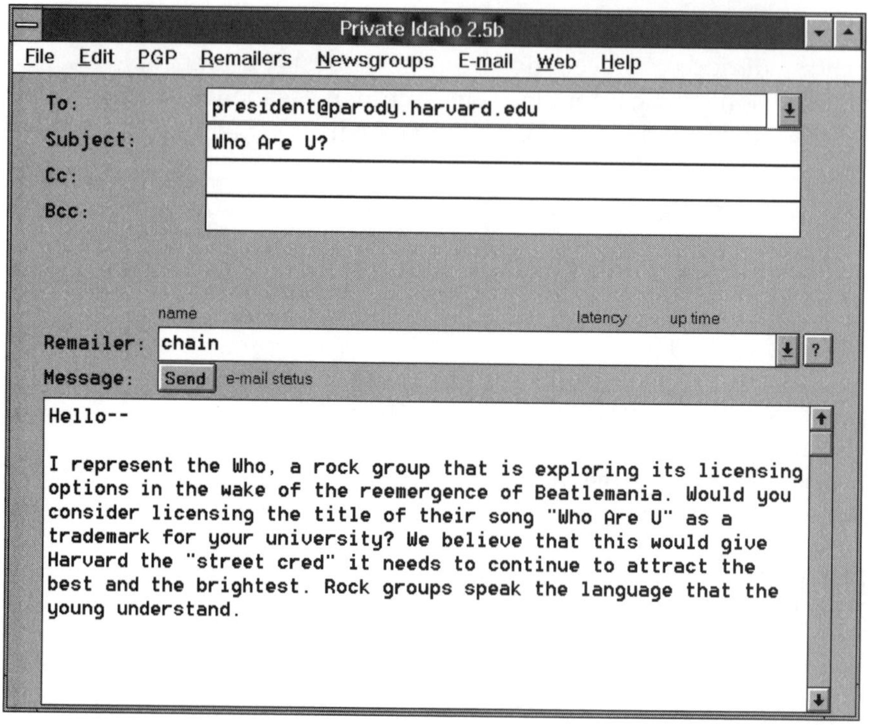

```
┌─────────────────────────────────────────────────────────────────────┐
│ ─                          Private Idaho 2.5b                   ▼  ▲  │
├─────────────────────────────────────────────────────────────────────┤
│ File   Edit   PGP   Remailers   Newsgroups   E-mail   Web   Help      │
├─────────────────────────────────────────────────────────────────────┤
│ To:          ┌──────────────────────────────────────────────────┬─┐  │
│              │ president@parody.harvard.edu                      │±│  │
│              └──────────────────────────────────────────────────┴─┘  │
│ Subject:     ┌─────────────────────────────────────────────────────┐ │
│              │ Who Are U?                                          │ │
│              └─────────────────────────────────────────────────────┘ │
│ Cc:          ┌─────────────────────────────────────────────────────┐ │
│              │                                                     │ │
│              └─────────────────────────────────────────────────────┘ │
│ Bcc:         ┌─────────────────────────────────────────────────────┐ │
│              │                                                     │ │
│              └─────────────────────────────────────────────────────┘ │
│                                                                       │
│              name                            latency    up time       │
│ Remailer:    ┌──────────────────────────────────────────────────┬─┐┌─┐│
│              │ chain                                             │±││?││
│              └──────────────────────────────────────────────────┴─┘└─┘│
│ Message:     ┌──────┐ e-mail status                                   │
│              │ Send │                                                 │
│              └──────┘                                                 │
│ ┌───────────────────────────────────────────────────────────────┬─┐ │
│ │ Hello--                                                        │↑│ │
│ │                                                                │ │ │
│ │ I represent the Who, a rock group that is exploring its licensing││ │
│ │ options in the wake of the reemergence of Beatlemania. Would you ││ │
│ │ consider licensing the title of their song "Who Are U" as a    │ │ │
│ │ trademark for your university? We believe that this would give │ │ │
│ │ Harvard the "street cred" it needs to continue to attract the  │ │ │
│ │ best and the brightest. Rock groups speak the language that the│ │ │
│ │ young understand.                                              │ │ │
│ │                                                                │↓│ │
│ └───────────────────────────────────────────────────────────────┴─┘ │
└─────────────────────────────────────────────────────────────────────┘
```

Figure 10.1. A screenshot of the Windows program Private Idaho. You can use it to send encrypted mail or anonymous mail.

Private Idaho works with the Cypherpunk remailers created by active codewriters of the Cypherpunk mailing list.

Private Idaho is just a shell for composing the e-mail message and encrypting it with the necessary steps. The final product can either be handed off directly to an SMTP server or another e-mail package like Eudora. Although the product is not a full-fledged e-mail package, it is a big help when you want to compose these messages. I hope someone will create a similar package for the Macintosh.

Private Idaho can handle many of the Cypherpunk remailer features including cut marks, reordering, and enhanced latency. The information about the various remailers is kept in the files CPMAILER.TXT and RMINFO.TXT. These are Raph Levien's automatically updated list of remailers and their performance. The file USENET.TXT contains a list of USENET gateways that will take mail and post it anonymously to newsgroups.

You can get copies of the software directly from `ftp://ftp.eskimo.com/u/j/joelm/pidaho21.zip`. Version 2.5 is in beta testing at the time this book was written.

Alpha.c2.org remailers

The Community ConneXion is an Internet service provider that also hopes to promote on-line privacy. As part of its efforts, it runs one of the more technically competent remailers available, alpha.c2.org. This remailer requires that all of the incoming messages be encrypted with PGP for the users' privacy. The remailer can decrypt the message before routing it through a network of other remailers.

Sameer Parekh founded c2.org.

If you want to use the Community ConneXion remailer, you need to set up PGP on your machine. You must use several passes of encryption to hide your return address and create your account. All transactions between you and the Alpha remailer are done with PGP encryption. This can be slightly complicated for the novice user because the file format is pretty unforgiving. You must use an ASCII text editor and make sure that the punctuation and blank lines are perfect. The instructions for the account can be found through the Community ConneXion's Web page, `http://www.c2.org/`.

When your account on the machine is set up, your remailer traffic will be encrypted with PGP. You must choose a password to set up your account just like the remailer at `anon.penet.fi` and you must specify this password to send an anonymous message. Alpha allows you to choose any pseudonym you want. If someone responds to that anonymous pseudonym, then the Alpha remailer will encrypt the response using PGP and your password.

This remailer offers a much greater degree of security because the traffic is encrypted between the host and the remailer. More sophisticated graphical interfaces will make it easier to use in the future because they'll be able to keep track of all of the details about blank lines and message formats.

Web Remailers

The World Wide Web promises to offer one of the best interfaces for anonymous remailers. Anyone can use the basic browsers available and any of the Web servers can be configured to act as proxies. It is quite easy, for instance, to write a remailer program in AppleScript for use with the very popular Macintosh Web server, MacHTTP and its commercial cousin, WebStar.

One of the more feature-rich Web sites is `http://www.c2.org/remail/by-www.phtml` which acts as a front end for Raph Levien's Premail program. Sending anonymous mail couldn't be easier. You simply fill out the form and press the button. The Premail software will route it through several different remailers to keep its destination secret.

Premail is discussed on page 193.

If you happen to be using Netscape or any other WWW browser that supports the Secure Sockets Layer (SSL), then the information you supply to the remailer at `c2.org` will be encrypted. The HTML page for this is quite similar: `https://www.c2.org/remail/by-www.html`. This is a good precaution to take if you intend to use the remailer for anything serious.

The Community ConneXion now asks for $.10 to remail a message which you can pay using the eCash system developed by David Chaum's DigiCash. This transfer is anonymous so the bank cannot tell who withdrew money from their account and spent it on sending anonymous messages. This is good technology and everyone who uses the system should consider supporting it by finding a way to pay anonymously.

Here's a sample of a letter that was created with this page:

```
Date: Wed, 6 Dec 1995 14:10:38 -0500
From: Amnesia Remailer <amnesia@chardos.connix.com>
Comments: This message did not originate from the
          address above. It was remailed by an anonymous
          remailing service. If you have questions or
          complaints, please direct them to
          <complaints@chardos.connix.com>
To: pcw@access.digex.net
Subject: Anon is not a nom.

Get thee to a nun, anon.
```

Reasons for Secrecy

There are many different reasons for using anonymous remailers and some are scurrilous. There is little doubt that the Four Horsemen of the

Infocalypse, drug dealers, terrorists, child pornographers, and money launders will find a way to use anonymous remailers to their benefit in the same way that they've found uses for telephones, cars, and video cameras. This introductory segment on remailers will close with a list of good reasons for fighting for anonymous communication in the world:

1. So you can seek counseling about deeply personal problems like suicide.

2. So you can inform colleagues and friends about a problem with odor or personal hygiene.

3. So you can meet potential romantic partners without danger.

4. So you can play roles and act out different identities for fun.

5. So you can explore job possibilities without revealing where you currently work and potentially losing your job.

6. So you can turn a person in to the authorities anonymously because you fear recriminations.

7. So you can leak information to the press about gross injustice or unlawful behavior.

8. So you can take part in a contentious political debate about, say, abortion, without losing the friendship of those who happen to be on the other side of the debate.

There are many other reasons, but I'm surprised that government officials don't recognize how necessary these freedoms are to the world. Much of government functions through back-corridor bargaining and power games. Anonymous communication is a standard part of this level of politics. I often believe that all governments would grind to a halt if information was as strictly controlled as some would like it to be. No one would get any work done. They would just spend hours arguing who should and should not have access to information.

The Central Intelligence Agency, for instance, has been criticized for missing the collapse of the former Soviet Union. They continued to issue pessimistic assessments of a burgeoning Soviet military while the country imploded. Some blame greed, power, and politics. I blame the sheer inefficiency of keeping information secret. Spymaster Bob can't share the secret data he got from Spymaster Fred because everything is compartmentalized. When people can't get new or solid information, they fall back to their basic prejudices—which in this case was that the Soviet Union is a burgeoning empire. There will always be a need for covert analysis for some problems, but it will usually be much more inefficient than overt analysis.

Anonymous dissemination of information is a grease for the squeaky wheel of society. As long as people question its validity and recognize that its source is not willing to stand behind the text, then everyone should be able to function with the information.

Remailer Guts

Designing the inside of a remailer is fairly easy. Most UNIX mail systems will take incoming mail and pass it along to a program that will do the necessary decoding. Repackaging it is just a matter of rearranging the headers and re-encrypting the information. This process can be accomplished with some simple scripts or blocks of C code. Moving this to any platform is also easy. There is an SMTP-compatible mail program for the Macintosh, for instance, known as the Apple Internet Mail Server (AIMS) that is currently given away free.

Designing better, smarter remailer systems is more of a challenge. Here are some of the standard attacks that people might use to try to follow messages through a web of remailers:

In and Out Tracking The attacker watches as messages go in and out of the remailer and match them up by either order or size. The defense against this is to keep n messages in an internal queue and dispense them in random order. The messages are either kept to be all the same size or they're randomly padded at each iteration.

Remailer Flooding Imagine that one remailer receives a letter and the attacker wants to know where it is going. The remailer keeps n letters in its queue and dispenses them randomly. One attack is to send n of the attacker's messages to the remailer just before the message in question arrives. The attacker knows the destination of her own n messages, so she can pick out the one different message from the flow. If the messages are sent out randomly, then the attacker must send another n messages to ensure that subsequent messages won't confuse her.

One defense against this approach is remailer broadcasting. Instead of sending each subsequent message to a particular remailer using one-to-one mail delivery, the remailer would broadcast it to a group of other remailers. Only one remailer would have the right key to decrypt the next address. The others would simply discard it.

Replay Attack An attacker grabs a copy of the message as it goes by. Then, it resends it awhile later. Eventually the letter will make its way through the chain of remailers until it arrives at the same destination as before. If the attacker keeps track of all of the mail going to all of the destinations and the attacker replays the message several times, then only one consistent recipient will emerge. This is the destination.

The best solution is to require each message to contain an individual ID number that is randomly generated by the sender. The remailer stores this ID in a large file. If it encounters another message with the same ID, then it discards the message. The size of this ID should be large enough to ensure that two IDs will almost certainly not match if they're chosen at random.

Forged Mail Attack It is relatively easy to fake mail sent to SMTP. Someone could pretend to be you when they sent the anonymous message containing something illegal. If the police were willing to pressure the remailer operator into revealing names, then you could be fingered for something you didn't do.

The passwords used by many remailers are a simple defense against this problem. The anonymous remailer won't send along mail that is supposed to be from a certain site unless the correct password is included. A more sophisticated system would require that the mail be signed with the correct digital signature.

Each of these solutions came from a paper by David Chaum [Cha81] that describes a process called a *mix*. The details of this paper were used as the architecture for the most sophisticated type of remailer currently operating on the Net. Lance Cottrell wrote Mixmaster, a UNIX-based program that will send anonymous mail packages using the more robust structure described in the paper.

The main difference is in the structure of the address information. The first class of remailers packaged their data up in nesting envelopes. Each remailer along the chain would open up an envelope and do the right thing with the contents. Mixmaster maintains a separate set of addressing blocks. Each travels through the entire chain of remailers. It is more like a distribution list that offices often use to route magazines through a list of different recipients. Each recipient crosses off its name after it receives it.

There are two advantages to arranging the contents of the messages in this form. The first is that there is no natural reason for the size of the messages to shrink. If the outer envelopes are merely stripped off, then the size of the letter will shrink. This can be compensated by adding padding, but getting the padding to be the right size may be complicated because of the different block sizes of ciphers like DES. The second advantage is reduced encryption time. The block of the encryption does not have to be encrypted or decrypted for each stage of the remailer chain. Only the address blocks need to be manipulated.

Imagine that a message will take five hops. Then the header for a Mixmaster will contain a table that looks something like this if all of the encryption was removed:

Remailer's Entry	Next Destination	Packet ID	Key
Bob	Ray	92394129	12030124
Ray	Lorraine	15125152	61261621
Lorraine	Carol	77782893	93432212
Carol	Gilda	12343324	41242219
Gilda	Final Location	91999201	93929441

The encryption was removed to show how the process works. This header specifies that the mail should go from the remailer run by Bob, to Ray to Lorraine to Carol to Gilda before heading to its final destination. The Packet ID is used by each remailer to defend against replay attacks.

There are two types of encryption used in Mixmaster. First, each entry in the header is encrypted with the public key of the remailer. So the Next Destination, the Packet ID, and the Key for Ray are encrypted

The State may, and does, punish fraud directly. But it cannot seek to punish fraud indirectly by indiscriminately outlawing a category of speech, based on its content, with no necessary relationship to the danger sought to be prevented.
—From the majority opinion by Justice Stevens in Joseph McIntyre v. Ohio Election Committee

I was the shadow of the waxwing slain by the false azure of the window pane.
—John Shade in Pale Fire

with Ray's public key. Only the rightful recipient of each remailer will be able to decode its entry.

The second encryption uses the keys stored in the table. The best way to understand it is to visualize what each remailer does. Here are the steps:

1. Decodes its packet using its secret key. This reveals the next destination, the ID, and the Key.
2. Uses its Key to decrypt every entry underneath it. Mixmaster uses triple DES to encode the messages.
3. Moves itself to the bottom of the list and replaces the remailer name, the destination information, and the ID with a random block of data. This obscures the trail.

If this is going to be repeated successfully by each remailer in the list, then the initial table is going to have to be encrypted correctly. Each entry in the header will need to be encrypted by the key of each of the headers above it. For instance, the entry for Carol should look something like this:

$$E_{12030124}(E_{61261621}(E_{93432212}(PK_{Carol}(\ldots)))).$$

Bob's remailer will strip off the first level of encryption indicated by the function $E_{12030124}$, Ray's will strip off the second and Lorraine's will strip off the third. The final block left is encrypted by Carol's public key.

When the header finally arrives at the last destination, each block will have been re-encrypted in reverse order. This forms something like the signature chain of a certified letter. Each step must be completed in order and each step can only be completed by someone holding the matching secret key. The final recipient can keep this header and check to see that it was processed correctly.

The last key in the chain, in this case the one in the entry for Gilda, is the one that was used to encrypt the message. There is no reason for the remailer to decrypt the message at each step.

Mixmaster currently appends a block of 20 header entries to the top of each entry. Each block takes 512 bytes. If the letter is only going through five remailers, for instance, then the others are filled with random noise. Each entry in the table contains a bit that identifies it as a "final" hop. If that bit is set, then the key is used to decrypt the main block.

The main block of each message is also kept the same size. If a current message is too short, then padding is added until it is 20k long. If it is too long, then it is broken into 20k blocks. This size is flexible, but it should be set to a constant for all messages. This prevents anyone from identifying the messages from their size or the change of size.

Mixmaster software can currently be found through anonymous ftp at obscura.com. The software cannot be exported so you must send a message certifying that you will comply with the U.S. government's export laws. More information can be found at Lance Cottrell's home page, http://obscura.com/loki/Welcome.html.

Other Remailer Packages

One of the nicest, feature-rich programs for UNIX-based machines is Mailcrypt, written in emacs-lisp for use with the popular GNU Emacs program distributed by the GNU project. The software, created by Patrick LoPresti, will handle all of the basic encryption jobs for mail including encrypting outgoing mail, decrypting incoming mail, and evaluating signatures. The software interacts with the major UNIX mail reading programs like MH-E, VM, and Rmail.

The software also includes a good implementation that will create chains of remailers. When you choose this option, it will automatically create a nested packet of encrypted envelopes that will be understood by the remailers on the list maintained by Raph Levien.

You can create lists of possible remailer chains for future use. These can either be hard coded lists or they can be flexible. You can specify, for instance, that Mailcrypt should choose a different random ordering of four remailers everytime it sends something along the chain. You could also request that Mailcrypt use the four most reliable remailers according to the list maintained by Raph Levien. This gives you plenty of flexibility in guiding the information. To get Mailcrypt, go to http://cag-www.lcs.mit.edu/mailcrypt/.

Mailcrypt also makes it simple to use pseudonyms very easily. You can create a PGP key pair for a secret identity and then publicize it. Then if you want to assume a name like Silence Dogood, you could send off your messages through a chain of remailers. The final readers would be able to verify that the message came from the one and only original Silence Dogood because they would be able to retrieve the right public key and check the signature. Some people might try and imitate him or her, but they would not own the corresponding secret key so they couldn't issue anything under this pseudonym.

Another program developed just for chaining together the necessary information for remailers is Premail written by Raph Levien. The software is designed as a replacement for Sendmail, the UNIX software that handles much of the low-level SMTP. Premail can take all of the same parameters that modify its behavior including an additional set of commands that will invoke chains of remailers. So you can drop it in place of Sendmail any place you choose.

Premail has several major options. If you simply include the line `key: user_id` in the header with the recipient's user_id, then Premail will look up the key in the PGP files and encrypt the file using this public key on the way out the door. If you include the header line `Chain: Bob; Ray; Lorraine`, then Premail will arrange it so that the mail will head out through Bob, Ray, and Lorraine's anonymous remailers before it goes to the final destination. You can also specify an anonymous return address if you like by adding the `Anon-From:` field to the header. Premail is very flexible because it will randomly select a chain of remailers from the list of currently operating remailers. Just specify the number of hops in a header field like this: `Chain:3`. Premail will find the best remailers from Raph Levien's list of remailers.

Splitting Paths

The current collection of remailers is fairly simple. A message is sent out one path. At each step along the line, the remailers strip off the incoming sender's name and add a new anonymous name. Return mail can follow this path back because the anonymous remailer will replace the anonymous name with the name of the original sender.

This approach still leaves a path—albeit one that is as strong as its strongest link. But someone can certainly find a way to discover the original sender if they're able to compromise every remailer along the chain. All you need to know is the last name in the chain, which is the first one in the return chain.

A better solution is to use two paths. The outgoing mail can
be delivered along one path that doesn't keep track of the mail
moving along its path. The return mail comes back along a path
specified by the original sender. For instance, the original message might go through the remailer `anon@norecords.com` which
keeps no records of who sends information through it. The recipient could send return mail by using the return address in the
encrypted letter. This might be `my-alias@freds.remailer.com`.
Only someone who could decode the message could know to attack `my-alias@freds.remailer.com` to follow the chain back to the
sender.

The approach defends against someone who has access to
the header which often gives the anonymous return address.
Now, this information can be encoded in the body. The plan is still
vulnerable because someone who knows the return address
`my-alias@freds.remailer.com` might be able to coerce Fred into
revealing your name.

A different solution is to split up the return address into a secret. When you opened an account at `freds.remailer.com`, you
could give your return address as R_1. This wouldn't be a working
return address, it would just be one half of a secret that would reveal your return address. The other half, R_2, would be sent along to
your friends in the encrypted body of the letter. If they wanted to
respond, they would include R_2 in the header of their return letter.
Then, `freds.remailer.com` could combine R_1 and R_2 to reveal the
true return address.

The sender's half of the return address can arrive at the anonymous
drop box at any time. The sender might have it waiting there so the
letter can be rerouted as soon as possible or the sender might send it
along three days later to recover the mail that happened to be waiting
there.

This split secret can be created in a number of different ways. The
simplest technique is to use the XOR addition described in Chapter 4.
This is fast, simple to implement, and perfectly secure. The only practical difficulty will be converting this into suitable ASCII text. E-mail
addresses are usually letters and some simple punctuation. Instead of
simply creating a full 8-bit mask to be XORed with the address, it is
probably simpler to think of offsets in the list of characters. You could
come up with a list of the 60-something characters used in all e-mail

addresses and call this string, C. Splitting an e-mail address would consist of doing the following steps on a character-by-character basis:

1. Choose a new character from C. Store this in R_1. Let x be its position in C.
2. To encode a character from the e-mail address, find the character's position in C and move x characters down x. If you get to the end, start again.
3. Store this character in R_2.

The reverse process is easy to figure out. This will produce a character-only split of the e-mail address into two halves, R_1 and R_2. R_1 is deposited at an anonymous remailer and attached to some pseudonym. R_2 is sent to anyone whom you want to respond to you. They must include R_2 in their letter so the remailer can assemble the return address for you.

An even more sophisticated approach can use the digital signature of the recipient. The initiator of the conversation could deposit three things at the return remailer: the pseudonym, one half of the return address, R_1, and the public key of the person who might be responding. When that person responds, they must send $f_e(R_2)$. This is the other half of the secret encoded with the private key. The remailer has the corresponding public key so it can recover R_2 and send the message on its way.

The systems can be made increasingly baroque. A remailer might want to protect itself against people banging down its door asking for the person who writes under a pseudonym. This can be accomplished by encrypting the remailer's files with the public keys of the recipient. This is better explained by example. Imagine that Bob wants to start up an anonymous communication channel with Ray through `freds.remailer.com`. Normally, `freds.remailer.com` would store Bob's return address, call it B, and match it with Bob's pseudonym, `maskT-AvEnGrr`. Naturally, someone could discover B by checking these files.

`freds.remailer.com` can protect itself by creating a session key, k_i, and encrypting it with Ray's public key, $f_{ray}(k_i)$. This value is sent along to Ray with the message. Then it uses k_i to encrypt B using some algorithm like triple DES before discarding k_i. Now, only Ray holds the private key that can recover k_i and thus B. `freds.remailer.com` is off the hook. It couldn't reveal B even if it wanted to.

This solution, unfortunately, can only handle one particular ongoing communication. It would be possible to create different session keys for each person to whom Bob sends mail. This increases the possibility that B could be discovered by the remailer who keeps a copy of B the next time that mail for `maskT-AvEnGrr` comes through with a session key attached.

The Future

In the short-term future, every machine on the Internet will be a first-class citizen that will be able to send and receive mail. The best solution for active remailers is to create tools that will turn each SMTP port into an anonymous remailer. To some extent, they already do this. They take the incoming mail messages and pass them along to their final destination. It would be neat, for instance, to create a plug-in MIME module for Eudora or another e-mail program that would recognize the MIME type "X-Anon-To:" and resend the mail immediately.

To a large extent, these tools are not the most important step. The tools are only useful if the remailer owner is willing to resist calls to reveal the hidden identity.

There is also a great need for anonymous dating services on the Net. Although many of the remailers are clothed in the cyberpunk regalia, there is no doubt that there are many legitimate needs for remailers. An upscale, mainstream remailer could do plenty of business and help people in need of pseudonymous communication.

Summary

The Disguise The path between sender and recipient is hidden from the recipient by having an intermediate machine remove the return address. More sophisticated systems can try to obscure the connection to anyone who is watching the mail messages entering and leaving the remailing computer.

How Secure Is It? Basic anonymous remailers are only as secure as the strongest link along the chain of remailers. If the person who runs the remailer chooses to log the message traffic, then that person can break the anonymity. This may be compelled by the law enforcement community through warrants or subpoenas.

The more sophisticated remailers that try to obscure traffic analysis can be quite secure. Anyone watching the network of remailers can only make high-level statements about the flow of information in and out of the network. Still, it may be quite possible to track the flow. The systems do not offer the unconditional security of the dining cryptographers networks described in Chapter 11.

Digital Mixes must also be constructed correctly. You cannot simply use RSA to sign the message itself. You must sign a hash of the message. [PP90] shows how to exploit the weakness.

How to Use the Software The Cypherpunks archive offers all of the software necessary to use chaining remailers or Mixmaster. The WWW pages are the easiest options available to most people.

Chapter 11

Secret Broadcasts

Secret Senders

How can you broadcast a message so everyone can read it, but no one can know where it is coming from? Radio broadcasts can easily be located with simple directional antenna. Anonymous remailers (see Chapter 10) can cut off the path back to its source, but they can often be compromised or traced. Practically any message on the Net can be traced because packets always flow from one place to another. This is generally completely impractical, but it is still possible.

None of these methods offers unconditional security, but there is one class of algorithms created by David Chaum that will make it impossible for anyone to detect the source of a message. He titled the system the "dining cryptographers" which is a reference to a famous problem in computer system design known as the "dining philosophers." In the Dining Philosophers problem, n philosophers sit around the table with n chopsticks set up so there is one between each pair. To eat, a philosopher must grab both chopsticks. If there is no agreement and schedule, then no one will eat at all.

Chaum phrased the problem as a question of principle. Three cryptographers were eating dinner and one was from the National Security Agency. The waiter arrives and tells them that one person at the table had already arranged for the check to be paid, but he wouldn't say who left the cash. The cryptographers struggle with the problem because neither of the two non-government employees want to accept even an anonymous gratuity from the NSA. But, because they respect the need for anonymity, they arrange to solve the problem with a simple, coin-tossing algorithm. When it is done, no one will know who paid the check, but they'll know if the payer was from the NSA.

This framing story is a bit strained, but it serves the purpose. In the abstract, one member will send a 1-bit message to the rest of the table. Everyone will be able to get the same message, but no one will be able to identify which person at the table sent it. There are many other situations that seem to lend themselves to the same problem. For instance, a father might return home to find the rear window smashed. He suspects that it was one of the three kids, but it could have been a burglar. He realizes that none will admit to doing it. Before calling the police and reporting a robbery, he uses the same dining cryptographer protocol so one of the kids can admit to breaking the window without volunteering for punishment.[1]

If a 1-bit message can be sent this way, then there is no reason why long messages cannot come through the same channel. One problem is that no one knows when someone else is about to speak since no one knows who is talking. The best solution is to never interrupt someone else. When a free slot of time appears, participants should wait a random amount of time before beginning. When they start broadcasting something, they should watch for corrupted messages caused by someone beginning at the same time. If that occurs, they should wait a random amount of time before beginning again.

Random protocols for sharing a communication channel are used by the ethernet developed at Xerox PARC.

The system can also be easily extended to create a way for two people to communicate without anyone being able to trace the message. If no one can pinpoint the originator of a message with the dining cryptographers protocol, then no one can also know who is actually receiving the message. If the sender encrypts the communication with a key that is shared between two members at the table, then only the intended recipient will be able to decode it. The rest at the table will see noise. No one will be able to watch the routing of information to and fro.

The system for the dining cryptographers is easy to understand. In Chaum's initial example, there are three cryptographers. Each cryptographer flips a coin and lets the person on his right see the coin. Now, each cryptographer can see two coins, determine whether they're the

---

[1]This may be progressive parenting, but I do not recommend that you try this at home. Don't let your children learn to lie this well.

same or different, and announce this to the rest of the table. If one of the three is trying to send a message—in this case that the NSA paid for dinner—then they swap their answer between same and different. A 1-bit message of "yes" or "on" or "the NSA paid" is being transmitted if the number of "different" responses is odd. If the count is even, then there is no message being sent.

There are only three coins, but they are all being matched with their neighbors so it sounds complex. It may be best to work through the problem with an example. Here's a table of several different outcomes of the coin flips. Each column shows the result of one diner's coin flip and how it matches that of the person on their right. An "H" stands for heads and a "T" stands for tails. Diner #1 is to the right of Diner #2, so Diner #1 compares the coins from columns #1 and #2 and reports whether they match or not in that subcolumn. Diner #2 is to the right of Diner #3 and Diner #3 is to the right of Diner #1.

Diner #1		Diner #2		Diner #3		
Coin	Match	Coin	Match	Coin	Match	Message
H	Y	H	Y	H	Y	none
T	N	H	Y	H	N	none
T	Y	H	Y	H	N	*yes*
T	N	H	N	H	N	*yes*
T	N	H	N	T	Y	none
T	Y	H	N	T	Y	*yes*

In the first case, there are three matches and zero differences. Zero is even so no message is sent. But "no message" could be considered the equivalent of 0 or "off." In the second case, there are two differences, which is even so no message is sent. In the third case, a message is sent. That is, a "1" or an "on" goes through. The same is true for the fourth and sixth cases.

There is no reason why the examples need to be limited to three people. Any number is possible and the system will still work out the same. Each coin flipped is added into the final count twice, once for the owner and once for the neighbor. So the total number of differences will only be odd if one person is changing the answer.

What happens if two people begin to send at once? The protocol fails because the two changes will cancel each other out. The total number of differences will end up even again. If three people try to send at once, then there will be success because there will be an odd number of changes. A user can easily detect if the protocol is failing. You try to broadcast a bit, but the final answer computed by everyone is the absence of a bit. If each person trying to broadcast stops and waits a random number of turns before beginning again, then the odds are that they won't collide again.

Is this system unconditionally secure? Imagine you're one of the people at the table. Everyone is flipping coins and it is clear that there is some message emerging. If you're not sending it, then can you determine who is? Let's say that your coin comes up heads. Here's a table with some possible outcomes:

	You		Diner #2		Diner #3	
Coin	Match		Coin	Match		Coin	Match
H	Y		H	N		?	Y
H	Y		*H*	N		H	Y
H	Y		H	N		*T*	Y
H	Y		H	Y		?	N
H	Y		*H*	Y		T	N
H	Y		H	Y		*H*	N
H	N		T	Y		?	Y
H	N		*T*	Y		H	Y
H	N		T	Y		*T*	Y
H	N		T	N		?	N
H	N		*T*	N		T	N
H	N		T	N		*H*	N

There are four possible scenarios reported here. In each case, your coin shows heads. You get to look at the coin of Diner #2 to your right. There are an odd number of differences appearing in each case so someone is sending a message. Can you tell who it is?

The first entry for each scenario in the table has a question mark for the flip of the third diner's coin. You don't know what that coin is. In the first scenario, if that hidden coin is heads then Diner #2 is lying and sending a message. If that hidden coin is tails, then Diner #3 is lying and sending the message. The message sender for each line is shown in *italics*.

As long as you don't know the third coin, you can't determine which of the other two table members is sending the message. If this coin flip is perfectly fair, then you'll never know. The same holds true for anyone outside the system who is eavesdropping. If they don't see the coins themselves, then they can't determine who is sending the message.

There are ways for several members of a dining cryptographers network to destroy the communications. If several people conspire, they can compare notes about adjacent coins and identify senders. If the members of the table announce their information in turn, the members at the end of the list can easily change the message by changing their answer. The last guy to speak, for instance, can always determine what the answer will be. This is why it is a good idea to force people to reveal their answers at the same time.

The dining cryptographers system offers everyone the chance to broadcast messages to a group without revealing their identity. It's like sophisticated anonymous remailers that can't be compromised by simply tracing the path of the messages. Unfortunately, there is no easy way to use system available on the Internet. Perhaps this will become more common if the need emerges.

Creating a DC Net

The dining cryptographers (DC) solution is easy to describe because many of the difficulties of implementing the solution on a computer network are left out of the picture. At a table, everyone can reveal their choices simultaneously. It is easy for participants to flip coins and reveal their choices to their neighbors using menus to shield the results. Both of these solutions are not trivial to resolve for a practical implementation.

The first problem is flipping a coin over a computer network. Obviously, one person can flip a coin and lie about it. The simplest solution is to use a one-way hash function like MD-5 or Sneferu.

The phone book is a good, practical one-way function but it is not too secure. It is easy to convert a name into a telephone number, but it is hard to use the average phone book to convert that number back into a name. The function is not secure because there are other ways around the problem. You could, for instance, simply dial the number and ask the identity of the person who answers. Or you could gain

Manuel Blum described how to flip coins over a network in [Blu82]. This is a good way to build up a one-time pad or a key.

access to a reverse phone directory or phone CD-ROM that offered the chance to look up a listing by the number, not the name.

The solution to using a one-way function to flip a coin over a distance is simple:

1. You choose x, a random number and send me $h(x)$ where h is a one-way hash function that is easy to compute but practically impossible to invert.

2. I can't figure out x from the $h(x)$ that you sent me. So I just guess whether x is odd or even. This guess is sent back to you.

3. If I guess correctly about whether x is odd or even, then the coin flip will be tails. If I'm wrong, then it is heads. You determine whether it is heads or tails and send x back to me.

4. I compute $h(x)$ to check that you're not lying. You can only cheat if it is easy for you to find two numbers, x that is odd and y that is even so that $h(x) = h(y)$. No one knows how to do this for good one-way hash functions.

The protocol can be made stronger if I provide the first n bits of x. A precomputed set of x and y can't be used.

This is the algorithm that the two neighbors can use to flip their coins without sitting next to each other at the dinner table. If you find yourself arguing with a friend over which movie to attend, you can use this algorithm with a phone book for the one-way function. Then the flip will be fair.

The second tool must allow for everyone to reveal at the same time whether their coin flips agree or disagree. Chaum's paper suggests allowing people to broadcast their answers simultaneously but on different frequencies. This requires more sophisticated electronics than computer networks currently have. A better solution is to require people to commit to their answers through a *bit commitment* protocol.

The solution is pretty simple. First, the entire group agrees upon a stock phrase or collection of bits. This should be determined as late as possible to prevent someone from trying to use computation in advance to game the system. Call this random set of bits B. To announce their answers, the n participants at the table:

1. Choose n random keys, $\{k_1, \ldots, k_n\}$ in secret.

2. Individually take their answers, put B in front of the answer, and encrypt the string with their secret key. This is $f_{k_i}(Ba_i)$ where f is

the encryption function, k_i is the key, and a_i is the answer to be broadcast.

3. Broadcast their encrypted messages to everyone in the group. It doesn't matter what order this happens.

4. When everyone has received the messages of everyone else, everyone begins sending their keys, k_i out to the group.

5. Everyone decrypts all of the packets, checks to make sure that B is at the beginning of each packet, and finally sums the answers to reveal the message.

These bit-commitment protocols make it nearly impossible for someone to cheat. If there was no B stuck at the beginning of the answers that were encrypted, a sophisticated user might be able to find two different keys that reveal different answers. If he wanted to tell the group that he was reporting a match, then he might show one key. If he wanted to reveal the other, then he could send out another key. This might be possible if the encrypted packet was only one bit long. But it would be near impossible if each encrypted packet began with the same bitstring B. Finding such a pair of keys would be highly unlikely. This is why the bitstring B should be chosen as late as practical.

The combination of these two functions makes it easy to implement a dining cryptographers network using asynchronous communications. There is no need for people to announce their answers in synchrony. Nor is there any reason for people to be adjacent to each other when they flip the coin.

Cheating DC Nets

There are a wide variety of ways that people can subvert the DC networks, but there are adequate defenses to many of the approaches. If people conspire to work together and reveal their information about bits to others around the table, then there is nothing that can be done to stop tracing. In these situations, anonymous remailers can be more secure because they're as secure as their strongest link.

Another major problem might be jamming. Someone on the network could just broadcast extra messages from time to time and thus disrupt the message of someone who is legitimately broadcasting. If, for instance, a message is emerging from the network, a malicious member of the group could start broadcasting at the same time and screw up the rest of the transmission. Unfortunately, the nature of DC networks means that the identity of this person is hidden.

If social problems become important, then it is possible to reveal who is disrupting the network by getting everyone on the network to reveal their coin flips. When this is done, it is possible to determine who is broadcasting. Presumably, there would be rules against broadcasting when another person is using the DC network so it would be possible to unwind the chain far enough to reveal who that person might be.

This can be facilitated if everyone sends out a digital signature of the block of coin flips. Each person in the network has access to two keys, theirs and their neighbor's. The best solution is to have someone sign the coin flips of their neighbor. When the process is unwound, this prevents them from lying about their coin flips to protect themselves. Forcing everyone to sign their neighbor's coin flips prevents people from lying about their own coin flips and changing the signature.

This tracing can be quite useful if only one person uses the DC network for a purpose that offends a majority of the participants—perhaps to send an illegal threat. If one person is trying to jam the communications of another, however, then it reveals both senders. The only way to determine which is legitimate is to produce some rules for when members can start broadcasting. The first sender would be the legitimate sender. The one who began broadcasting afterward would be the jammer.

Summary

Dining Cryptographers networks offer a good opportunity to provide unconditional security against traffic analysis. No one can detect the broadcaster if the nodes of the network keep their coin flips private. Nor can anyone determine the recipient if the messages are encrypted.

The major limitation to DC nets is the high cost of information traffic. Every member of the network must flip coins with their neighbor and then broadcast this information to the group. This must be done for each bit and this overhead can be quite painful.

The Disguise DC nets offer an ideal way to obscure the source of a transmission. If this transmission is encrypted, then only the intended recipient should be able to read it.

How Secure Is It? The system is secure if all of the information about the coin flips are kept secret. Otherwise, the group can track down the sender by revealing all of this information.

How to Use the Software The dining cryptographer net software is for people with access to UNIX workstations and full Internet packet capabilities.

Chapter 12

Coda

As I've been writing this book, I've been haunted by the possibility that there may be something inherently evil or wrong in these algorithms. If criminals are able to hide information so effectively, justice becomes more elusive. There is less the police can do before a crime is committed and there is less evidence after the fact. All of the ideas in this book, no matter how philosophical or embellished with allegory or cute jokes, carry this implicit threat.

The U.S. Federal Bureau of Investigation or at least its senior officers are clearly of the opinion that they need ready access to all communications. If someone is saying it, writing it, mailing it, or faxing it, the Bureau would like to be able to listen in so they can solve crimes. This is a sensible attitude. More information can only help make sure that justice is fair and honest. People are convicted on the basis of their own words—not the testimony of stoolpigeons who often point the finger in order to receive a lighter sentence.

The arguments against giving the FBI and the police such power are more abstract and anecdotal. Certainly, the power can be tamed if everyone follows proper procedures. If warrants are filed and chains of evidence are kept intact, the power of abuse is minimized. But even if the police are 100 times more honest than the average citizen, there will still be rogue cops on the force with access to the communications of everyone in the country. This is a very powerful tool and the corruption brought by power is one of the oldest themes.

Both of these scenarios are embodied in one case that came along in the year before I began writing this book. The story began when a

New Orleans woman looked out the window and saw a police officer beating her son's friend. She called the internal affairs department to report the officer. By lunchtime, the officer in question knew the name of the person making the accusation, her address, and even what she was wearing. He allegedly ordered a hit and by the end of the day, she was dead.

How do we know this happened? How do we know it wasn't a random case of street violence? Federal authorities were in New Orleans following the officer and bugging his phone. He was a suspect in a ring of corrupt cops who helped the drug trade remain secure. They audiotaped the order for the hit.

There is little doubt that secure communications could have made this case unsolvable. If no one heard the execution order except the killer, there would be no case and no justice.

There is also little doubt that a secure internal affairs office could have prevented the murder. That leak probably came from a colleague, but the corrupt cops could have monitored the phones of the internal affairs division. That scenario is quite conceivable. At the very least, the murder would have been delayed until a case was made against the officer. The right to confront our accusers in court means that it would be impossible to keep her identity secret forever.

Which way is the right way? Total openness stops many crimes but it encourages others forms of fraud and deceit. Total secrecy protects many people, but it gives the criminals a cover.

The FBI and other parts of the law enforcement community would like to believe that the Clipper system and other forms of "key escrow" systems are a viable compromise. These systems broadcast a copy of the session key in an encrypted packet that can only be read

One solution is to encrypt the session key with a special public key. Only the government has access to the private key.

by designated people. Although Department of Justice officials have described extensive controls on the keys and access to them, I remain unconvinced that there will not be abuse. If the tool is going to be useful to the police on the streets, they'll need fast access to keys. The audit log will only reveal a problem if someone complains that their phone was tapped illegally. But how do you know your phone was tapped? Only if you discover the tapes in the hands of someone.

There really is no way for technology to provide any ultimate solution to this problem. At some point, law-enforcement authorities must be given the authority to listen in to solve a crime. The more this ability is concentrated in a small number of hands, the more powerful it becomes and the more alluring the corruption associated with breaking the rules. Even the most dangerous secret owned by the United States, the technology for building nuclear weapons, was compromised by an insider. Is there any doubt that small-time criminals with needs won't be able to pull off small-time corruption across the country?

The technology described in this book offers a number of ways for information to elude the police dragnets. Encrypted files may look like secrets and secrets can look damning. Although the Fifth amendment to the U.S. Constitution gives each person the right to refuse to incriminate themselves, there is little doubt that invoking that right can look suspicious.

At the time this essay is being written, the Clinton administration is refusing to hand over files to a Republican Senate committee. Earlier, the President vowed to cooperate with the investigation. Now, the Republicans seem to want to amplify the image of a President with something to hide.

The mimic functions, anonymous remailers, and photographic steganography allow people to create files and hide them from sight. If no one can find them, no one can demand the encryption key. This may offer a powerful tool for the criminal element.

There are some consolations. Random violence on the street really can't be stopped by phone taps. Muggers, rapists, robbers, and many other criminals don't rely upon communications to do their job. These are arguably some of the most important problems for everyone and something that requires more diligent police work. None of the tools described in this book should affect the balance of power on the street.

Other crimes can only really be solved through wiretaps because some crime only exists through communications. Bribery of officials, for instance, is only committed when two people sit down in private and make an agreement. If the money can't be traced (as it so often can't be), then the only way to prove the crime happened is to record the conversation or get someone to testify. Obviously, the recorded conversation is much more convincing evidence. State and local police in some states are not allowed to use wiretaps at all. Some police officers suggest that this isn't an accident. The politicians in those states recognized that the only real targets for wiretaps were the politicians. They were the primary ones who broke laws in conversation. Almost all other lawbreaking involved some physical act that might leave other evidence.

But in the end it doesn't matter what they see or think they see. The terminals are equipped with holographic scanners, which decode the binary secret of every item, infallibly. This is the language of the waves and radiation, or how the dead speak to the living. And this is where we wait together, regardless of age, our carts stocked with brightly colored goods.
—Don DeLillo in White Noise

The power for creating secret deals that this technology offers is numbing. The only consolation is that these deals have been made in the past and only a fool would believe that they won't be made in the future. All of the wiretap laws didn't stop them before cryptography became cheap. Meeting people face to face to conduct illegal business also has other benefits. You can judge people better in person. Also, the locations like bars where such deals may be made offer drinks and often food. You can't get that in cyberspace.

The fact that crooks have found ways to elude wiretaps in the past can be easily extended to parallel a popular argument made by the National Rifle Association. If cryptography is outlawed, only outlaws will have cryptography. People who murder, smuggle, or steal will probably not feel much hesitation to violate a law that simply governs how they send bits back and forth. Honest people who obey any law regulating cryptography will find themselves easy marks for those who want to steal their secrets.

Clint Brooks, a senior official at the National Security Agency, recognizes that any law won't prevent outlaws from using cryptography, but he argues that any law will still be worth the trouble. Criminals won't be able to purchase secure phones off-the-shelf from companies like Radio Shack. This is a fair argument. The Clipper wiretaps may only catch the stupid crooks, but that's still not bad.

I mulled over all of these thoughts while I was writing this book. I've almost begun to feel that the dispute is not really about technology. If criminals can always avoid the law, this wasn't really going to change with more technology. The police have always been forced to adapt to new technology and they would have to do the same here.

In the end, I began concentrating on how to balance the power relationships. If power can be dispersed successfully, then the results of abuse can be limited. If individuals can control their affairs, then they are less likely to be dominated by others. If they're forced to work in the open, then they're more likely to be controlled.

The dishonest will never yield to the law that tells them not to use any form of steganography. The cliché of gangsters announcing the arrival of a shipment of 10,000 bananas will be with us forever. The question is whether the honest should have access to the tools to protect their privacy. Cryptography and steganography give individuals this power.

Appendix A

Mimic Code

Here is the source code for a Pascal version of the mimic software described in Chapter 7. A C version is also available from the author. You are welcome to use this in any noncommercial way that you choose.

MimicGlobals.p

```
unit MimicGlobals;
{This section contains all of the global definitions that are}
{necessary to run the Mimic Function Generator/Parser. }
interface
 const
  MaxLettersPerWord = 40;
        {The maximum letters in each word. This might be better}
        {left large , although it does waste space in these cases . }
  StoppingCharacter = '/';
        {In the definition of section where the grammar is defined,}
        {this character is used to separate the different}
        {productions that could occur. When it occurs twice, }
        {it signifies the end of the production...}
  VariableSignifier = '*';
        {If the first character of a word equals this then the }
        {program shall treat the word as a variable which }
        {will undergo more transformations. Note the program }
        {ASSUMES that a variable is one word.}
  EqualityCharacter = '=';
        {There is a character which signifies the equality }
        {between a variable and set of productions.}
  EndOfFileSignifier = chr(0);
```

```
        {This is passed back from NextWord when it finds it }
        {is at the end of the file...}
  NullWord = ' ';
        {This is what comes back from NextWord if it can't }
        {find something...}
  Space = ' ';
        {This is something different, but the same. It is the }
        {same thing, but used in a different fashion. }
  ReserveBits = $55;
        {When MimicMan runs out of bits in the file, he }
        {still might need to finish up a production.}
        {ReserveBits let this be done...}
type
  Word = string[MaxLettersPerWord];
        {This is the standard unit...}
  ScanTableResponses = (Normal, Stopper, Spacer);
        {Used in NextWord to make quick decisions about character.}
{These are the node types constructed }
{for the table which holds the grammar.}
  WordNodePtr = ^WordNode;
  WordNode = record
    w1: word;
            {The word stored at this point...}
    next: WordNodePtr;
            {The Next in the list...}
   end;
  ProductionNodePtr = ^ProductionNode;
  BitNodePtr = ^BitNode;
  BitNode = record
    BitNumber: integer;
            {This is the number of a central registers of bits .}
    Polarity: boolean;
            {If True, then it is the same as Bits[BitNumber] }
            {otherwise it is reversed.}
    probability: real;
            {This is the total probability of all subordinate nodes.}
    Up: BitNodePtr;
            {This is the precursor...}
  Left, Right: BitNodePtr;
            {Because This is a tree...}
    TheProductionNode: ProductionNodePtr;
            {Well, technically, I could get away with storing }
            {this pointer in either left or }
            {right because left and right will equal nil if and }
            {only if TheProductionNode <> nil, but}
```

```
                {I don't feel like packing this too tightly right now. }
                {I'm being lavish with memory.}
     end;
   ProductionNode = record
     probability: real;
                {The Probability that this particular }
                {production will be chosen.}
       ItsBit: BitNodePtr;
                {Follow this up to the root to find the bits }
                {associated with this production.}
       TheWords: WordNodePtr;
                {This is the list of words that come from the }
                {Production. Variables are at the end.}
       next: ProductionNodePtr;
                {This is the next in the list...}
     end;
   VariableNodePtr = ^VariableNode;
   VariableNode = record
     w1: word;
                {This is the identity of the variable...}
       Productions: ProductionNodePtr;
                {This is the list of productions....}
       ItsBitRoot: BitNodePtr;
                {This is the top of the bit tree. When random }
                {characters are being generated, it follows this down to}
                {the bottom...}
       next: VariableNodePtr;
                {One thing before the other...}
     end;
   MimicProdNodePtr = ^MimicProdNode;
   MimicProdNode = record
     ww: WordNodePtr;
            {This is where the next word to be dealt with...}
       next: MimicProdNodePtr;
            {The next one down.}
     end;
   MimicParseFramePtr = ^MimicParseFrame;
   MimicParseFrame = record
     TheVariable: VariableNodePtr;
            {This is the variable that is being considered at this}
            {point...}
       TheWordsToMatch: WordNodePtr;
            {Once a production is matched, this baby is loaded }
            {with words to check.}
     end;
```

```
var
  OpenGrammarFile: text;
      {This is the file that is opened at the time.}
  OpenGrammarName: str255;
      {This is the name of the file.}
  OpenMimicryFile: text;
      {This is the file that Mimicry will either be read out of or}
      {pushed into in the process of parsing or producing text.}
  OpenMimicryName: str255;
      {This is the name of the file.}
  OpenSourceFile: packed file of QDbyte;
      {This is the file of data that is used to
         generate the mimicry. this was a file of
         long integers but sometimes there are an
         odd number of bytes in a file and this
         got munged. For some reason, the type "byte"
         doesn't work here. "QDbyte" seems to work,
         even though I can't seem to find the word
         in the documentation.}
  OpenSourceName: str255;
      {This is the name of the file.}
  ScanTable: array[0..255] of ScanTableResponses;
      {Used by NextWord to speed up the classification procedure.}
  VariableListRoot: VariableNodePtr;
      {This is the list of variables contained in the list...}
  CurrentVariable: variableNodePTr;
      {This is a global containing the current variable that
         productions are being added to...}
  LastCharacter: char;
      {This is last character read in NextWord.}
  GoodTable: boolean;
      {This signifies that a table has been loaded without errors.}
  AddCarriageReturns: boolean;
      {Set to true if the program should insert carriage returns
         in the output.}
  RightMargin: integer;
      {When this boundary is crossed, the carriage returns will
         b e included.}
 procedure Error (str: str255);
implementation
 procedure Error; {(str: str255)}
  var
   temp: str255;
 begin
  writeln(str);
```

```
 writeln('Continue? (Type quit to say good bye)');
 readln(input, temp);
 writeln(str);
 if temp = 'quit' then
  ExitToSHell;
 end;
end.
```

Randomness.p

```
unit Randomness;
{This is a customized version of a random number generator.}
{It is based on a cellular automaton version of a random number}
{generator written by Stephen Wolfram. The generator is now}
{known to be INSECURE. I should REPLACE it.}
{$SETC NoRandomness=false}
interface
 uses
  MimicGlobals;
 procedure SetKey;
    {This is just a routine to turn a password into a key.}
 procedure InitRandomBits;
    {This is just for setting everything up at the beginning.}
 procedure SyncRandomBits;
    {Starts the ball rolling.}
 function RandomBit (bitter: integer): boolean;
    {Returns a specific random bit.}
 procedure UpdateRandomBits;
    {This cycles the random number generator.}
implementation
 const
  MaxRandomBit = 32;
        {This is just a local boundary. This should not }
        {effect the user of this module.}
 var
  RandomBits: longint;
        {This is the register.}
  InitialKey: longint;
        {This is for resetting...}
 procedure SetKey;
    {This is just a routine to turn a password into a key.}
  var
   i: integer;
   tempor: longint;
  begin
```

```
  InitialKey := $deadbeef;
  writeln('Please input a pass number.');
  write('::');
  read(input, tempor);
  InitialKey := BXOR(InitialKey, tempor);
 end;{SetKey}
procedure InitRandomBits;
   {Starts the ball rolling.}
 begin
  InitialKey := $baadfaad;
  RandomBits := InitialKey;
 end;{InitRandomBits}
procedure SyncRandomBits;
   {Starts the ball rolling.}
 begin
{$IFC NoRandomness}
  RandomBits := 0;
{$ELSEC}
  RandomBits := InitialKey;
{$ENDC}
 end;{SyncRandomBits}
 procedure UpdateRandomBits;
   {This cycles the random number generator.}
 begin
{$IFC NoRandomness}
  RandomBits := 0;
{$ELSEC}
  RandomBits := BXOR(BROTL(RandomBits, 1),
                     BOR(RandomBits,
                     BROTR(RandomBits, 1)));
{$ENDC}
 end;{UpdateRandomBits}
 function RandomBit (bitter: integer): boolean;
   {Returns a specific random bit.}
 begin
  bitter := bitter mod MaxRandomBit;
  if BTST(RandomBits, bitter) then
   RandomBit := true
  else
   RandomBit := false;
{writeln('Testing bit:', bitter : 3, ' and the result is:',
          BTST(RandomBits, bitter));}
 end;{RandomBit}
end.
```

WordEater.p

```
unit WordEater;
{I've named this section Wordeater because}
{it contains the basic file operations that must }
{be done to look around and keep}
{pulling off words.}
interface
 uses
  MimicGlobals;
 function NextWord (var StopChar: char): word;
    {This function reads the next word from the currently opened
     file. }
 function OpenOneUp: boolean;
    {This function goes through what needs to be done to open up a
     file for reading.}
 function CloseOneDown: boolean;
    {This one does the other end. Ashes to Ashes.}
 procedure InitializeScanHashTable;
    {The Scanning Hash Table has 256 entries. They identify a }
    {character as either, letter, stop character,}
    {a space or a comment.}
implementation
 function OpenOneUp: boolean;
    {This function goes through what needs to be }
    {done to open up a file for reading.}
    {This uses a MacIntosh Version...Actually, }
    {a THINK Pascal specific function...}
 begin
  OpenGrammarName := OldFileName('Give Me the file...');
        {A THINK function.}
  if OpenGrammarName <> '' then begin
    OpenOneUp := true;
    Open(OpenGrammarFile, OpenGrammarName)
   end
  else
   OpenOneUp := false;
 end;{OpenOneUp}
 function CloseOneDown: boolean;
    {This one does the other end. Ashes to Ashes.}
 begin
  Close(OpenGrammarFile);
 end;{CloseOneDown}
 procedure InitializeScanHashTable;
    {The Scanning Hash Table has 256 entries. }
    {They identify a character as either, letter, stop character,}
```

```
      {a space or a comment.}
    var
      i: integer;
   begin
    LastCharacter := Space;
    for i := 14 to 255 do
     ScanTable[i] := Normal;
    for i := 0 to 13 do
     ScanTable[i] := Spacer;
    ScanTable[13] := Spacer;
    ScanTable[ord(EqualityCharacter)] := Stopper;
    ScanTable[ord(StoppingCharacter)] := Stopper;
    ScanTable[ord(' ')] := Spacer;
   end;{InitializeScanHashTable}
   function NextWord (var StopChar: char): word;
      {Find the next word...}
    const
     Space = ' '; {For clarity?}
    var
     CurPos: integer;
         {This is the current position to be filled in the answer....}
     CurLet: char;
         {What comes out of the read.}
     answer: word;
         {Because we can't always assign to NextWord }
         {very easily because of the semantics.}
   begin
    if eof(OpenGrammarFile) then begin
      StopChar := EndOfFileSignifier;
      NextWord := ' ';
    end
    else begin
      CurPos := 1;
      answer := '';
      CurLet := LastCharacter;
      while not (eof(OpenGrammarFile))
            & (ScanTable[Ord(CurLet)] = Spacer) do
       read(OpenGrammarFile, CurLet);
      while not (eof(OpenGrammarFile))
            & (ScanTable[Ord(CurLet)] = Normal)
            & (CurPos < MaxLettersPerWord) do begin
        answer := concat(answer, CurLet);
        CurPos := CurPos + 1;
        read(OpenGrammarFile, CurLet);
       end;
```

```
      answer := concat(answer, space);
      while (ScanTable[Ord(CurLet)] = Spacer)
            and not (eof(OpenGrammarFile)) do
       read(OpenGrammarFile, CurLet);
      if eof(OpenGrammarFile) then begin
        StopChar := EndOfFileSignifier;
        {If it is an end of file, return that as the end....}
       end
      else if CurPos = MaxLettersPerWord then {Ignore The Extra}
       begin
        while not (eof(OpenGrammarFile)) & (CurLet <> Space) do
         read(OpenGrammarFile, CurLet);
        StopChar := Space;
       end
      else begin
        if ScanTable[Ord(CurLet)] = Normal then begin
         LastCharacter := CurLet;
         StopChar := Space
          {Just in case a return or line-feed enters the process.}
         end
        else begin
         LastCharacter := space;
         StopChar := CurLet
         end;
       end;
     NextWord := answer;
{$IFC DebugNextWord}
     writeln('NW:', answer : 20, ' SC:', stopchar);
{$ENDC}
   end;
 end;{NextWord}
end.
```

TableSetter.p

```
unit TableSetter;
    {Reads in the grammars from a file and fills
       it up so that everything is fine.}
interface
 uses
  MimicGlobals, WordEater, SANE;
 function LoadTable: boolean;
    {This function tries to load the }
    {information from the currently opened file into table.}
    {Returns true if it succeeds. False if it signals an error.}
```

```
function FindVariable (Name: word): VariableNodePtr;
  {Looks up the list and finds the variable corresponding to it.}
  {Note that everything is extremely slow
    to just keep this in a list!}
procedure PrintTable;
  {Prints out the grammar table so people can see }
  {what got read in correctly and what wasn't.}
function CompareStrings (st1, st2: word): integer;
  {Returns -1 if st1<st2, 0 if st1=st2 and 1 }
  {if st1>st2. Assumes they end with a space.}
function GetStartVariable: VariableNodePtr;
  {This returns the variable that starts out
    every production. This is just set to be
    the first one in the list. The first alphabetically.
    It would be possible to put some sort of random
    selection here too if you wanted to add an additional
    signifier that said "I'm a good candidate to
    start a production."}
implementation
 var
  WasThereNoError: boolean;
        {Kept locally to determine if there was an error or not.}
procedure PrintWordList (w: WordNodePtr);
begin
 while w <> nil do begin
   write(w^.w1, ',');
   w := w^.next;
  end;
 writeln;
end;{PrintWordList}
procedure PrintProductionList (p: ProductionNodePtr);
begin
 while p <> nil do begin
   write('Production with P=', p^.probability : 6, ':');
   PrintWordList(p^.TheWords);
   p := p^.next;
  end;
 writeln('-----------------------------');
end;{PrintProductionList}
procedure PrintVariableList (v: VariableNodePtr);
begin
 while v <> nil do begin
   writeln('<><>Starting Variable:', v^.w1 : 20, '<><><><><><><><>');
   PrintProductionList(v^.Productions);
   v := v^.next;
```

```
  end;
 writeln('<><><><><><><><><><><><><><><><><><>');
end;{PrintProductionList}
procedure PrintTable;
   {Prints out the grammar table so people can }
   {see what got read in correctly and what wasn't.}
begin
 PrintVariableList(VariableListRoot);
end;
procedure InitLoader;
begin
 VariableListRoot := nil;
 WasThereNoError := true;
end;
procedure SkipToEnd;
   {This procedure just keeps hitting NextWord until }
   {it hits the double StoppingCharacter, which when}
   {I wrote this line was defined to be '//'.}
 var
  wa: word;
       {For local reasons...}
  Previous, Stopper: char;
       {To see why it ended...}
begin
 WasThereNoError := false;
 wa := NextWord(Stopper);
 repeat
  Previous := Stopper;
  wa := NextWord(Stopper);
 until ((wa = ' ') and (Previous = StoppingCharacter)
                   and (Stopper = StoppingCharacter))
                   or (stopper = EndOfFileSignifier);
end;{SkipToEnd}
procedure LocalMinorError (message: str255);
   {This procedure prints out the message and }
   {then prints out the rest of the line.}
 var
  wa: word;
       {For local reasons...}
  Previous, Stopper: char;
       {To see why it ended...}
begin
 WasThereNoError := false;
 writeln(message);
 wa := NextWord(Stopper);
```

```
 repeat
  write(wa, stopper);
  Previous := Stopper;
  wa := NextWord(Stopper);
 until ((wa = ' ') and (Previous = StoppingCharacter)
                   and (Stopper = StoppingCharacter))
                or (stopper = EndOfFileSignifier);
  write(wa, stopper);
  writeln;
  writeln('That line was ignored.');
 end;{LocalMinorError}
procedure LocalMinorErrorNoPrint (message: str255);
   {This procedure prints out the message
      and then prints out the rest of the line.}
  var
   wa: word;
        {For local reasons...}
   Previous, Stopper: char;
        {To see why it ended...}
begin
 WasThereNoError := false;
 writeln(message);
 wa := NextWord(Stopper);
 repeat
  Previous := Stopper;
  wa := NextWord(Stopper);
 until ((wa = ' ') & (Previous = StoppingCharacter)
                 & (Stopper = StoppingCharacter))
                | (stopper = EndOfFileSignifier);
  writeln('The rest of the line was ignored.');
 end;{LocalMinorErrorNoPrint}
function CompareStrings (st1, st2: word): integer;
   {Returns -1 if st1<st2, 0 if st1=st2 and 1 }
   {if st1>st2. Assumes they end with a space.}
  var
   i, last: integer;
begin
 i := 1;
 while (st1[i] = st2[i]) and (st1[i] <> ' ') do
  i := i + 1;
 if st1[i] = st2[i] then
  CompareStrings := 0
 else if st1[i] < st2[i] then
  CompareStrings := -1
 else
```

```
  CompareStrings := 1;
end;
procedure AddVariable (v: variableNodePtr);
   {This adds it to the root.}
 var
  Previous, Node: variableNodePtr;
       {For scanning along the list.}
  Relativity: integer;
begin
 Node := VariableListRoot;
 if (VariableListRoot = nil) then begin
   VariableListRoot := v;
   v^.next := nil;
  end
 else if CompareSTrings(node^.w1, v^.w1) = 1 then begin
   VariableListRoot := v;
   v^.next := node;
  end
 else begin
   while (node <> nil) do begin
     Relativity := CompareStrings(node^.w1, v^.w1);
     if Relativity = -1 then begin
      Previous := node;
      node := node^.next
      end
     else if Relativity = 0 then
      LocalMinorError(concat('"', v^.w1, '" has Been previously
                    defined.'))
     else begin
      previous^.next := v;
      v^.next := node;
      node := nil;
      v := nil;{To signal that it was added...}
       end;
     end;
    if v <> nil then begin
      previous^.next := v;
      v^.next := nil;
     end;
   end;
end;{AddVariable}
function FindVariable (Name: word): VariableNodePtr;
   {Looks up the list and finds the variable corresponding to it.}
   {Note that everything is extremely }
   {slow to just keep this in a list!}
```

```
label
 152;
var
 temp: VariableNodePtr;
      {Sort of a stunt double for FindVariable.}
  relativity: integer;
      {Just for storing the relative differences between strings.}
begin
 temp := VariableListRoot;
      {Start at the very beginning.}
 while temp <> nil do begin
   relativity := CompareStrings(name, temp^.w1);
   if relativity > 0 then
    temp := temp^.next
   else if relativity = 0 then begin
     FindVariable := temp;
     goto 152
    end
   else begin
     FindVariable := nil;
     goto 152
    end
  end;
 FindVariable := nil;
152:
end;{FindVariable}
function HandleFirst: boolean;
   {The first word in a line must be a variable. }
   {This will be used to set up the variable list...}
 var
 V: variableNodePtr;
      {This is what is going to get built...}
  wa, wb: word;
      {For local reasons...}
  Stopper: char;
      {To see why it ended...}
begin
 HandleFirst := true;
 wa := NextWord(stopper);
 if stopper = EndOfFileSignifier then begin
   if wa <> NullWord then
    Error('Unexpected end of the file.');
   HandleFirst := false;
   exit(HandleFirst)
  end;
```

```
      if (wa = ' ') or (wa[1] <> VariableSignifier) then
        LocalMinorError('Expected a variable name at
                        the beginning of the line:')
      else begin
        new(v);
        with V^ do begin
          w1 := wa;
          Productions := nil;
          ItsBitRoot := nil
        end;
{Now add it to the list in the right place...}
        AddVariable(v);
        CurrentVariable := v;
      end;
    if stopper <> EqualityCharacter then begin
      repeat
        wa := NextWord(stopper)
      until (stopper <> Space) or (wa <> NullWord);
      if wa <> NullWord then
        LocalMinorError(concat('The Variable should only be one word. "',
                                wa, '" is too much. Error in line:'))
    end
  end;{HandleFirst...}
  function WordToValue (w: word;
        var Error: Boolean): real;
      {Returns the real value of the string contained in w. }
      {Signals an error if there is a problem.}
    var
      temp: real;
  begin
    Error := false;
    temp := Str2Num(w);{This uses a MacIntosh SANE routine.}
      {I can't seem to find my copy of Inside
        Macintosh so I can't seem to figure out
        how to correctly figure out if an error
        has been generated. It turns out that the bad
        values are less than zero.}
    if (temp >= 0) then
      WordToValue := temp
    else begin
      WordToValue := 0;
      Error := true;
    end;
  end;
  function HandleProduction: boolean;
```

```
      {Keeps Adding Production until it encounters
         a double Stopping Character.}
   var
     LastAddedWord: wordNodePtr;
           {This is just a place keeper which
              points to the last word added so the
              next can be updated when another one is added.}
     TheProduction: productionNodePTr;
           {This is where the info goes...}
     wa: word;
           {For local reasons...}
     Stopper: char;
           {To see why it ended...}
     startedVariables: boolean;
           {Variables can only come at the end of productions...}
     IsError: boolean;
           {If there is a problem this get's set to be true.}
   begin
   HandleProduction := true;
   LastAddedWord := nil;
   TheProduction := nil;
   repeat
    repeat
     wa := NextWord(stopper);
     if (stopper = EndOfFileSignifier) then begin
       if (LastAddedWord <> nil) then begin
        writeln('Just parsed something left incomplete by the end of
                 the file:');
        PrintWordList(LastAddedWord);
        Error('Unexpected end of the file.');
        HandleProduction := false;
        end;
       exit(HandleProduction)
      end;
     if wa <> NullWord then begin
       if LastAddedWord = nil then {Start a new production...}
       begin
       if wa[1] = VariableSignifier then begin
       Error(concat('The first word of a production, "', wa, '"
                     cannot be a variable. Ignoring Production.'));
       SkipToEnd;
       stopper := StoppingCharacter;
       wa := NullWord;
       end
       else begin
```

```
      new(TheProduction);
      TheProduction^.next := CurrentVariable^.Productions;
      CurrentVariable^.Productions := TheProduction;
        {Put it at the beginning of the list...}
      New(LastAddedWord);
      TheProduction^.TheWords := LastAddedWord;
      LastAddedWord^.w1 := wa;
      StartedVariables := false;
      end
      end
    else begin
     New(LastAddedWord^.next);
     LastAddedWord := LastAddedWord^.next;
     LastAddedWord^.w1 := wa;
     if wa[1] = VariableSignifier then begin
     if not (startedVariables) then
     startedVariables := true;
     end
     else if startedVariables then begin
     LocalMinorError('The format of a production is terminal,
                      terminal ... terminal, variable... varable.
                      A terminal comes before the variable in
                      line:');
     CurrentVariable^.Productions := nil;
        {Clean out this baby to signal a problem.}
     end
     end;
   end;
until stopper = StoppingCharacter;
if LastAddedWord <> nil then begin
 LastAddedWord^.next := nil;
 LastAddedWord := nil
 end;
if wa <> NullWord then
 {At this point a production has been stored away.
   Now get its probability...}
 begin
 wa := NextWord(Stopper);
 if stopper = EndOfFileSignifier then begin
   Error('Unexpected end of the file.');
   HandleProduction := false;
   exit(HandleProduction)
   end;
 TheProduction^.probability := WordToValue(wa, Iserror);
 if Iserror then begin
```

```
            LocalMinorErrorNoPrint(concat('The word "',
                      wa, '" does not translate into a number.'));
            write('The error occurs in production:');
            PrintWordList(LastAddedWord)
           end
         else if Stopper <> StoppingCharacter then begin
           wa := NextWord(Stopper);
           LocalMinorErrorNoPrint(concat('The word "',
               wa, '" does not belong in the probability field . '));
           write('The error occurs in production:');
           PrintWordList(LastAddedWord)
          end;
       end;
 until wa = NullWord;
end;{HandleProduction}
procedure InsertIntoBitList (node: BitNodePtr;
      var ListStart: BitNodePtr);
   {This is just a temporary procedure that maintains }
   {a list of BitNodes Sorted by Probability.}
 var
  Previous, Scanner: BitNodePtr;
       {For scanning along the list.}
begin
 if (ListStart = nil) then begin
   ListStart := node;
   node^.up := nil;
  end
 else if node^.probability <= ListStart^.probability then begin
   node^.up := ListStart;
   ListStart := node;
  end
 else begin
   Scanner := ListStart;
   while (Scanner <> nil) do begin
     if node^.probability > Scanner^.probability then begin
      Previous := Scanner;
      Scanner := Scanner^.up
      end
     else begin
      previous^.up := node;
      node^.up := Scanner;
      Scanner := nil;
      node := nil;{To signal that it was added...}
      end;
    end;
```

```pascal
      if node <> nil then begin
        previous^.up := node;
        node^.up := nil;
      end;
    end;
end;{InsertIntoBitList}
procedure BuildBitTable;
    {It is important that there be a tree that describes }
    {how the bits are assigned to each production...}
  var
    IntermediateBitList: BitNodePtr;
        {This contains the list of bit nodes that }
        {don't have a root. When there is only}
        {one left, then this is crowned king and }
        {assigned to the variable's ItsBitRoot.}
    TempBit: BitNodePtr;
        {Used in the building...}
    ProductionList: ProductionNodePtr;
        {This is the list of productions that }
        {the bit list will be built out of...}
    NExtBitNumber: integer;
        {This is used for assigning a unique }
        {number to each node...}
    v: VariableNodePtr;
        {This is so the list can do this for every variable...}
  begin
   v := VariableListRoot;
   while v <> nil do begin
     productionList := V^.productions; {This is the list...}
     IntermediateBitList := nil;
     NextBitNumber := 0;
     while productionList <> nil do begin
       new(TempBit);
       with TempBit^ do begin
        probability := ProductionList^.probability;
        left := nil;
        right := nil;
        polarity := true;
        BitNumber := -1;
        TheProductionNode := ProductionList;
        end;
       ProductionList^.itsBit := TempBit;
       InsertIntoBitList(TempBit, IntermediateBitList);
       ProductionList := ProductionList^.next;
     end;
```

```
{Now one bit for each production list, let's start making pairs...}
while IntermediateBitList^.up <> nil do
{While there is more than one node in the list...}
 begin
  new(TempBit);
  with TempBit^ do begin
   probability := IntermediateBitList^.probability +
                  IntermediateBitList^.up^.probability;
   left := IntermediateBitList;
   right := IntermediateBitList^.up;
   BitNumber := NextBitNumber;
   polarity := true;
   NextBitNumber := NextBitNumber + 1;
   TheProductionNode := nil;
   end;
  IntermediateBitList := IntermediateBitList^.up^.up;
       {Get Rid of the top two...}
  with TempBit^.left^ do begin
   polarity := false;
        {Flip one... One son should be true and the other false.}
   up := TempBit;
   end;
  TempBit^.right^.up := TempBit;
  InsertIntoBitList(TempBit, IntermediateBitList);
  end;
 {There should only be one left at this point...}
 v^.ItsBitRoot := IntermediateBitList;
 IntermediateBitList^.up := nil;
 v := v^.next;
 end;
end;{BuildBitTable}
function GetStartVariable: VariableNodePtr;
  {This returns the variable that starts
   out every production. This is just set
   to be the first one in the list. The
   first alphabetically. It would be possible
   to put some sort of random selection here
   too if you wanted to add an additional signifier
   that said "I'm a good candidate to start a production."}
begin
 GetStartVariable := VariableListRoot;
end;{GetStartVariable}
function LoadTable: boolean;
  {This function tries to load the information from }
  {the currently opened file into table.}
```

```
    {Returns true if it succeeds. False if }
    {it signals an error.}
  var
   looping: boolean;
begin
 InitLoader;
 if OpenOneUp then begin
   VariableListRoot := nil;
   looping := true;
   while looping do
    if HandleFirst then
     looping := HandleProduction
    else
     looping := false;
   BuildBitTable;
   PrintVariableList(VariableListRoot);
   LoadTable := WasThereNoError
  end;
 if CloseOneDown then
  ; {Don't really care about this...}
 end;{LoadTable}
end.
```

OutSpitter.p

```
unit OutSpitter;
{This unit uses the structures built in TableSetter }
{to produce output from the grammar.}
interface
 uses
  MimicGlobals, WordEater, TableSetter, Randomness;
 procedure DoSomeMimicry;
    {This produces some randomness and }
    {keeps it all going until the end...}
 procedure SetProcessingFilesIn;
 procedure SetProcessingFilesOut;
    {These get the files from the user.}
implementation
 var
  AtTheEndOfFile: boolean;
        {This is set to be true when we get to the end...}
  SourceBits: longint;
        {The current longint read in from the file.}
  SourcePosition: integer;
        {The next bit to be read.}
```

```pascal
TheOutputStack: MimicProdNodePtr;
        {This is the stack of variables that are un produced...}
CarriagePosition: integer;
        {This is the location of the last character }
        {printed out on the page. For justification.}
procedure SetProcessingFilesIn;
 var
  Err: OSErr;
        {A Mac Error Code...}
begin
 writeln('Okay, please tell me the file you wish to
          covert into mimicry using the grammar.');
 OpenSourceName := OldFileName('Give Me the file...');
   {A THINK function.}
 writeln('Now where would you like the output to go?');
 OpenMimicryName := NewFileName('Give Me the file...');
    {A THINK function.}
 if OpenMimicryName <> '' then begin
   Err := Create(OpenMimicryName, 0, 'Mmmk', 'TEXT');
       {Ignore the Error if it already exists...}
   if (Err <> NoErr) and (Err <> DupFNErr) then
    Error('Macintosh File Error ');
   end
end;{SetProcessingFiles}
procedure SetProcessingFilesOut;
 var
  Err: OSErr;
       {A Mac Error Code...}
begin
 writeln('Now where would you like the data to go?');
 OpenSourceName := NewFileName('Give Me the file...');
       {A THINK function.}
 writeln('Okay, please tell me the file you wish to covert out
          of mimicry using the grammar.');
 OpenMimicryName := OldFileName('Give Me the file...');
       {A THINK function.}
 if OpenSourceName <> '' then begin
   Err := Create(OpenSourceName, 0, 'Mmmk', 'TEXT');
       {Ignore the Error if it already exists...}
   if (Err <> NoErr) and (Err <> DupFNErr) then
    Error('Macintosh File Error ');
   end
end;{SetProcessingFilesOut}
procedure OpenForOutput;
   {This opens up a pair of files for producing mimicry.}
```

```
begin
 Open(OpenSourceFile, OpenSourceName);
 read(OpenSourceFile, SourceBits);
 SourcePosition := 7;
 CarriagePosition := 0;
 AtTheEndOfFile := false;
 TheOutputStack := nil;
 ReWrite(OpenMimicryFile, OpenMimicryName);
end;{OpenForOutput}
procedure CloseUpOutput;
   {This closes up a pair of files for producing mimicry.}
begin
 Close(OpenSourceFile);
 Close(OpenMimicryFile);
end;{CloseUpOutput}
function NextBit: boolean;
   {Pulls off the next bit...}
begin
 if SourcePosition = -1 then
  if eof(OpenSourceFile) then begin
    SourceBits := ReserveBits;
    AtTheEndOfFile := true;
    SourcePosition := 7
   end
  else begin
    read(OpenSourceFile, SourceBits);
    SourcePosition := 7;
   end;
 if BTST(SourceBits, SourcePosition) then
  NextBit := true
 else
  NextBit := false;
 SourcePosition := SourcePosition - 1;
end;{NextBit}
function VariableToProduction (v: VariableNodePtr): ProductionNodePtr;
   {This baby takes a variable and follows
     its way down to the production using the bit tree.}
 var
  Bitto: BitNodePtr;
       {This is the position that the bit tree should follow.}
begin
 UpdateRandomBits;
       {Cycle the random number generator.}
 Bitto := v^.ItsBitRoot;
 while Bitto^.TheProductionNode = nil do begin
```

```
   if NextBit then begin
     if RandomBit(Bitto^.BitNumber) then
       Bitto := Bitto^.right
     else
       Bitto := Bitto^.left
     end
   else begin
     if RandomBit(Bitto^.BitNumber) then
       Bitto := Bitto^.left
     else
       Bitto := Bitto^.right
     end;
   end;
 VariableToProduction := Bitto^.TheProductionNode; {TheAnswer.}
end;{VariableToProduction}
procedure DoStack (s: MimicProdNodePtr);
   {This just goes through the list of words on
     the stack until they are gone.}
forward;
procedure DoWord (w: WordNodePtr);
   {This will do the correct thing with the word node w.}
   {If it is a terminal, it will write it out.
     Otherwise it will start a new frame...}
 var
  StackFrame: MimicProdNodePtr;
       {For creating new ones...}
begin
 if w^.w1[1] = VariableSignifier then begin
   new(StackFrame);
   StackFrame^.next := TheOutputStack;
   TheOutputStack := StackFrame;
   StackFrame^.ww :=
     VariableToProduction(FindVariable(w^.w1))^.TheWords;
   DoStack(StackFrame);
  end
 else begin
       {Write it out...}
   write(OpenMimicryFile, w^.w1);
      {Assuming there is a space at the end of each word.}
   if AddCarriageReturns then begin
     CarriagePosition := CarriagePosition + length(w^.w1);
     if CarriagePosition > RightMargin then begin
      write(OpenMimicryFile, chr(13));
      CarriagePosition := 0
      end
```

```
        end;
      end;
  end;{DoWord}
  procedure DoStack (s: MimicProdNodePtr);
       {This just goes through the list of
          words on the stack until they are gone.}
    var
      wurds: WordNodePtr;
  begin
    wurds := s^.ww;
    while wurds <> nil do begin
       DoWord(wurds);
       wurds := wurds^.next
      end;
    TheOutputStack := TheOutputStack^.next;
  end;{DoStack}
  procedure DoSomeMimicry;
       {This keeps it all going until the end...}
  begin
    SyncRandomBits;
    OpenForOutput;
    while not (AtTheEndOfFile) do begin
       new(TheOutputStack);
       TheOutputStack^.ww :=
          VariableToProduction(GetStartVariable)^.TheWords;
       DoStack(TheOutputStack);
      end;
    CloseUpOutput;
  end;{DoProduction}
end.
```

MimicParser.p

```
unit MimicParser;
{This section will try and parse output that
  should have come from the  table built in
  TableSetter. Of course if it doesn't correspond,
  there will be problems. }
{}
{Right now its limitations are:}
{}
{1) Each production of the grammar must begin with a terminal. }
{2) A fixed amount of look-ahead specified at compile time.}
{3) A host of compromises that get in the way of making the files}
{completely flexible as they could or should be. }
```

```
interface
uses
 MimicGlobals, WordEater, TableSetter, Randomness;
procedure DoItAllLoop;
    {This sucker just keeps going...}
    {This routine is called to get everything moving along...}
implementation
const
 MaxLookAhead = 10;
 StandardLookAhead = 3;
        {MaxLookAhead is the absolute maximum }
        {permitted by the sizes of the array.}
        {StandardLookAhead is the usual amount to }
        {search. Note that the running time is }
        {potentially exponential in the LookAhead... }
        {Don't be greedy. Sorry I didn't write a better }
        {algorithm.}
type
 LookAheadAddress = 0..MaxLookAhead;
        {This is the range of numbers kept for the lookahead table.}
var
 LookaheadTable: array[0..MaxLookAhead] of word;
        {The next MaxLookAhead words are kept in this circular array.}
        {When the end of file is found, the table contains NullWord.}
 LookaheadOffset: integer;
        {Keeps track of where the first word will be.}
 TempWord: longint;
        {This is where the bits are stored before
           they are written away...}
 TempPosition: integer;
        {Starts at zero and works up to 31.}
 FoundAmbiguity: boolean;
        {When the machine starts to do some
           parsing and discovers that there}
        {are two different paths for each
           production, this baby is set to true.}
 SoftMaxLookAhead: integer;
        {This allows the parser to set its }
        {lookahead on the fly if it wants to increase it.}
 ReachedEndOfFile: boolean;
        {Set true when everything is exhausted...}
procedure InitLookahead;
   {Sets up the lookahead buffer to keep all of the words in place.}
 var
  i: integer;
```

```
  stopper: char;
       {to be ignored.}
begin
 LookAheadOffset := 0;
 for i := 0 to MaxLookAhead - 1 do
  LookAheadTable[i] := NextWord(Stopper);
end;{InitLookahead}
function TimeDelayNextWord: word;
   {This returns the next word in time delay.}
 var
  stopper: char;
       {The end...}
begin
 TimeDelayNextWord := LookAheadTable[LookAheadOffset];
 LookAheadTable[LookAheadOffset] := NextWord(stopper);
 if stopper = EndOfFileSignifier then
  ReachedEndOfFile := true;
 LookAheadOffset := (LookAheadOffset + 1) mod MaxLookAhead;
end;{TimeDelayNextWord}
procedure OpenOutputFile;
   {Sets up the file where the outputted bits will go...}
begin
 rewrite(OpenSourceFile, OpenSourceName);
 TempWord := 0;
 TempPosition := 7;
 ReachedEndOfFile := false;
 Open(OpenGrammarFile, OpenMimicryName);
       {Set to be OpenGrammarFile because that is }
       {what the WordEater is programmed to recognize.}
 LastCharacter := Space;
       {This is for initializing the WordEater. }
       {It must come BEFORE InitLookAHEAD}
 InitLookAhead;
end;{OpenOutputFile}
procedure CloseOutputFile;
   {Clean up the file where the outputted bits went...}
begin
 close(OpenSourceFile);
 close(OpenGrammarFile);
end;{CloseOutputFile}
procedure StoreBit (b: boolean);
   {This stores the next bit. Note that they are coming off in
     reverse order this time...}
begin
 if tempPosition = 8 then begin
```

```
      write(OpenSourceFile, TempWord);
       TempWord := 0;
       TempPosition := 0;
      end;
   if b then
    BSET(TempWord, TempPosition);
   TempPosition := TempPosition + 1;
 end;{StoreBit}
 procedure StoreWord (TheBits: longint;
        LastPos: integer);
      {This stores away a word in the right place...}
 begin
   if LastPos < TempPosition then begin
     TempWord := BOR(TempWord, BSL(TheBits, TempPosition - LastPos));
     TempPosition := TempPosition - LastPos - 1
    end
   else begin
     TempWord := BOR(TempWord, BSR(TheBits, LastPos - TempPosition));
     if TempWord = $74202f2f then
      Error('Weird');
     writeln('If Tempword=', ptr(TempWord), ' then a smaller
                version is:', QDbyte(TempWord));
     write(OpenSourceFile, QDbyte(TempWord));
     TempWord := BSL(BAND($ff, TheBits), 8 - LastPos + TempPosition);
     TempPosition := 7 - LastPos + TempPosition;
    end;
 end;{StoreWord}
 procedure ProductionToBits (p: ProductionNodePtr);
      {This returns the bits associated with a particular
       production by following the path up the root to
       the variable. Note that the bits will come off
       in the reverse order in which they were generated.}
   var
    BitPointer: BitNodePtr;
        {This will lead the way.}
    TempBit: longint;
        {This will hold the bits...}
    BitCounter: integer;
        {This is position of the next bit to be stored.}
 begin
   UpdateRandomBits;
        {Get a new group of random bits for the random generator...}
   TempBit := 0;
   BitCounter := 0;
   BitPointer := p^.ItsBit;
```

```
    {We're not concerned about the first node }
    {because it is just an interface.}
  while BitPointer^.up <> nil do begin
    with BitPointer^ do
     if polarity then begin
       if RandomBit(up^.BitNumber) then
       BSet(TempBit, BitCounter);
      end
     else begin
       if not (RandomBit(up^.BitNumber)) then
       BSet(TempBit, BitCounter);
      end;
    BitPointer := BitPointer^.up;
    BitCounter := BitCounter + 1;
    if BitCounter = 8 then begin
      StoreWord(TempBit, BitCounter - 1);
      TempBit := 0;
      BitCounter := 0;
     end
   end;
 StoreWord(TempBit, BitCounter - 1);
end;{ProductionToBits}
function TokenInVariable (var MoreOffset: LookAheadAddress;
      v: VariableNodePtr): ProductionNodePtr;
   {Imagine this case. You are now trying to decide }
   {whether the next token, say "Ernest" came}
   {for the production of a variable "*Dudes" or }
   {"*Duds". It could be from either. This tries }
   {to lookahead and see if there is any clue that }
   {says, "Hey, it can't be "*Dudes" because the}
   {production of the token "Ernest" is always }
   {followed by the token "Rex" to indicate his stature.}
forward;
function CheckWordList (MoreOffset: LookAheadAddress;
      www: wordNodePtr): boolean;
   {This compares the words in the word }
   {list with the words in the lookahead buffer.}
   {If they all match, then BINGO!}
 label
  188;
begin
 CheckWordList := true;
 while (MoreOffset < SoftMaxLookAhead) and (www <> nil) do begin
   if www^.w1[1] = VariableSignifier then begin
    if (TokenInVariable(MoreOffset, FindVariable(www^.w1)) = nil)
```

```
         then begin
         CheckWordList := false;
         goto 188
         end;
       MoreOffset := MoreOffset + 1;
       www := www^.next;
      end
    else if CompareStrings(LookAheadTable[(MoreOffset +
          LookAheadOffset)
          mod MaxLookAhead], www^.w1) <> 0 then begin
       CheckWordList := false;
       goto 188;
      end
    else begin
      MoreOffset := MoreOffset + 1;
      www := www^.next;
     end;
   end;
188:
end;{CheckWordList}
function TokenInVariable (var MoreOffset: LookAheadAddress;
      v: VariableNodePtr): ProductionNodePtr;
   {Imagine this case. You are now trying to decide }
   {whether the next token, say "Ernest" came}
   {for the production of a variable "*Dudes" or }
   {"*Duds". It could be from either. This tries }
   {to lookahead and see if there is any clue that }
   {says, "Hey, it can't be "*Dudes" because the}
   {production of the token "Ernest" is always }
   {followed by the token "Rex" to indicate his stature.}
  var
   ProductionNumber: ProductionNodePtr;
       {Well not as much a number as a pun.}
   TheWordInQuestion: word;
       {This is pulled out to save array references...}
   OneFound: boolean;
       {This is just set to look for ambiguities...Problems,
        you know....}
begin
 TokenInVariable := nil;
 ProductionNumber := v^.Productions;
 OneFound := false;
 while ProductionNumber <> nil do begin
   if OneFound then begin
     if CheckWordList(MoreOffset, ProductionNumber^.TheWords)
```

```
      then begin
      Error('Parsing Ambiguity Here!!!');
      FoundAmbiguity := true;
      TokenInVariable := nil;
      exit(TokenInVariable)
      end
    end
  else if CheckWordList(MoreOffset, ProductionNumber^.TheWords)
    then begin
    OneFound := true;
    TokenInVariable := ProductionNumber;
    end;
   ProductionNumber := ProductionNumber^.next;
  end;
end;{TokenInVariable}
procedure DoItAllLoop;
  {This sucker just keeps going...}
 label
  199;{To get out of here...}
 var
  BaseFrame: MimicParseFramePtr;
      {This is the first frame allocated.}
 procedure DoFrame (f: MimicParseFramePtr);
  {This routine takes the frame and figures out which pointer
   would match...}
  var
  Prod: ProductionNodePtr;
      {This is the location of the pointer...}
  NewFrame: MimicParseFramePtr;
      {If a new frame is needed...}
  CurrentDepth: LookAheadAddress;
      {Used to halt the spread of the search.}
 begin
  FoundAmbiguity := false;
  SoftMaxLookAhead := StandardLookAhead;
  CurrentDepth := 0;
  Prod := TokenInVariable(CurrentDepth, f^.TheVariable);
      {I realize that it is a bit of an overkill to use a }
      {big hammer like TokenInVariable, but it is}
      {late at night and I don't want to bother writing }
      {an elegant method that uses breadth first }
      {instead of depth-first.}
  if FoundAmbiguity then begin
    FoundAmbiguity := false;
    SoftMaxLookAhead := MaxLookAhead;
```

```
                         {This just doubles the lookahead for the fun of it...}
                 CurrentDepth := 0;
                 Prod := TokenInVariable(CurrentDepth, f^.TheVariable)
               end;
             if Prod = nil then begin
               Error('Problems in parsing.');
               goto 199
             end
           else if not (FoundAmbiguity) then
                 {We've found something....}
             begin
               ProductionToBits(Prod); {Store the bits...}
               with f^ do begin
                 new(NewFrame);
                 TheWordsToMatch := Prod^.TheWords;
                 while TheWordsToMatch <> nil do begin
                 if TheWordsToMatch^.w1[1] = VariableSignifier then begin
                 NewFrame^.TheVariable := FindVariable(TheWordsToMatch^.w1);
                 DoFrame(NewFrame)
                 end
                 else
                   if CompareStrings(TheWordsToMatch^.w1, TimeDelayNextWord) <> 0
                   then
                   begin
                     Error(concat('Problem in parsing the file.  The Word "'
                                  , TheWordsToMatch^.w1, '" doesn'' t belong
                                  here . '));
                       goto 199;
                   end;
                 TheWordsToMatch := TheWordsToMatch^.next;
                 end;
                 dispose(NewFrame);
               end
           end
    end;{DoFrame}
  begin
  SyncRandomBits;
  OpenOutputFile;
  new(BaseFrame);
  BaseFrame^.TheVariable := GetStartVariable;
  repeat
   DoFrame(BaseFrame);
  until (ReachedEndOfFile) & (LookAheadTable[LookAheadOffset] =
                              NullWord);
  dispose(BaseFrame);
```

```
199:
  CloseOutputFile;
 end;{DoItAllLoop}
end.
```

MimicMaster.p

```
program MimicMaster;
    {The Top, The Tower of Pizza, The Top, The Smile on the Mona Lisa.}
 uses
  MimicGlobals, WordEater, TableSetter, SANE, Randomness, OutSpitter,
  MimicParser;
 var
  ww: word;
 procedure InitEverything;
    {Does the openning headaches.}
 begin
  InitRandomBits;
  InitializeScanHashTable;
  AddCarriageReturns := true;
  RightMargin := 50;
  OpenGrammarName := '';
  OpenMimicryName := '';
  OpenSourceName := '';
  GoodTable := false;
        {We don't know of anything set correctly yet...}
 end;{InitEverything}
 procedure CheckCool (procedure p);
    {Checks to make sure that the grammar is
      cool enough to allow this to happen.}
 begin
  if GoodTable & (OpenSourceName <> '') & (OpenMimicryName <> '') then
   p
  else
   error('An error-free grammar has not been loaded yet.')
 end;{CheckCool}
 procedure ControlLoop;
    {This is an interface built around that old standby, text. }
    {In fact since plain text is the purpose of this}
    {exercise it is probably fitting that I haven't }
    {bothered with any of that GUI stuff.}
  var
   choice: integer;
 begin
  InitEverything;
```

```
  repeat
   writeln('---------------------------------------------');
   writeln('Input Grammar File:', OpenGrammarName);
   writeln('Mimicry File:', OpenMimicryName);
   writeln('Data File:', OpenSourceName);
   writeln('---------------------------------------------');
   writeln('0=Read In Grammar File, 1= Set Mimic
            and Data File Names for Encoding');
   writeln('2=Set Mimic and Data File Names for
            Decoding, 3= Data -> Mimicry');
   writeln('4= Mimicry -> Data, 5=Set Special Password,
            6=Print out Grammar');
   writeln('99=Quit');
   write('?');
   read(choice);
   case choice of
    0:  begin
      GoodTable := LoadTable;
      end;
    1:
     SetProcessingFilesIn;
    2:
     SetProcessingFilesOut;
    3:
     CheckCool(DoSomeMimicry);
    4:
     CheckCool(DoItAllLoop);
    5:  begin
      SetKey;
      SyncRandomBits;
      end;
    6:
     PrintTable;
    otherwise
      ;
   end;
  until choice = 99;
 end;{ControlLoop}
begin
 ShowText;
 ControlLoop;
end.
```

Appendix B

Baseball CFG

This appendix contains a sample context-free grammar designed to simulate the voiceover from a baseball game. The grammar is printed in the format required by the program in Appendix A.

Each variable begins with an asterisk. Each production has two components that are broken up by forward slashes. The first part is the mixture of variables and terminals that will replace the variable in question during the production. The second is the weight given to one production in the random selection process. The final production for each variable is ended with a double forward slash.

```
*period = ./1//
*questionmark = ?/1//
*WeatherComment = Hmm . Do you think it will rain ? /.1/
     What are the chances of rain today ? /.1/
     Nice weather as long as it doesn't rain . /.1/
     Well, if rain breaks out it
       will certainly change things . /.1/
     You can really tell the mettle
       of a manager when rain is threatened . /.1//
*BlogsOutfielder = Orville Baskethands /.1/
                   Robert Liddlekopf /.1/
                   Harrison "Harry" Hanihan /.1//
*BlogsInfielder = Gerry Johnson /.1/
                  Lefty Clemson /.1/
                  Robby Rawhide /.1/
                  Alberto Juan Turbosino /.1//
*BlogsManager = Billy Martin /.1/
```

```
                    Hanson Haversham /.1//
*BlogsCatcher = Bloaty Von Ripple /.1//
*BlogsPitcher = Mark Markinson /.1/
                    Andy Anteriority /.1//
*BlogsPlayer= Orville Baskethands /.1/
                    Robert Liddlekopf /.1/
                    Harrison "Harry" Hanihan /.1/
                    Gerry Johnson /.1/
                    Lefty Clemson /.1/
                    Robby Rawhide /.1/
                    Alberto Juan Turbosino /.1/
                    Bloaty Von Ripple /.1/
                    Mark Markinson /.1/
                    Andy Anteriority /.1//
*WhapperOutfielder = Prince Albert von Carmicheal /.1/
                        Parry Posteriority /.1/
                        Herbert Herbertson /.1//
*WhapperInfielder = Johnny Johanesberger /.1/
                    Frank Gavi /.1/
                    Harry Dolcetto /.1/
                    Sal Sauvignon /.1//
*WhapperManager = Bob Von Bittle /.1/
                    Hank Von Bittle /.1//
*WhapperCatcher = Mark Cloud /.1//
*WhapperPitcher = Jerry Johnstone /.1/
                    Albert Ancien-Regime /.1//
*WhapperPlayer = Prince Albert von Carmicheal /.1/
                    Parry Posteriority /.1/
                    Herbert Herbertson /.1/
                    Johnny Johanesberger /.1/
                    Frank Gavi /.1/
                    Harry Dolcetto /.1/
                    Sal Sauvignon /.1/
                    Jerry Johnstone /.1/
                    Albert Ancien-Regime /.1/
                    Mark Cloud /.1//
*Announcer= Bob /.1/
            Ted /.1/
            Mike /.1/
            Rich /.1//
*DumbComment = Some kind of Ballplayer, huh ? /.1/
        These guys came to play ball ./.1/
        What a game so far today ./.1/
        How about those players ./.1/
        Got to love baseball ./.1/
```

```
              Hey, they're playing the organ ./.1//
*WhapperOutfieldOut = He pops one up into deep left field . /.1/
          He lifts it back toward the wall where it is caught
          by *BlogsOutfielder *period/.1/
          He knocks it into the glove of
           *BlogsOutfielder *period /.1/
          He gets a real piece of it and
           drives it toward the wall
           where it is almost ... Oh My God! ... saved by
           *BlogsOutfielder *period /.1/
          He pops it up to *BlogsOutfielder *period /.2//
*WeirdOutfield = who is too deep to get it. Basehit! /.1/
      who bobbles the catch! /.05/
      who trips on his Nikes! Time for a new sponsor. /.05/
      who loses it in the sun. It drops in the warning track. /.1/
      whose mind seems lost thinking of investments. He starts
      moving too late! Hit. /.1//
*OutfieldResult = for a double! /.1/ for a stand-up double. /.1/
      for a stand-up double ... wait he's going to stretch
      it for a triple and ... he's safe. /.1/
      to grab another hit . /.1/
      to bump his average up . His salary is up for renegotiation
      this year . /.1//
*WhapperOutfieldHit = knocks it toward *BlogsOutfielder
          *WeirdOutfield /.1/
          line-drives toward the outfield where *BlogsOutfielder
          *WeirdOutfield /.1/
          puts it into the back corner of right field. /.1/
          lifts it over the head of *BlogsOutfielder
          *OutfieldResult /.1/
          drives it into the stands for a HomeRun! /.1/
          lifts it toward heaven ! HomeRun !/.1/
          sends it to the man upstairs . HomeRun !/.1/
          clears the stadium wall . Whoa ! HomeRun !/.1/
          and it's ... La Bomba ! HomeRun !/.1//
*BlogsOutfieldHit = knocks it toward *WhapperOutfielder
          *WeirdOutfield /.1/
          line-drives toward the outfield where *WhapperOutfielder
          *WeirdOutfield /.1/
          puts it into the back corner of right field. /.1/
          lifts it over the head of *WhapperOutfielder
          *OutfieldResult /.1/
          drives it into the stands for a home-run! /.1/
          lifts it toward heaven ! /.1/
          sends it to the man upstairs . /.1/
```

```
                  clears the stadium wall . Whoa ! /.1/
                  and it's ... La Bomba ! /.1//
*BlogsOutfieldOut = He pops one up into deep left field . /.1/
                  He lifts it back toward the wall where it is caught
                  by *WhapperOutfielder *period/.1/
                  He knocks it into the glove of
                   *WhapperOutfielder *period /.1/
                  He gets a real piece of it and
                   drives it toward the wall
                  where it is almost ... Oh My God! ... saved by
                  *WhapperOutfielder *period /.1/
                  He pops it up to *WhapperOutfielder *period /.2//
*BuntResponseHit = bobbles it ./.1/
       trips on it . /.1/
       scoops it up and realizing that he's too late
       signs it and throws it to a kid in the stands . / .01 /
       gets to, but the throw is ... late! /.1/
       grabs it, but the throw is too low ! /.1//
*BuntResponseOut = grabs it and makes the out . /.1/
       scoops it up and tosses him out . /.1/
       passes it on to first . /.1/
       nabs it ./.1/
       picks it up, laughs and tosses him out . /.1/
       grabs it and tosses it to first . /.1//
*InfieldLocation = first base /.1/
                      second base/.1/
                       the pitcher's mound/.1/
                   short stop/.1/
                   third base/.1/
                   third base foul line/.1/
                   first base foul line/.1//
*BadThrow = in the dirt ./.1/
           digging a ditch ./.1/
           too wide ./.1/
           into the umpire's head ! Whoa ! /.01/
           way too wide to make the tag ./.1/
         too high ./.1/
         too high to make the tag ./.1/
         in his chest ./.1//
*BaseReached = for a single ./.1/
               for a double ./.1/
               for a triple ./.1/
               for a easy single ...
                  Wait he's going to try for more and the
                  throw is *BadThrow /.1/
```

```
                    for a standup double. But is that young
                    Charlie Hustle going to wait ?
                    No . He's going for the triple and
                    the throw is *BadThrow /.1/
                    for a close single and the the toss is
                    *BadThrow /.1/
                  for a dangerous double and the
                    throw is *BadThrow /.1//
*HitResult = into short right field *BaseReached /.1/
        into short left field *BaseReached / .1/
        and the ball bounces past the shortstop *BaseReached/.1/
        and the ball takes a weird bounce at *InfieldLocation
        *BaseReached /.1/
        and the ball flies down the foul line .
         It stays fair *BaseReached/.1/
        in the short left field where it
        bounces into the stands . Ground rule
         double for the young man ./.1//
*WhapperInfieldHit = He tries to bunt, and *BlogsInfielder
        *BuntResponseHit /.1/
        He knocks it down the line between
        the legs of *BlogsInfielder *period /.1/
        He waps it into the short-stops glove,
        but he can't control it . Safe at first . /.1/
        He lifts it over the head of *BlogsInfielder
         *HitResult /.1/
        The batter gets a piece of it *HitResult /.1/
        It's contact time  *HitResult /.1/
        Nice hit *HitResult /.1/
        Whoa ! That swing was on the money  *HitResult /.1/
        Nice job *HitResult /.1/
        Great hit *HitResult /.1/
        Super looper for a hit /.1/
        He knocks a line-drive into the head of
         *BlogsInfielder /.05//
*WhapperInfieldOut = He grounds out to *BlogsInfielder *period/.1/
        He pops it up to *BlogsInfielder *period/.1/
        He tries to bunt, and *BlogsInfielder
         *BuntResponseOut /.1/
        He knocks a line-drive into the glove of
         *BlogsInfielder /.1/
        He knocks an easy bouncer to *BlogsInfielder
         *period /.1/
        He bounces one of the ground into the
         first-baseman's glove ./ .1//
```

```
*BlogsInfieldHit = He tries to bunt, and *WhapperInfielder
            *BuntResponseHit /.1/
        He knocks it down the line between the legs of
          *WhapperInfielder *period /.1/
        He lifts it over the head of *WhapperInfielder
          *HitResult /.1/
        The batter gets a piece of it *HitResult /.1/
        Nice job *HitResult /.1/
        Great hit *HitResult /.1/
        It's contact time  *HitResult /.1/
        Nice hit *HitResult /.1/
        He waps it into the short-stops glove,
        but he can't control it . Safe at first . /.1/
        Whoa ! That swing was on the money  *HitResult /.1/
        Super looper for a hit /.1/
        He knocks a line-drive into the head of
          *WhapperInfielder /.05//
*BlogsInfieldOut =
        He grounds out to *WhapperInfielder *period/.1/
        He  knocks a line-drive into the glove of
          *WhapperInfielder /.1/
        He tries to bunt, and
          *WhapperInfielder *BuntResponseOut /.1/
        He knocks an easy bouncer to
          *WhapperInfielder *period /.1/
        He  pops it up to *WhapperInfielder *period/.1/
        He  bounces one of the ground into the
          first-baseman's glove ./ .1//
*EndOfInning =
      Well, that's the end of their chances in
      this inning, *Announcer *period *Commercial/.1/
      No more at bats left in this inning. *Commercial /.1/
      The inning's over . Some kind of ballplayer, huh,
       *Announcer *period *Commercial /.1/
      Yowza! End of the inning . Hard to imagine
       life without baseball? Right, *Announcer
      *questionmark *Commercial /.1/
      That inning proves why baseball is
      the nation's game . *Commercial /.1//
*Return = Back to the game, *Announcer *period /.1/
      We now return to the game between the Blogs and
      the Whappers . /.1/
      Now back to the game . /.1/
      Just wanted to say thanks to our sponsors for
       those great messages . /.1//
```

```
*Commercial = This is WZZZ-TV bringing you the ballgame!
        *BeerCom *BeerCom
        *CarCom *Return/.1/
    We're here at WZZZ-TV bringing you the ballgame!
        *CarCom *CarCom
        *BeerCom *Return /.1/
    This is the WZZZ baseball network!
        *BeerCom *CarCom *CarCom
        *BeerCom *BeerCom *Return /.1/
    Now a message from our sponsors. *BeerCom *BeerCom
        *BeerCom *Return /.1/
    Now a very special message from our sponsors.
        *CarCom *BeerCom
        *CarCom *Return /.1//
*BeerOne = Imported Name . / .1/
            Imported Label ./.1/
            Imported Aura . /.1/
            Imported Concept ./.1/
            Imported Danger Warning in German . /.1//
*BeerTwo = American Taste . /.1/
            American Flavor . /.1/
            Clean American Taste ./.1/
            No Overly-flavorful Assault on your tongue . /.1//
*BeerThree = fermentation is natural ? /.1/
        yeast is one of Mother Nature's Creatures ? /.1/
        yeast is a beast of Nature ? /.1/
        beer is natural ? /.1//
*BeerFour = Support Mother Nature and drink. /.1/
        Go green and support the environment . /.1/
        Support Natural Things and drink another ! /.1/
        Live a natural life and drink some more ! /.1//
*BeerCom = St. Belch . *BeerOne *BeerTwo /.1/
        Longing for adventure ? Open a bottle of St. Belch ! /.1/
        Did you know that *BeerThree *BeerFour /.1/
        Hey! *BeerFour /.1/
        Man comes up to Bob on the street and says,
        ''Want a St. Belch ?" and his friend says, "Sure, I'm a man
        and I love to drink ." It turns out the Man was the head of
        a Fortune 500 company looking for a new Chairman of the
        Board of Directors . He hires Bob for
        $350,000 a year . /.1/
        St. Belch Beer: Especially tailored for men who watch
        ballgames . /.1//
*Car = Chevy Cordon-Bleu / .1 /
        Chevy Coq-au-Van /.1/
```

```
          Ford Platzer /.1/
          Ford Wienerschnitzel / .1/
          Chevy Choucroute /.1/
          Ford Weisswurst /.1/
          Chevy Crouton /.1//
*CarFoodAdj = Scrumptious ! /.1/
              Delicious ! /.1/
              Mouth-watering !/.1/
              Tasty! /.1/ Rich ! /.1/
              Sinfully Sweet ! /.1/
              Organically-Grown/.1//
*CarRegAdj = Fast ! / .1/
             Bold ! / .1/ Ambitious ! /.1/
             Nocturnal ! /.1/ Adiabatic ! /.1/
             Anti-establishmentary !/.1/ Plenary ! /.1/
             Easy ! /.1/ Capitalistic ! /.1//
*CarLink = That's the new /.1/
           What a car, the /.1/
           How about that /.1/
           That's it. The new /.1//
*CarCom = Wow! *CarFoodAdj *CarRegAdj *CarFoodAdj *CarRegAdj
      *CarLink *Car *period /.1/
   What do these words mean? *CarRegAdj *CarFoodAdj *CarRegAdj
      *CarLink *Car *period /.1/
   Yowza! *CarFoodAdj *CarRegAdj *CarFoodAdj *CarLink
      *Car *period /.1/
   The way to a man's heart is through his stomach. Ergo we want
      you to think of our car as *CarFoodAdj *period *CarLink *Car
      *period /.1//
*PlateAction = comes to the plate ./.1/
          swings the bat to get ready and enters
           the batter's box ./.1/
          adjusts the cup and enters the batter's box ./.1/
          swings the baseball bat to stretch and enters
          the batter's box ./.1//
*NewBlogsBatter = Now, *BlogsPlayer *PlateAction /.1/
      Here we go. *BlogsPlayer *PlateAction /.1/
      The pitcher spits. *BlogsPlayer *PlateAction /.1/
      The crowd is nervous. *BlogsPlayer *PlateAction /.1//
*NewWhapperBatter = Now, *WhapperPlayer *PlateAction /.1/
      Here we go. *WhapperPlayer *PlateAction /.1/
      The pitcher spits. *WhapperPlayer *PlateAction /.1/
      The crowd is nervous. *WhapperPlayer *PlateAction /.1//
*Strike = Swings and misses ! /.1/ Fans the air ! /.1/
   No contact in Mudsville ! /.1/
```

```
        Whooooosh! Strike ! /.1/ Steeeriiiiike ! /.1/
        No wood on that one . /.1/
        He just watched it go by ./.1/ No contact on that one . /.1/
        Nothing on that one ./.1/
        He swings for the stands, but no contact . /.1//
*BallCall = Ball ./.1/The umpire calls a ball ./.1/
        Definitely a ball ./.1/
        No strike this time . /.1//
*Ball = High and outside . *BallCall /.1/
        Whoa, he's brushing him back . *BallCall/.1/
        Short and away . *BallCall/.1/
        OOOh, that's almost in the dirt . *BallCall/.1/
        No good. *BallCall /.1/
        High and too inside. *BallCall/.1//
*ThePitchType = a curve ball ./.1/
        a flaming fast ball ./.1/
        a screaming fast ball ./.1/
        a change-up ./.1/
        a knuckler ./.1/
        what looks like a spitball ./.1/
        a spitter ./.1/
        a split-fingered fastball ./.1/ a rising fast ball ./.1/
        a fast one that looked like it was rising ./.1/
        a screamer ./.1/
        a torcher ./.1/ a blaster ./.1/a knuckball ./.1/
        a breaking curve ./.1/
        a slow change-up ./.1/ a toaster ./.1/
        a rattling corkscrew ./.1/
        a curvaceous beauty ./.1/
        a wobbling knuckler ./.1/
        a bouncing knuckleball ./.1/
        a smoking gun ./.1/a blazing comet ./.1/
        a rattler ./.1/
        a heckraising fast ball ./.1/
        a rocket booster ./.1/a fastball with wings ./.1//
*ThePitch = Checks first base . Nothing. Winds up and pitches
        *ThePitchType /.1/
        Here's the pitch It's *ThePitchType /.1/
        Here comes the pitch It's *ThePitchType/.1/
        He's winding up . What *ThePitchType /.1/
        And the next pitch is *ThePitchType /.1/
        The next pitch is *ThePitchType /.1/
        A full windup and it's *ThePitchType /.1/
        He's uncorking *ThePitchType /.1/
        It's *ThePitchType /.1//
```

```
*StrikeOut = He's out of there . / .1/
        Strike out . He's swinging at the umpire .
        The umpire reconsiders until
        the security guards arrive . /.1/
        Strike out ! /.1/
        Yes. Another wiffer ./.1/
        Strike out . There goes his batting average . /.1/
        Strike three . Some sports writer figured that
        each strike cost the ball
        player about $1,530 at today's average rate . /.1/
        The last strike . Only three chances in this game . /.1//
*BlogsHit = Here we go. *ThePitch *Ball *ThePitch *BlogsInfieldHit /.1/
        Okay. *ThePitch *Ball *Strike *Strike *BlogsInfieldHit /.1/
        The crowd is roaring . *ThePitch *Ball *ThePitch
         *Ball *BlogsOutfieldHit/.1/
        Here we go . *Ball *ThePitch *Ball
         *ThePitch *BlogsOutfieldHit /.1/
        Here's the pitch . *Strike *ThePitch *Strike *ThePitch
         *BlogsOutfieldHit /.1//
*BlogsOut = Yeah. *ThePitch *Strike *ThePitch *Strike *ThePitch
        *Strike *StrikeOut /.1/
        The pitchers is winding up to throw. *Strike
         *ThePitch *Ball *ThePitch
        *BlogsInfieldOut /.1/
        Here's the fastball . *BlogsInfieldOut /.1/
        He's trying the curveball . *BlogsOutfieldOut /.1/
        Love that Baseball game. *ThePitch *Ball
         *ThePitch *Ball *ThePitch
        *Strike *ThePitch *Strike *ThePitch *Strike *StrikeOut /.1/
        Another fastball . *Strike *ThePitch
         *BlogsOutfieldOut /.1//
*WhapperHit = Here we go. *ThePitch *Ball *ThePitch
        *WhapperInfieldHit /.1/
        Okay. *ThePitch *Ball *Strike *Strike *WhapperInfieldHit /.1/
        The crowd is roaring . *ThePitch *Ball *ThePitch
        *Ball *WhapperOutfieldHit/.1/
        Here we go . *Ball *ThePitch *Ball
         *ThePitch *WhapperOutfieldHit /.1/
        Here's the pitch . *Strike *ThePitch
         *Strike *ThePitch
         *WhapperOutfieldHit /.1//
*WhapperOut = Yeah. *ThePitch *Strike *ThePitch *Strike
        *ThePitch *Strike *StrikeOut /.1/
        The pitchers is winding up to throw. *Strike *ThePitch *Ball
        *ThePitch
```

```
        *WhapperInfieldOut /.1/
        Here's the fastball . *WhapperInfieldOut /.1/
        He's trying the curveball . *WhapperOutfieldOut /.1/
        Love that Baseball game. *ThePitch *Ball
         *ThePitch *Ball *ThePitch
         *Strike *ThePitch *Strike *ThePitch
         *Strike *StrikeOut /.1/
        Another fastball . *Strike *ThePitch
         *WhapperOutfieldOut /.1//
*OneWhapperLeft = Only one more out needed . *NewWhapperBatter
     *WhapperHit
     *OneWhapperLeft /.1/
    The Blogs only need to get one more out . *NewWhapperBatter
    *WhapperHit *OneWhapperLeft /.1/
    The Blogs are trying for the last out .  *NewWhapperBatter
    *WhapperHit *OneWhapperLeft /.1/
    The crowd is looking for the last out !   *NewWhapperBatter
    *WhapperHit *OneWhapperLeft /.1/
    Before the last out, let's get a message in from our
    sponsors. *Commercial   *NewWhapperBatter
    *WhapperHit *OneWhapperLeft /.05/
    Only one out left.   *NewWhapperBatter
    *WhapperHit *OneWhapperLeft /.1/
    Yup, the Blogs only need to get one more out.
     *NewWhapperBatter
    *WhapperHit *OneWhapperLeft /.1/
    Hey, two down, one to go. *NewWhapperBatter
    *WhapperOut *EndOfInning /.1/
    Only one chance left for the Whapper . *NewWhapperBatter
    *WhapperOut *EndOfInning /.1/
    Two big outs for the Blogs. *NewWhapperBatter
    *WhapperOut *EndOfInning /.1/
    What a game ! *NewWhapperBatter
    *WhapperOut *EndOfInning /.1/
    These are the times that make baseball special .
      *NewWhapperBatter
    *WhapperOut *EndOfInning /.1/
    One more thin out stands between the Whappers and the end of
    this inning's chances . *NewWhapperBatter
    *WhapperOut *EndOfInning /.1/
    Yowza. *NewWhapperBatter
    *WhapperOut *EndOfInning /.1/
    He's hefting some wood . *NewWhapperBatter
    *WhapperOut *EndOfInning /.1//
*TwoWhappersLeft = Hey, one down, two to go.   *NewWhapperBatter
```

```
        *WhapperHit *TwoWhappersLeft /.1/
The Whappers have only one out .        *NewWhapperBatter
        *WhapperHit *TwoWhappersLeft /.1/
One down, two to go.  *NewWhapperBatter
        *WhapperHit *TwoWhappersLeft /.1/
Only one out into the inning.  *NewWhapperBatter
        *WhapperHit *TwoWhappersLeft /.1/
One out against the Whappers.  *NewWhapperBatter
        *WhapperHit *TwoWhappersLeft /.1/
The Blogs need two more outs. *NewWhapperBatter
        *WhapperOut *OneWhapperLeft /.1/
Two more outs to go. *NewWhapperBatter
        *WhapperOut *OneWhapperLeft /.1/
The Whappers have two outs to spare. *NewWhapperBatter
        *WhapperOut *OneWhapperLeft /.1/
Plenty of room. Only one out. *NewWhapperBatter
        *WhapperOut *OneWhapperLeft /.1/
How about those ballplayers.
  One out so far. *NewWhapperBatter
        *WhapperOut *OneWhapperLeft /.1/
Some day for a ballgame, huh? *WeatherComment *NewWhapperBatter
        *WhapperOut *OneWhapperLeft /.1/
Wow. Only one out. *NewWhapperBatter
        *WhapperOut *OneWhapperLeft /.1/
Somekind of ballgame, huh, *Announcer
  *questionmark *NewWhapperBatter
        *WhapperOut *OneWhapperLeft /.1/
Yup, got to love this stadium. *NewWhapperBatter
        *WhapperOut *OneWhapperLeft /.1//
*ThreeWhappersLeft = No damage yet, *Announcer *period
        *NewWhapperBatter
        *WhapperHit *ThreeWhappersLeft /.1/
No outs . *NewWhapperBatter
        *WhapperHit *ThreeWhappersLeft /.1/
No outs yet for the Whappers . *NewWhapperBatter
        *WhapperHit *ThreeWhappersLeft /.1/
No trouble yet . *NewWhapperBatter
        *WhapperHit *ThreeWhappersLeft /.1/
Check out the Whapper's mascot a Weasel.
  He's biting a 7-year old !
  Some kind of mascot, huh, *Announcer *questionmark
  *NewWhapperBatter
        *WhapperOut *TwoWhappersLeft /.01/
Nobody out yet . *NewWhapperBatter
        *WhapperOut *TwoWhappersLeft /.1/
```

```
          Whappers are up with no outs . *NewWhapperBatter
          *WhapperOut *TwoWhappersLeft /.1/
          Nothing's happened yet to the Whappers . *NewWhapperBatter
          *WhapperOut *TwoWhappersLeft /.1/
          No outs yet . *NewWhapperBatter
          *WhapperOut *TwoWhappersLeft /.1/
          What a day . *NewWhapperBatter
          *WhapperOut *TwoWhappersLeft /.1/
          I could go for a home run,
           *Announcer *period *NewWhapperBatter
          *WhapperOut *TwoWhappersLeft /.1/
          Baseball and Apple Pie . *NewWhapperBatter
          *WhapperOut *TwoWhappersLeft /.1/
          Yup. *DumbComment *NewWhapperBatter
          *WhapperOut *TwoWhappersLeft /.2//
*OneBlogsLeft = Only one more out needed . *NewBlogsBatter *BlogsHit
    *OneBlogsLeft /.1/
    The Whapper only need to get one more out . *NewBlogsBatter
    *BlogsHit *OneBlogsLeft /.1/
    The Whappers are trying for the last out . *NewBlogsBatter
    *BlogsHit *OneBlogsLeft /.1/
    The crowd is looking for the last out !   *NewBlogsBatter
    *BlogsHit *OneBlogsLeft /.1/
    Before the last out, let's get a message in from our
    sponsors. *Commercial   *NewBlogsBatter
    *BlogsHit *OneBlogsLeft /.05/
    Only one out left.   *NewBlogsBatter
    *BlogsHit *OneBlogsLeft /.1/
    Yup, the Whappers only need to get
     one more out.   *NewBlogsBatter
    *BlogsHit *OneBlogsLeft /.1/
    Hey, two down, one to go. *NewBlogsBatter
    *BlogsOut *EndOfInning /.1/
    Only one chance left for the Blogs . *NewBlogsBatter
    *BlogsOut *EndOfInning /.1/
    Two big outs for the Whappers. *NewBlogsBatter
    *BlogsOut *EndOfInning /.1/
    What a game ! *NewBlogsBatter
    *BlogsOut *EndOfInning /.1/
    These are the times that make baseball
     special . *NewBlogsBatter
    *BlogsOut *EndOfInning /.1/
    One more thin out stands between the Blogs and the end of
    this inning's chances . *NewBlogsBatter
    *BlogsOut *EndOfInning /.1/
```

```
          Yowza. *NewBlogsBatter
        *BlogsOut *EndOfInning /.1/
          He's hefting some wood . *NewBlogsBatter
        *BlogsOut *EndOfInning /.1//
*TwoBlogsLeft = Hey, one down, two to go.    *NewBlogsBatter
          *BlogsHit *TwoBlogsLeft /.1/
          The Blogs have only one out .        *NewBlogsBatter
          *BlogsHit *TwoBlogsLeft /.1/
          One down, two to go. *NewBlogsBatter
          *BlogsHit *TwoBlogsLeft /.1/
          Only one out into the inning. *NewBlogsBatter
          *BlogsHit *TwoBlogsLeft /.1/
          One out against the Blogs.  *NewBlogsBatter
          *BlogsHit *TwoBlogsLeft /.1/
          The Whappers need two more outs. *NewBlogsBatter
        *BlogsOut *OneBlogsLeft /.1/
          Two more outs to go. *NewBlogsBatter
        *BlogsOut *OneBlogsLeft /.1/
          The Blogs have two outs to spare. *NewBlogsBatter
        *BlogsOut *OneBlogsLeft /.1/
          Plenty of room. Only one out. *NewBlogsBatter
        *BlogsOut *OneBlogsLeft /.1/
          How about those ballplayers. One out so
           far. *NewBlogsBatter
        *BlogsOut *OneBlogsLeft /.1/
          Some day for a ballgame, huh?
           *WeatherComment *NewBlogsBatter
        *BlogsOut *OneBlogsLeft /.1/
          Wow. Only one out. *NewBlogsBatter
        *BlogsOut *OneBlogsLeft /.1/
          Somekind of ballgame, huh, *Announcer
           *questionmark *NewBlogsBatter
        *BlogsOut *OneBlogsLeft /.1/
          Yup, got to love this stadium. *NewBlogsBatter
        *BlogsOut *OneBlogsLeft /.1//
*ThreeBlogsLeft = No damage yet, *Announcer *period *NewBlogsBatter
          *BlogsHit *ThreeBlogsLeft /.1/
          No outs . *NewBlogsBatter
          *BlogsHit *ThreeBlogsLeft /.1/
          No outs yet for the Blogs . *NewBlogsBatter
          *BlogsHit *ThreeBlogsLeft /.1/
          No trouble yet . *NewBlogsBatter
          *BlogsHit *ThreeBlogsLeft /.1/
          Check out the Blogs Weasel. He's biting a 7-year old !
          Some kind of mascot, huh, *Announcer *questionmark
```

```
              *NewBlogsBatter
              *BlogsOut *TwoBlogsLeft /.01/
              Nobody out yet . *NewBlogsBatter
              *BlogsOut *TwoBlogsLeft /.1/
              Blogs are up with no outs . *NewBlogsBatter
              *BlogsOut *TwoBlogsLeft /.1/
              Nothing's happened yet to the Blogs .
               *NewBlogsBatter
              *BlogsOut *TwoBlogsLeft /.1/
              No outs yet . *NewBlogsBatter
              *BlogsOut *TwoBlogsLeft /.1/
              What a day . *NewBlogsBatter
              *BlogsOut *TwoBlogsLeft /.1/
              I could go for a home run,
               *Announcer *period *NewBlogsBatter
              *BlogsOut *TwoBlogsLeft /.1/
              Baseball and Apple Pie . *NewBlogsBatter
              *BlogsOut *TwoBlogsLeft /.1/
              Yup.  *DumbComment *NewBlogsBatter
              *BlogsOut *TwoBlogsLeft /.2//
*BlogsHalf = Time for the Blogs to see what they can do .
         *ThreeBlogsLeft /.1/
         It's the Blogs turn at bat . *ThreeBlogsLeft /.1/
         Bottom half of the inning .
         The Blogs must prove their stuff .
         *ThreeBlogsLeft /.1/
         Let's get on with the inning . *ThreeBlogsLeft /.1/
         Well, another half of the inning, *Announcer *period
         *DumbComment
         *ThreeBlogsLeft /.1/
         Let's get moving  with this half of the inning, but first,
         another message from our sponsors . *Commercial
         *ThreeBlogsLeft /.1//
*WhapperHalf = Top of the inning. *ThreeWhappersLeft /.1/
      Another new inning . Ain't life great, *Announcer *questionmark
      *ThreeWhappersLeft /.1/
      Start of another inning . *ThreeWhappersLeft /.1/
      Yes, it's time for the Whappers to lead off the inning .
      *ThreeWhappersLeft /.1/
      Time for another inning . The Whappers will be leading off .
      *ThreeWhappersLeft /.1//
*NineInnings = Let's get going ! *WhapperHalf *BlogsHalf
         *WhapperHalf *BlogsHalf
         *WhapperHalf *BlogsHalf
         *WhapperHalf *BlogsHalf
```

```
                *WhapperHalf *BlogsHalf
                *WhapperHalf *BlogsHalf
                *WhapperHalf *BlogsHalf
                *WhapperHalf *BlogsHalf
                *WhapperHalf *BlogsHalf /.1/
                The Umpire throws out the ball . *WhapperHalf *BlogsHalf
                *WhapperHalf *BlogsHalf
                *WhapperHalf *BlogsHalf
                *WhapperHalf *BlogsHalf
                *WhapperHalf *BlogsHalf
                *WhapperHalf *BlogsHalf
                *WhapperHalf *BlogsHalf
                *WhapperHalf *BlogsHalf /.1/
                Play Ball ! *WhapperHalf *BlogsHalf
                *WhapperHalf *BlogsHalf
                *WhapperHalf *BlogsHalf
                *WhapperHalf *BlogsHalf
                *WhapperHalf *BlogsHalf
                *WhapperHalf *BlogsHalf
                *WhapperHalf *BlogsHalf
                *WhapperHalf *BlogsHalf
                *WhapperHalf *BlogsHalf /.1/
                It's a fine day for a game . *WhapperHalf *BlogsHalf
                *WhapperHalf *BlogsHalf
                *WhapperHalf *BlogsHalf
                *WhapperHalf *BlogsHalf
                *WhapperHalf *BlogsHalf
                *WhapperHalf *BlogsHalf
                *WhapperHalf *BlogsHalf
                *WhapperHalf *BlogsHalf
                *WhapperHalf *BlogsHalf /.1//
*OneInning = Let's get going !
                *WhapperHalf *BlogsHalf/.1/
                The Umpire throws out the ball .
                *WhapperHalf *BlogsHalf/.1/
                Play Ball ! *WhapperHalf *BlogsHalf/.1/
                It's a fine day for a game . *WhapperHalf
                *BlogsHalf/.1//
*AAStart = Well Bob, Welcome to yet another game between the
        Whappers and the Blogs here in scenic downtown
        Blovonia . I think it is fair to say that there is
        plenty of BlogFever brewing in the stands as the
        hometown comes out to root for its favorites.
        *OneInning /.1/
```

It's time for another game between the Whappers and
the Blogs in scenic downtown Blovonia . I've just got
to say that the Blog fans have come to support their
team and rant and rave . *OneInning /.1//

Appendix C

Reversable Grammar Generator

Here is the LISP source code for the reversible grammar generator described in Chapter 8. It was written for the XLISP version of lisp that can be found in many archives throughout the Internet. The SIMTEL site is one popular location.

```
;;; Reversable Grammar Machine
;;; Copyright 1996 Peter Wayner
;;; All rights reserved.
;;; Permission is granted to copy the file as long as no charge
;;; is made. Permission is also granted to make changes as long
;;; the author of the changes is indicated in the comments.
;;;
;;;
;;; This code is designed to implement a reversible computer. If
;;; it can be reversed then, the data used to create it can be extracted.
;;;
;;;
;;; constant-list contains constant values that are left unchanged.
;;; Var-list contains variables that are changed by the person.
;;; Procedure list includes all of the procedures that are executed.
(setq constant-list
        '(
                (c1 ("Bob " "Ray " "Loraine " "Carol " "Gilda "))
                (c2 ("Lucy " "Ricky " "Ethel " "Fred "))
                (c3 ("Fred " "Barney " "Wilma " "Betty "))
                (v1 ("considered insubordination "
```

```
                        "redirected commercial inertia "
                        "smiled knowingly "
                        "reundeconstructed comedic intent "
                        "ladled laugh slop "
                        "insinuated a nervous satire "))
                  (cs 1) (ci 1) (ce 5)
        ))
(setq var-list
        '(
                  (va 3) (vb 4) (vc 45) (vd 1) (ve 41) (vf 11)
        ))
(setq procedure-list
        '(
                  (main ((add va vb)
                          (whi vf cs ci (gt vf ce) t1)
                          (chz (c1)) (chz (c1 c2)) (add vb vc)
                          (chz (v1)) (chz (c2 c3)) (mul vc va)
                          (chz (v1))))
                  (t1          ((add va vb)
                          ;;(add vb vc) (mul vd va) (mul vc vd)
                          (if (gt va vb) b1 b2) (add vc vd) (add vd ve)))
                  (b1    ((mul vd ve) (mul vb ve)))
                  (b2    ((add vd vc) (add vc ve)))
          )
)
(defun Record-Error (error-string)
;;; If something goes wrong, this indicates the error.
        (print error-string))
(defun eval-tag (tag)
;;; Finds the right match for the tag.
        (setq temp nil)
        (setq temp (assoc tag constant-list))
        (cond ((not temp)
                        (setq temp (assoc tag var-list))))
        (cond ((not temp)
                        (Record-Error (concatenate 'string
                                        "Missing Tag:"
                                        (symbol-name tag)))))
        temp)
(defun test-change (tag new-value)
        (setq temp (assoc tag var-list))
        (cond (temp
                        (setf (cdr temp) new-value))))
(defun do-addition (tag1 tag2)
;; Add tag2+tag1 and store in tag1
```

```
            (setq temp (eval-tag tag2))
            (setq temp2 (assoc tag1 var-list))
            (cond ((not temp2)
                        (Record-Error (concatenate 'string
                                            "Missing Variable Tag:"
                                            (symbol-name tag1))))
                    ((and temp (numberp (cadr temp))
                            (numberp (cadr temp2)))
                        (setf (cdr temp2)
                            (list (+ (cadr temp) (cadr temp2)))))
                    (t
                      (Record-Error (concatenate 'string
                                        "Problems with adding:"
                                        (symbol-name tag1)
                                        (symbol-name tag2))))))
(defun do-subtraction (tag1 tag2)
;; Subtract tag1-tag2 and store in tag1
            (setq temp2 (eval-tag tag2))
            (setq temp1 (assoc tag1 var-list))
            (cond ((not temp1)
                        (Record-Error (concatenate 'string
                                            "Missing Variable Tag:"
                                            (symbol-name tag1))))
                    ((and temp2 (numberp (cadr temp1))
                            (numberp (cadr temp2)))
                        (setf (cdr temp1)
                            (list (- (cadr temp1) (cadr temp2)))))
                    (t
                      (Record-Error (concatenate 'string
                                        "Problems with subtracting:"
                                        (symbol-name tag1)
                                        (symbol-name tag2))))))
(defun do-multiplication (tag1 tag2)
;; Add tag2+tag1 and store in tag1
            (setq temp (eval-tag tag2))
            (setq temp2 (assoc tag1 var-list))
            (cond ((not temp2)
                        (Record-Error (concatenate 'string
                                            "Missing Variable Tag:"
                                            (symbol-name tag1))))
                    ((and temp (numberp (cadr temp))
                            (numberp (cadr temp2)))
                    (cond ((or (= 0 (cadr temp2)) (= 0 (cadr temp)))
                                (Record-Error (concatenate 'string
                                        "Multiply by zero error: "
```

```
                                        (symbol-name tag1) " by "
                                        (symbol-name tag2))))
                        (t
                         (setf (cdr temp2)
                         (list (* (cadr temp) (cadr temp2)))))))))
                (t
                 (Record-Error (concatenate 'string
                                 "Problems with multiplying: "
                                 (symbol-name tag1) " by "
                                 (symbol-name tag2))))))
(defun do-division (tag1 tag2)
;; Add tag2+tag1 and store in tag1
        (setq temp (eval-tag tag2))
        (setq temp2 (assoc tag1 var-list))
        (cond ((not temp2)
                        (Record-Error (concatenate 'string
                                         "Missing Variable Tag: "
                                         (symbol-name tag1))))
               ((and temp (numberp (cadr temp))
                        (numberp (cadr temp2)))
                (cond ((or (= 0 (cadr temp2)) (= 0 (cadr temp)))
                        (Record-Error (concatenate 'string
                                         "Divide by zero error: "
                                         (symbol-name tag1) " by "
                                         (symbol-name tag2))))
                      (t
                       (setf (cdr temp2)
                       (list (/ (cadr temp2) (cadr temp)))))))
                (t
                 (Record-Error (concatenate 'string
                                 "Problems with Dividing: "
                                 (symbol-name tag1) " by "
                                 (symbol-name tag2))))))
(defun Do-Swap (var1 var2)
;;; Swap the values stored here.
        (setq temp (cdr (assoc var1 var-list)))
        (setf (cdr (assoc var1 var-list)) (cdr (assoc var2 var-list)))
        (setf (cdr (assoc var2 var-list)) temp))
;;;;;;;;;;;;;;;;;;;;;;;;;;;;;;;;;;;;;;
;;;; Eval Operations.
;;;;   used to step through lists of ops.
(defvar Forbidden-List nil)
;;; This is the list of variables that can't be touched.
;;; This feature is used when progressing down paths chosen
;;; by an if statement. If the variable used to choose the
```

```
;;; path is changed along the path, then bad things can happen
;;; and the world can't be reversed correctly.
(defun check-if-test (if-test)
;;; Evaluate test.
 (setq ans nil)
   (setq side1 (cadr (eval-tag (cadr if-test))))
   (setq side2 (cadr (eval-tag (caddr if-test))))
   (cond ((eq (car if-test) 'lt) ;; less-than
          (setq ans (< side1 side2)))
         ((eq (car if-test) 'gt) ;; greater-than
          (setq ans (> side1 side2)))
               ((eq (car if-test) 'eq) ;; equal-than
          (setq ans (= side1 side2)))
         ((eq (car if-test) 'le) ;; less-or-equal
          (setq ans (<= side1 side2)))
         ((eq (car if-test) 'ge) ;; greater-or-equal
          (setq ans (>= side1 side2)))
         (t
          (Report-Error (concatenate 'string
                         "Error evaluating If-then:"
                         (symbol-name (car if-test))))))
         ans)
(defun Do-If (if-test if-clause else-clause)
;;; Evaluate an if-then branch.
;;;
;;; This current version can CREATE bugs when
;;; the program takes one path and then CHANGES
;;; the value of one of the variables used to
;;; choose the path. Reversing this is filled
;;; with ambiguitities and is prohibited.
;;;
         (setq ans (check-if-test if-test))
      (setq Forbidden-List (append
                            (list (cadr if-test) (caddr if-test))
                            Forbidden-List))
    (cond (ans
           (Do-Op-List if-clause))
          (t
           (Do-Op-List else-clause)))
    (setq Forbidden-List (cdr (cdr Forbidden-List)))
    )
(defun Do-Reverse-If (if-test if-clause else-clause)
;;; Evaluate an if-then branch.
;;; This goes backwards. I could remove some of this
;;; extra code by embedding a strategic reverse, but I
```

```lisp
;;; think it might be better to build the separate code
;;; now.
   (setq ans (check-if-test if-test))
   (cond (debug
          (print (list "In Rev If. Taking path:" ans))))
    (cond (ans
           (Do-Reverse-Op-List if-clause))
          (t
           (Do-Reverse-Op-List else-clause)))))
(defun Do-While (var init-const inc-const if-test branch)
;;; A while operation looks like this: '(whi var init-const inc-const
;;; test branch) var is the variable that is used to keep track of the
;;; progress of the loop. The first pass through the loop, var is set
;;; to init-const. Then if-test is checked. When it becomes true, then
;;; the loop breaks out. Otherwise the branch is executed. Then
;;; inc-const is ADDed to var and we go back to if-test.
;;;
;;; There is something irreversable going on here!!! The prior contents
;;; of var are destroyed. This is only bad if you use the variable
;;; before it gets to the loop. The solution is to use a new variable
;;; for each loop. This is, alas, a requirement. Something must keep
;;; track of the number of passes through the loop.
        (setf (cdr (assoc var var-list))
              (append (cdr (assoc init-const constant-list)) nil))
        (setq ans (check-if-test if-test))
        (do () (ans)
            (Do-Op-List branch)
                (Do-Addition var inc-const)
                (setq ans (check-if-test if-test)))
)
(defun Do-Reverse-While (var init-const inc-const if-test branch)
;;; The While Loop run in reverse!
        (do () ((= (cadr (assoc var var-list))
                   (cadr (assoc init-const constant-list))))
            (Do-Reverse-Op-List branch)
                (Do-Subtraction var inc-const)
        )
)
(defun Do-Operation (op)
;;; An operation looks like this: '(op var1 var2)
;;; Do the right thing.
        (cond (debug
                     (print (list "Doing Op:" op))))
        (cond ((member (cadr op) Forbidden-List)
               (Record-Error (concatenate 'string
```

```
                              "Attempt to influence op on Forbidden List:"
                              (symbol-name (cadr op)))))
           ((eq (car op) 'add)
            (Do-Addition (cadr op) (caddr op)))
           ((eq (car op) 'sub)
            (Do-Subtraction (cadr op) (caddr op)))
           ((eq (car op) 'mul)
            (Do-Multiplication (cadr op) (caddr op)))
           ((eq (car op) 'div)
            (Do-Division (cadr op) (caddr op)))
           ((eq (car op) 'swp)
            (Do-Swap (cadr op) (caddr op)))
           ((eq (car op) 'if)
            (Do-If (cadr op) (caddr op) (cadddr op)))
           ((eq (car op) 'chz)
            (Do-Choice (cadr op)))
           ((eq (car op) 'whi)
            (Do-While (cadr op) (caddr op) (cadddr op)
                    (nth 4 op) (nth 5 op)))
              (t
                    (Record-Error (concatenate 'string
                                   "Undefined Operation: "
                                   (symbol-name (car op)))))))
        ))
(defun Do-Reverse-Operation (op)
;;; An operation looks like this: '(op var1 var2)
;;; Do the right thing.
     (cond (debug
                    (print (list "Doing Reverse Op:" op))))
      (cond ((eq (car op) 'add)
             (Do-Subtraction (cadr op) (caddr op)))
            ((eq (car op) 'sub)
             (Do-Addition (cadr op) (caddr op)))
            ((eq (car op) 'mul)
             (Do-Division (cadr op) (caddr op)))
            ((eq (car op) 'div)
             (Do-Multiplication (cadr op) (caddr op)))
            ((eq (car op) 'swp)
             (Do-Swap (cadr op) (caddr op)))
            ((eq (car op) 'if)
             (Do-Reverse-If (cadr op) (caddr op) (cadddr op)))
                ((eq (car op) 'chz)
             (Do-Reverse-Choice (cadr op)))
            ((eq (car op) 'whi)
             (Do-Reverse-While (cadr op)
```

```
                                  (caddr op) (cadddr op)
                                  (nth 4 op) (nth 5 op)))
                (t
                            (Record-Error (concatenate 'string
                                          "Undefined Operation: "
                                          (symbol-name (car op)))))
          ))
(defun Do-Op-List (ls)
;;; Look up the tag in the procedure list.
    (do ((l (cadr (assoc ls procedure-list)) (cdr l)))
        ((null l))
      (Do-Operation (car l))))
(defun Do-Reverse-Op-List (ls)
;;; Look up the tag in the procedure list.
    (do ((l (reverse (cadr (assoc ls procedure-list))) (cdr l)))
        ((null l))
      (Do-Reverse-Operation (car l))))
;;;;;;;;;;;;;;;;;;;;;;;;;;;;;;;;;;;;;;;;
;;;; File Operations
;;;; Used for going backwards.
(defvar Backwards-Text nil)
;;; This file is where the text will be removed.
(defvar Backwards-Buffer "")
;;; This holds the reversed version of the string.
(defun File-To-String (name)
;;; Reads in a file. Might be faster if AREF is used
;;; to index the string.
        (setq temp "")
        (setq Backwards-Text
          (open name))
        (setq a (read-char backwards-text))
        (do ()
              ((null (peek-char 'nil backwards-text)))
            (setq temp (concatenate 'string temp (string a)))
            (setq a (read-char backwards-text)))
        (setq temp (concatenate 'string temp (string a)))
        (close backwards-text)
        temp)
(defun File-To-BitString (name)
;;; Reads in a file and converts it into a bitstring.
;;; Might be faster if AREF is used
;;; to index the string.
;;;
;;; This is a really inefficient way to do things. It
;;; is silly to load an entire file into memory. But,
```

```
;;; I'm getting lazy in these days of cheap memory.
;;; If this isn't changed to buffer things, then I
;;; didn't have time to be efficient.
      (setq temp "")
      (setq temp-file
        (open name))
      (setq a (read-byte temp-file))
      (do ()
            ((null (peek-char 'nil temp-file)))
          (setq temp (concatenate 'string temp (Num-To-Bits a 256)))
          (setq a (read-byte temp-file)))
      (close temp-file)
      (setq BitSourcePointer 0)
      (setq MaxBitSourcePointer (length temp))
      temp)
(defun BitString-To-File (str name)
;;; Take a bit string and convert it into bytes.
      (setq out-file (open name :direction :io ))
      (setq tot-bytes (ceiling (/ (length str) 8)))
      (setq ptr 0)
      (do ((i 0 (+ 1 i))) ((= tot-bytes i))
            (setq cur-byte 0)
            (setq cur-value 128)
            (do ((j 0 (+ 1 j))) ((= j 8))
                  (cond ((eq (aref str ptr) #)
                          (setq cur-byte (+ cur-byte cur-value))))
                  (setq cur-value (/ cur-value 2))
                  (setq ptr (+ 1 ptr)))
            (write-byte cur-byte out-file))
      (close out-file))
(defun write-string (st stream)
  (do ((i 0 (+ 1 i))) ((= i (length st)))
    (write-char (aref st i) stream)))

;;;;;;;;;;;;;;;;;;;;;;;;;;;;;;;;;;;
;;;; Choose Operation and its reverse.
(defun Flatten-Choice-List (ls)
;;; ls is presented as a list of variables and constants.
;;; Some of these variables and constants might be lists
;;; of variables and constants.
;;; This current version is NOT recursive. It can
;;; handle ONE level of indirection.
      (setq answer nil)
      (do ((l ls (cdr l))) ((null l))
        (cond ((stringp (car l))
                (setq answer (cons (car l) answer)))
```

```
                  ((atom (car l))
                   (setq answer (append
                                     (cadr (eval-tag (car l)))
                                     answer)))
                  (t
                   (Report-Error (concatenate 'string
                                     "Something wrong with: "
                                     (symbol-name (car l))))))))
            answer)
(defun Stringify (i)
;;; Make sure that i is a string.
        (cond ((listp i)
                (Flatten-Choice-List i))
               ((stringp i) i)
               ((integerp i)
                (format nil "~d" i))
               ((floatp i)
                (format nil "~g" i))
               ((rationalp i)
                (format nil "~d" i))))
(defun Find-Reverse-Choice (ls)
;;; Scans down ls and looks for the first complete match with
;;; the Backwards-Buffer.
        (setq answer nil)
        (setq counter 0)
        (do ((l (car ls) (cdr l)))
               ((null l))
           (setq ttt (reverse (car l)))
           (cond ((string= ttt Backwards-Buffer :end2 (length ttt))
                    ;;; We have a match!!!
                    (setq answer counter)
                    (setq l nil)
                    )
                  (t (setq counter (+ 1 counter))))))
            answer)
(defun Num-To-Bits (value top)
;;; There are top choices between 0 and top-1.
;;; Find the bits to this value.
        (setq bot 0)
        (setq top (- top 1))
        (setq answer "")
        (do ()
               ((= top bot))
        ;;  (print (list bot top))
          (cond ((> value (+ (/  (- top bot) 2) bot))
```

```
                    (setq bot (ceiling (+ (/ (+ 1 (- top bot)) 2) bot)))
                    (setq answer (concatenate 'string answer "1")))
                   (t
                    (setq top (floor (+ (/  (- top bot) 2) bot)))
                    (setq answer (concatenate 'string answer "0")))))
            answer)
(defun test-num (j)
  (setq answer nil)
  (do ((i 0 (+ 1 i))) ((= i j))
    (setq temp (num-to-bits i j))
    (cond ((not (= i (Bits-To-Num temp j)))
          (print (list i (Bits-To-Num temp j) j))))))
(defun Bits-To-Num (bits top )
;;; Reverse Num-To-Bits.
;;; This consumes bits from the BitFile.
;;; Choose them at random if the file is finished.
    (setq bot 0)
    (setq top (- top 1))
        (do ((i BitSourcePointer (+ 1 i))) ((= top bot))
            (setq BitSourcePointer (+ 1 BitSourcePointer))
            (cond (debug
                    (print (list "taking bit: " (aref bits i) i))))
                (cond ((> BitSourcePointer MaxBitSourcePointer)
                        (cond ((= 0 (rand 1))
                         (setq top (floor (+ (/  (- top bot) 2) bot))))
                        (t
                         (setq bot
                         (ceiling (+ (/ (+ 1 (- top bot)) 2) bot))))))
                ((eq (aref bits i) #)
                (setq top (floor (+ (/  (- top bot) 2) bot))))
                (t
                (setq bot (ceiling (+ (/ (+ 1 (- top bot)) 2) bot))))))
    bot)
(defun Old-Bits-To-Num (bits top )
;;; Reverse Num-To-Bits.
    (setq bot 0)
    (setq top (- top 1))
        (do ((i 0 (+ 1 i))) ((= top bot))
                (cond ((eq (aref bits i) #)
                (setq top (floor (+ (/  (- top bot) 2) bot))))
                (t
                (setq bot (ceiling (+ (/ (+ 1 (- top bot)) 2) bot))))))
    bot)
(defun Do-Choice (ls)
;;; This is presented by the Do-Op function.
```

```
;;; Make a choice and spit it out the right stream.
  (setq temp (Flatten-Choice-List ls))
  (setq t1 (Bits-To-Num BitSource (length temp)))
  (cond (debug
         (print (list "In Do Choice with choice:" t1))))
   (write-string
     (nth t1
          temp)
     output-stream))
(defun Do-Reverse-Choice (ls)
;;; Reverse the effects of do-choice.
  (setq answer nil)
  (setq temp (Flatten-Choice-List ls))
  (setq len (length temp))
  (setq counter 0)
  (do ((l temp (cdr l))) ((null l))
      (cond (debug
             (print (list "Checking :" counter (reverse (car l))))))
      (cond ((string= TextSource (reverse (car l))
                      :start1 TextSourcePointer
                      :end1 (+ TextSourcePointer (length (car l))))
             (setq answer
                   (Num-To-Bits counter len))
             (setq TextSourcePointer
                   (+ TextSourcePointer (length (car l))))
             (setq l nil)))
      (setq counter (+ 1 counter)))
   (cond (debug
          (print (list "Found bits: " (reverse answer)))))
   (setq output-bits (concatenate 'string output-bits (reverse answer)))
   answer)
;;;;;;;;;;;;;;;;;;;;;;;;;;;;;;;;;;;;
;;;; Main Code Section
;;;;
;;;;    This is the mastermind.
;;;;    It must open up the correct files and start processing.
;;;;
(defun Encode (In-Data-Name Out-Text-Name &optional (Grammar-File nil))
;;; Encode information so it ends up in a funky grammar file.
        (cond (Grammar-File
               (load Grammar-File))) ;;; If Grammar-File is declared,
                                     ;;; then load more information.
        (setq BitSource (File-To-BitString In-Data-Name))
        (setq output-stream (open Out-Text-Name
                                  :direction :output
```

```
                                          :if-does-not-exist :create))
     (setq Forbidden-List nil)
        (Do-Op-List  'main)
        (close output-stream))
(defun Decode (In-Data-Name Out-Text-Name &optional (Grammar-File nil))
;;; Decode information so it comes out in the correct format.
        (cond (Grammar-File
               (load Grammar-File))) ;;; If Grammar-File is declared,
                                     ;;; then load more information.
        (setq TextSource (reverse (File-To-String In-Data-Name)))
        (setq output-bits "")
        (setq TextSourcePointer 0)
        (Do-Reverse-Op-List  'main)
        (BitString-To-File output-bits Out-Text-Name)
)
```

Bibliography

This book is quite incomplete because it only offers the reader an introduction to many of the topics. Other topics are simply left out because of time and space constraints. This preface to the bibliography is intended to offer some suggestions for further reading and exploration.

A good place to begin is with history. David Kahn's *Codebreakers* is an excellent survey of the history of cryptology [Kah67]. There are numerous descriptions of steganographic solutions like secret inks and microdots. More recent histories are published in *Cryptologia*.

Other more specific information can be found in these areas.

Error-Correcting Codes The chapter in this book can not do justice to the wide field. There are many different types of codes with different applications. Some of the better introductions are: [LJ83] and [Ara88]. There are many others.

Compression Algorithms Compression continues to be a hot topic and many of the latest books aren't current any longer. The best solution is to combine books like [Bar88a, Bar88b] with papers from the the procedings from academic conferences like [Kom95].

Subliminal Channels This idea is not covered in the book, but it may be of interest to many readers. Much of the work in the area was done by Gus Simmons who discovered that many digital signature algorithms had a secret channel that could be exploited to send an extra message. [Sim84, Sim85, Sim86, Sim93, Sim94] This is pretty easy to understand in the abstract. Many of the algorithms like the El Gamal signature scheme [ElG85] or the Digital Signature Algorithm [NCSA93] create a new digital signature at random. Many different valid signatures exist and the algorithm simply picks one at random. It is still virtually impossible for someone without the secret key to generate one, but the algorithms were intended to offer authentication without secrecy.

Imagine that you want to send a one bit message to someone. The only encryption software you can use is a DSA signature which is designed not to hide secrets. You could simply send along a happy message and keep recomputing the digital signature of this message until the last bit is the bit of your message. Eventually, you should find one because the algorithm chooses amoung signatures at random.

This abstract technique only shows how to send one bit. There are many extra bits available for use and the papers describe how to do the mathematics and exploit this channel.

The algorithms form an important example for political discussions about cryptography. The U.S. Government would like to allow people to use authentication, but they would like to restrict the use of secrecy-preserving encryption. Algorithms like the DSA appear to be perfect compromises. The existence of subliminal channels, however, shows how the current algorithms are not an perfect compromise.[1]

Covert Channels These are another popular subject for investigation in the world of computer security. Imagine that you run a computer system which has an operating system that is supposed to be secure. That means the OS can keep information from travelling between two users. Obviously, you can implement such an OS by shutting down services like file copying or electronic mail. It is not clear, however, that you can completely eliminate every way of communicating.

The simplest example for sending a message is to tie up some shared resource like a printer. If you want to send a '1' to a friend, then you print a file at 12:05 and tie up the printer. If you want to send a '0', then you print the file at 12:30. The other person checks the availability of the printer. This may not be a fast method, but it could work. The speed of the channel depends upon the shared

---

[1]They may be a perfectly adequate practical compromise because implementing the software to use this additional channel is time consuming.

system resources and the accuracy of detection. Obviously one way to defend against covert channels is to create timing errors.

Some beginning sources are [NCSA93, PN93, MM92]

Text Permutation Many people are interested in modulating the position of text on the page to encode secret messages. If you shift a line of text up or down a small amount, the change might not be noticed by the reader, but it could be measured by a calibrated device. Many people see this as an ideal way to catch document leakers. If thirty copies of a document are printed, then each of the thirty could be printed with the recipeant's name encoded in the line positions. A leaker could be identified from a photocopy.

Naturally, there are any number of ways that information could be hidden in this manner. The word spacing in justified text is also fairly changeable and just waiting for a subtextual message. Some papers on the topic are:[BLMO94, Max94].

Digital Cash There are many different ways to exchange money over digital wires, but some of the most interesting systems offer complete anonymity. People are able to spend their money without fear of records being kept. This is a fairly neat trick because digital cash must be counterfeit-resistant. Paper cash achieves this goal when it is printed with a sophisticated press. Digital copies, on the other hand, are easy to make. If people can copy files of numbers meant to represent cash, then anonymity would seem to allow people the freedom to counterfeit without being caught.

The cleverest schemes involve a complicated spending system that forces the spender to reveal part of their identity. If the spender tries to use a bill twice, enough of the identity should be revealed to expose the criminal.

Readers should explore the original works by visionaries like David Chaum [Cha81, Cha83, Cha85, Cha88] and Stefan Brands [Bra93]. My book, *Digital Cash*, gives an introduction to these anonymous systems and other approaches to the problem [Way95b].

Anonymous Voting People often want to cast their votes anonymously because this can prevent coercision. Paper ballots are generally successful if no one checks the ballot before they enter the box. Providing the same accountability and security is no simple feat.

K. Sako and J. Killian [SK95], for instance, modified the Mixmaster protocol described in Chapter 10 to provide a simple way for people to cast their vote. Each person can check the tally and compare their vote to the recorded vote to guarantee that the election was fair. Other systems include [BY86, Boy90, FOO93].

[18694]   NIST FIPS PUB 186. Digital signature standard. Technical report, National Institute of Standards and Technology, U.S. Department of Commerce, May 1994.

[Age95]   National Security Agency. N.s.a. press release: Venona documents released. Technical report, National Security Agency, July 1995.

[AHU83]   A.V. Aho, J.E. Hopcroft, and J.D. Ullman. *Data Structures and Algorithms.* Addison-Wesley, Reading, Massachusetts, 1983.

[AK91]   Dana Angluin and Michael Kharitonov. When won't membership queries help? In *Proceedings of the Twenty-Third Annual ACM Symposium on Theory of Computing,* pages 444–454. ACM Press, 1991. to appear in *JCSS.*

[Ara88]   Benjamin Arazi. *A Commonsense Approach to the Theory of Error Correcting Codes.* MIT Press, Cambridge, Massachusetts, 1988.

[Aur95]   Tuomas Aura. Invisible communication. Technical report, Helsinki University of Technology, November 1995.

[Bar88a]   Michael F. Barnsley. Fractal modelling of real world images. In Heinz-Otto Peitgen and Dietmar Saupe, editors, *The Science of Fractal Images,* chapter 5, pages 219–239. Springer-Verlag, 1988.

[Bar88b]   Michael F. Barnsley. *Fractals Everywhere.* Academic Press, San Diego, 1988.

[BH92]   M. Barnsley and L. Hurd. *Fractal Image Compression.* AK Peters, Ltd., Wellesley, Ma., 1992.

[BFHMV84] I.F. Blake, R. Fuji-Hara, R.C. Mullin, and S.A. Vanstone. Computing logarithms in finite fields of characteristic two. *SIAM Journal on Algebraic Discrete Methods*, 5, 1984.

[BJNW57] F.P. Brooks, A.L Hopkins Jr., Peter G. Neumann, and W.V. Wright. An experiment in musical composition. EC-6(3), September 1957.

[BL85] Charles Bennett and Rolf Landauer. The fundamental physical limits of computation. *Scientific American*, pages 48–56, July 1985.

[BLMO94] J Brassil, S Low, N Maxemchuk, and L O'Garman. Electronic marking and identification techniques to discourage document copying. In *Proceedings of IEEE Infocom 94*, pages 1278 – 1287, 1994.

[Blu82] M. Blum. Coin flipping by telephone: A protocol for solving impossible problems. *Proceedings of the 24th IEEE Computer Conference (CompCon)*, 1982.

[Boy90] C. Boyd. A new multiple key cipher and an improved voting scheme. In *Advances in Cryptology–EUROCRYPT '89 Proceedings*. Springer-Verlag, 1990.

[Bra93] S.A. Brands. An efficient off-line electronic cash system based on the representation problem. Technical Report CSR9323, Computer Science Department, CWI, Mar 1993.

[Bri82] E.F. Brickell. A fast modular multiplication algorithm with applications to two key cryptography. In *Advances in Cryptology: Proceedings of Crypto 82*. Plenum Press, 1982.

[Bur] William S. Burroughs. *The Ticket that Exploded*.

[BY86] J.C. Benaloh and M. Yung. Distributing the power of government to enhance the privacy of voters. *Proceedings of the 5th ACM Symposium on the Principles in Distributed Computing*, 1986.

[Cha81] D. Chaum. Untraceable electronic mail, return addresses, and digital pseudonyms. *Communications of the ACM*, 24(2), Feb 1981.

[Cha83]   D. Chaum. Blind signatures for untraceable payments. In *Advances in Cryptology: Proceedings of Crypto 82*. Plenum Press, 1983.

[Cha85]   D. Chaum. Security without identification: Transaction systems to make big brother obsolete. *Communications of the ACM*, 28(10), Oct 1985.

[Cha88]   D. Chaum. Blinding for unanticipated signatures. In *Advances in Cryptology–EUROCRYPT '87 Proceedings*. Springer-Verlag, 1988.

[Cha95a]   David Charlap. The bmp file format, part i. *Dr. Dobbs Journal*, Mar 1995.

[Cha95b]   David Charlap. The bmp file format, part ii. *Dr. Dobbs Journal*, Apr 1995.

[CM58]   Noam Chomsky and G.A. Miller. Finite state languages. *Information and Control*, 1:91–112, 1958.

[CW93]   K.W. Campbell and M.J. Wiener. DES is not a group. In *Advances in Cryptology–CRYPTO '92 Proceedings*. Springer-Verlag, 1993.

[ed.92]   G.J. Simmons ed. *Contemporary Cryptology: The Science of Information Integrity*. IEEE Press, Piscataway, N.J., 1992.

[ElG85]   T. ElGamal. A public-key cryptosystem and a signature scheme based on discrete logarithms. In *Advances in Cryptology: Proceedings of CRYPTO 84*. Springer-Verlag, 1985.

[FOO93]   A. Fujioka, T. Okamoto, and K. Ohta. A practical secret voting scheme for large scale elections. In *Advances in Cryptology–AUSCRYPT '92 Proceedings*. Springer-Verlag, forthcoming, 1993.

[Fre82]   Ed Fredkin. Conservative logic. *International Journal of Theoretical Physics*, 21, 1982.

[FT82]   Edward Fredkin and Tommaso Toffoli. Conservative logic. *International Journal of Theoretical Physics*, 21:219–253, 1982.

[Gro]   Wendy Grossman. alt.scientology.war. *Wired*.

[Gun88]   C.G. Gunther. A universal algorithm for homophonic coding. In *Advances in Cryptology–Eurocrypt '88 Lecture Notes in Computer Science*, number 330, pages 405–414, New York, 1988. Springer-Verlag.

[Hec82]   Paul Heckbert. Color image quantization for frame buffer display. In *Proceedings of SIGGRAPH T82*, 1982.

[Hil91a]   D Hillman. The structural of reversible one-dimensional cellular automata. *Physica D*, 52(2 / 3):277, sep 1991.

[Hil91b]   David Hillman. The structure of reversible one-dimensional cellular automata. *Physica D*, 54:277–292, 1991.

[HU79]   John Hopcroft and Jeffrey Ullman. *Introduction to Automata Theory, Languages and Computation*. Addison-Wesley, Reading, Massachusetts, 1979.

[JKM90]   H.N. Jendal, Y. J. B. Kuhn, and J. L. Massey. An information-theoretic treatment of homophonic substitution. In *Advances in Cryptology–Eurocrypt '89*, New York, 1990. Springer-Verlag, Lecture Notes in Computer Science.

[Kah67]   David Kahn. *The Codebreakers*. MacMillan, New York City, 1967.

[Kea89]   Michael Kearns. *The Computational Complexity of Machine Learning*. PhD thesis, Harvard University Center for Research in Computing Technology, May 1989.

[Knu81]   D. Knuth. *The Art of Computer Programming: Volume 2, Seminumerical Algorithms*. 2nd edition, Addison-Wesley, 1981.

[KO84]   Hugh Kenner and Joseph O'Rourke. A travesty generator for micros. *BYTE*, page 129, November 1984.

[Kob87]   Neal Koblitz. *A Course in Number Theory and Cryptography*. Springer-Verlag, New York, Berlin, Heidelberg, London, Paris, Tokyo, 1987.

[Kom95]   John Kominek. Convergence of fractal encoded images. In James Storer, editor, *IEEE Data Compression Conference*, pages 242–251, 1995.

[KV89]   Michael Kearns and Leslie Valient. Cryptographic limitations on learning boolean formulae and finite automata. In *Proceedings of the Twenty-First Annual ACM Symposium on Theory of Computing*, pages 433–444, Seattle,Washington, May 1989.

[Leh82]   D.J. Lehmann. On primality tests. *SIAM Journal on Computing*, 11(2), May 1982. ((page numbers are wrong)).

[Lia95]   Wilson MacGyver Liaw. Reading gif files. *Dr. Dobbs Journal*, Feb 1995.

[LJ83]   Shu Lin and Daniel J. Costello Jr. *Error Control Coding: Fundaments and Applications*. Prentice Hall, Englewood Cliffs, NJ, 1983.

[Mar84]   N. Margolus. Physics-like models of computation. *Physica D*, 10:81–95, 1984.
           Discussion of reversible cellular automata illustrated by an implementation of Fredkin's Billiard-Ball model of computation.

[Max94]   NF Maxemchuk. Electronic document distribution. *AT&T Technical Journal*, 73(5):73 – 80, September 1994.

[Mer93]   Ralph Merkle. Reversible electronic logic using switches. *Nanotechnology*, 4:21–40, 1993.

[MM92]   IS Moskovitz and AR Miller. The channel capacity of a certain noisy timing channel. *IEEE Trans. on Information Theory*, IT-38(4):1339 – 43, 1992.

[Mon85]   P.L. Montgomery. Modular multiplication without trial division. *Mathematics of Computation*, 44(170), 1985.

[NCSA93]   NCSA. A guide to understanding covert channel analysis of trusted systems. Technical Report TG-030, NCSC, November 1993.

[Neu62]   Peter G. Neumann. Efficient error-limiting variable-length codes. *IRE Transactions on Information Theory*, IT-8:292–304, July 1962.

[Neu64]   P.G. Neumann. Error-limiting coding using information-lossless sequential machines. *IEEE Transactions on Information Theory*, IT-10:108–115, April 1964.

[NY89]   M. Naor and M. Yung. Universal one-way hash functions and their cryptographic applications. In *Procedings of the 21nd Annual ACM Symposium on Theory of Computing*, pages 33–43. ACM, 1989.

[NY90]   M. Naor and M. Yung. Public-key cryptosystems provably secure against chosen ciphertext attacks. In *Procedings of the 22nd Annual ACM Symposium on Theory of Computing*, pages 427–437. ACM, 1990.

[PN93]   N Proctor and P Neumann. Architectural implications of covert channels. In *Proceedings of the 15th National Computer Security Conference*, 1993.

[PP90]   B Pfitzmann and A Pfitzmann. How to break the direct rsa-implementation of mixes. In *Advances in Cryptology–Eurocrypt '89*, number 434. Springer-Verlag, 1990.

[QC82]   J.-J. Quisquater and C. Couvreur. Fast decipherment algorithm for rsa public-key cryptosystem. *Electronic Letters*, 18, 1982.

[Rob62]   L. G. Roberts. Picture coding using pseudo-random noise. *IRE Trans. on Information Theory*, IT-8, Feb 1962.

[Sch94]   Bruce Schneier. *Applied Cryptography*. John Wiley and Sons, New York, 1994.

[Sha79]   A. Shamir. How to share a secret. *Communications of the ACM*, 24(11), Nov 1979.

[Sim84]   G.J. Simmons. The prisoner's problem and the subliminal channel. In *Advances in Cryptology: Proceedings of CRYPTO '83*. Plenum Press, 1984.

[Sim85]   G.J. Simmons. The subliminal channel and digital signatures. In *Advances in Cryptology: Proceedings of EUROCRYPT 84*. Springer-Verlag, 1985.

[Sim86]   G.J. Simmons. A secure subliminal channel (?). In *Advances in Cryptology–CRYPTO '85 Proceedings*. Springer-Verlag, 1986.

[Sim93]   G.J. Simmons. The subliminal channels of the U.S. Digital Signature Algorithm (DSA). In *Proceedings of the Third Symposium on: State and Progress of Research in Cryptography*, Fondazone Ugo Bordoni, Rome, 1993.

[Sim94]   G.J. Simmons. Subliminal communication is easy using the DSA. In *Advances in Cryptology–EUROCRYPT '93 Proceedings*. Springer-Verlag, 1994.

[SK95]   K Sako and J Killian. Receipt-free mix-type voting schemes. In *Advances in Cryptology– Eurocrypt '95*, pages 393–403. Springer-Verlag, 1995.

[Sto88]   James Storer. *Data Compression*. Computer Science Press, Rockville, Maryland, 1988.

[TM87]   Tommaso Toffoli and Norman Margolus. *Cellular Automata Machines*. MIT Press, London, 1987.

[Tof77a]   Tommaso Toffoli. *Cellular Automata Mechanics*. Ph.D. thesis, University of Michigan, 1977.

[Tof77b]   Tommaso Toffoli. Computation and construction universality of reversible cellular automata. *Journal of Computer and System Sciences*, 15:213–231, 1977.

[Tur36a]   Alan Turing. On computable numbers with an application to the entscheidungsproblem. *Proceedings of the London Math Soceity*, 2(42):230–265, 1936.

[Tur36b]   Alan Turing. On computable numbers with an application to the entscheidungsproblem. *Proceedings of the London Math Soceity*, 2(43):544–546, 1936.

[Val84]   Leslie G. Valient. A theory of the learnable. *Communications of the ACM*, 27:1134–1142, 1984.

[Wal95]   Steve Walton. Image authentification for a slippery new age. *Dr. Dobbs Journal*, Apr 1995.

[Way85]   Peter Wayner. Building a travesty tree. *BYTE*, page 183, September 1985.

[Way95a]   Peter Wayner. Strong theoretical steganography. *Cryptologia*, 19(3):285–299, July 1995.

[Way95b]   Peter C. Wayner. *Digital Cash: Commerce on the Net*. AP Professional, Boston, 1995.

[Wei76]   Joseph Weizenbaum. *Computer power and human reason: from judgment to calculation*. W.H. Freeman, San Fransisco, 1976.

Index